ADVANCED POWERPOINT

MORE THAN PRESENTATIONS!

Wei-Chieh Wayne Yu
Anthony A. Olinzock
Chun Fu Charlie Lin

Copyright © 2018 Wei-Chieh Wayne Yu
Anthony A. Olinzock
Chun Fu Charlie Lin
All rights reserved
First Edition

PAGE PUBLISHING, INC.
New York, NY

First originally published by Page Publishing, Inc. 2018

ISBN 978-1-64214-002-6 (Paperback)
ISBN 978-1-64214-003-3 (Digital)

Printed in the United States of America

Introduction

PowerPoint® is a comprehensive software application that has a variety of uses beyond presentations because of its advanced features, flexibility, and coding capabilities. It is an excellent software application for developing more advanced and interactive presentations, training and instructional materials, games, and apps.

Advanced PowerPoint: More Than Presentations! does not require users to have VBA coding experience. The coding needed to complete applications is gradually integrated, step-by-step, throughout the text. Users learn to write basic code, and to understand and modify more complex code, thus greatly expanding the capabilities of this media application. Most users have some basic experience using PowerPoint; however, most of them do not know the capabilities of this software application, and do not see it as an application for more than presentations.

This textbook provides hands-on experience and step-by-step instructions for developing a variety of applications. Just a few examples include 3-D drawings, analog and digital timers, animated photos, calculators, electronic books, electronic games and game boards, drag and drop, image mapping, gifs, interactive instructional materials and presentations, morphing, simulations, tutorials, games, and a variety of apps.

The directions and images in this book refer to the Windows® 10 ribbon framework and Microsoft® Office and PowerPoint 2016. However, you can complete the applications, with some minor adjustments, using early versions of the software.

Accompanying the textbook are a set of *data files* and *solutions files* for each of the eighteen lessons. In each lesson, you are instructed to open a data file, when needed. The data files reduce the amount of keyboarding and formatting required to complete the applications. The solution files show you a completed example of the application.

Accessing Data and Solution Files

There are three ways you can download the data and solution files.
To access the file on *Facebook*®, you would complete four steps:
1. Log in to Facebook or create a new account.

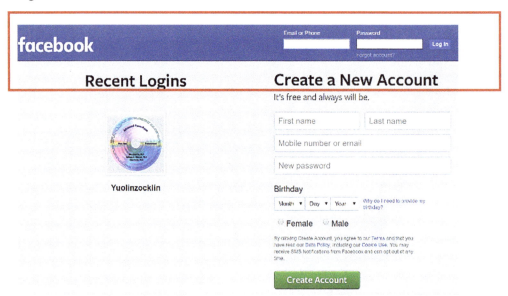

2. Enter *Yuolinzocklin* in the search box and press return or click Search.

3. Click on the CD image to view the post, which allows you to access the data and solution files.

4. Click on the *Google® Drive* hyperlink or See More to access *Dropbox®* containing data and solution files.

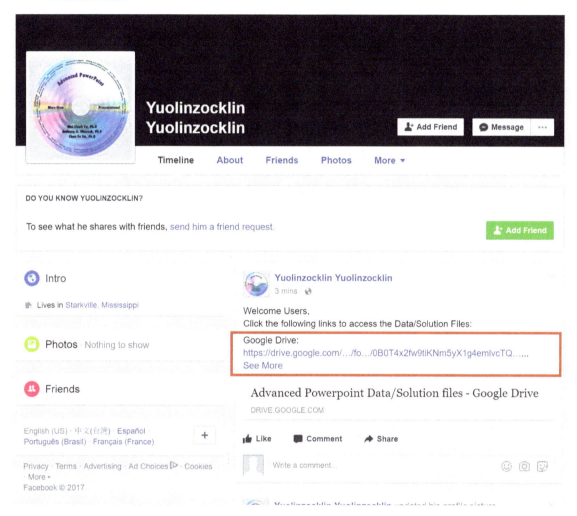

To access the files on *Google+®*, you would complete four steps:

1. Enter the URL, https://plus.google.com/, in any browser window, and Sign-in with your Google account information, or create a new account.

2. Enter adv.pptx@gmail.com in the search box and press Enter.

3. Click on the icon displayed under People and Pages.

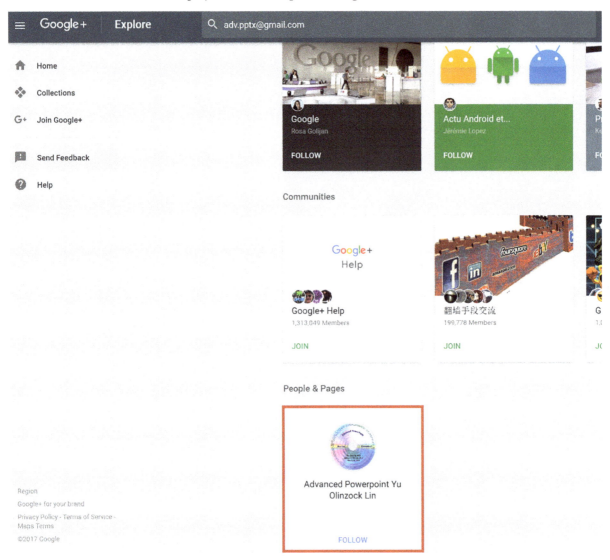

4. Click on the *Google Drive* or *Dropbox* hyperlink to access the data and solution files.

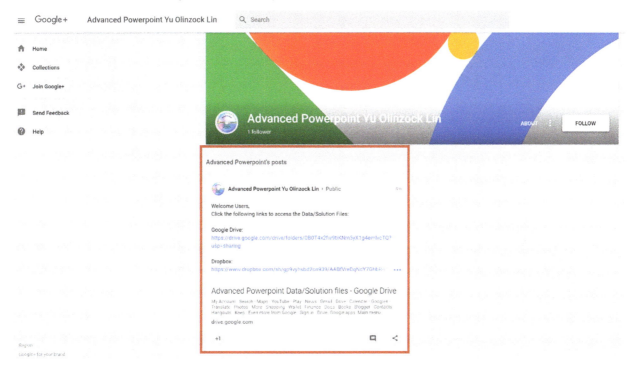

To receive a *link* to the files by sending an e-mail request to the authors, use the following e-mail address: Adv.pptx@gmail.com.

Dropbox is either a registered trademark or a trademark of Dropbox Inc. in the United States and/or other countries.

Facebook is either a registered trademark or a trademark of Facebook Inc. in the United States and/or other countries.

Google, Google Drive, and Google+ are either registered trademarks or trademarks of Google Inc. in the United States and/or other countries.

UnFREEz is either a registered trademark or a trademark of WhitSoft Development in the United States and/or other countries.

Windows, Microsoft, and PowerPoint are either registered trademarks or trademarks of Microsoft Corporation in the United States and/or other countries.

YouTube is either a registered trademark or a trademark of Alphabet Inc. in the United States and/or other countries.

LESSON 1

ActiveX Text Box Control, Analog Clock, and Drag and Drop

Data Files

Lesson 1 ActiveX Text Box Control
Lesson 1 Analog Clock or Timer
Lesson 1 Application 1 Presentation Application
Lesson 1 Application 2 Instructional Materials Application
Lesson 1 Application 3 Gaming Application

Overview

In Lesson 1, you will learn to add ActiveX Text Box Controls to create interactive presentations and to enable *drag and drop* behavior. You will also learn to create analog clocks and timers and apps that use these features.

ActiveX Text Box Control

ActiveX Controls are small programs, *macros*, that you can use to expand the capabilities of the software application you are using. You do not have to know how to program to use these controls. The ActiveX Text Box Control enables you to create an interactive presentation where the user can key in information in Slide Show view. You can also adjust the *properties* of the ActiveX Text Box Control to change the font size and color, to allow for multiple lines, to enable word wrap, to add scroll bars, and much more. *Properties* enable you to specify aspects of the program you can adjust.

Prior to working with ActiveX Text Box Controls, you need to do two things:

- Make sure the Developer tab is displayed.
- Check the Trust Center Settings for macros.

Windows Ribbon Framework

Directions in this book refer to the *Windows ribbon framework and Microsoft Office* and PowerPoint *2016*. However, you can compete the applications with some minor adjustments in early versions of the software. The ribbon includes the Quick Access Toolbar, which lists common commands and a *Tab row* that lists the application menu, standard or Contextual Tab, and a Help button. Groups appear for each tab at the bottom of the ribbon, and various button appear above each group. *Contextual tabs* are hidden tabs that contain one or more commands that are applicable to a selected or highlighted object only, and are displayed as needed. Figure 1–1 shows an example of the ribbon.

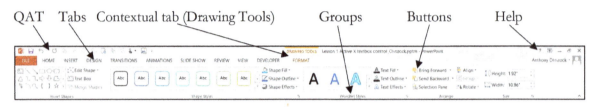

Figure 1–1

When prompts for completing an action are provided in this book, the prompt follows the format Tab/Group/Button. For example, if you wanted to insert a shape, the prompt would be Insert/Illustrations/Shapes—that is, click the Insert tab, and in the Illustrations group, click Shapes button. Prompts are withdrawn as you move through the book.

Developer Tab

Launch PowerPoint and open the data file **Lesson 1 ActiveX Text Box Control**. (Refer to the Introduction section in the beginning of this book for steps for downloading data and solution files.)

To display the Developer tab:

- Click File/Options/Customize Ribbon. This abbreviated instruction means that you should click the File tab on the ribbon, then click Options from the drop-down menu, and then click Customize Ribbon from the next drop-down menu.
- Under the Customize the Ribbon column, place a check mark in front of Developer and click OK.

Enable Macros

A *macro* is a saved sequence of commands or keyboard strokes that can be stored and then recalled with a single command or keyboard stroke. *Macros* are very useful, but can also be the source for harmful code that someone could use to perform a destructive act to your computer. Unless you change the trust center settings, macros are probably disabled on your computer.

To enable *macros*, click File/Options/Trust Center/Trust Center Settings/Enable all macros/OK. You should only do this when you are working with your own presentations or when you trust the person sending you a presentation with a macro in it.

You need to save a presentation containing a *macro* as a *PowerPoint Macro-Enabled Presentation*.

Inserting an ActiveX Text Box Control

If you have not already opened the data file **Lesson 1 ActiveX Text Box Control** from the folder that contains your data files, do so now. Verify that the Design applied is *Parallax* (Design/Themes/Parallax) and the theme color is *blue* (Design/Variants/More button/Colors/blue). *Note: For this and other textbook assignments, if you do not have a specified theme, color, or font available on the software you are using, make a substitution from those available on your system.* The theme and color for Lesson 1 ActiveX Text Box Control have already been applied.

Controls

Slide 1

On slide 1, Title Layout, add your name to the subtitle placeholder. Save the file to the location where you will be saving all work. Add your last name at the end of the file name such as **Lesson 1 ActiveX Text Box Control Your Name.** Be sure to save it as a *PowerPoint Macro-Enabled Presentation*. Your Save As dialog box will look like figure 1–2.

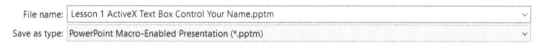

Figure 1–2

Slide 2

On slide 2 you will add a Text Box Control as shown in figure 1–3. Add gridlines to facilitate placement of objects (View/Show/Gridlines). This abbreviated instruction means that you should click the View tab on the ribbon, and in the Show group, click the Gridlines button. The gridlines are, height 1" and width 1", and do not display in Slide Show view.

Click the Developer tab, and in the Controls group, click the Text Box icon. *Drag and draw* the text box, height ½" and width 5", as shown in figure 1–3. You have created a text box object where users viewing the Slide Show will be able to enter text; thus, making the presentation interactive. You will only be able to use the control during Slide Show view.

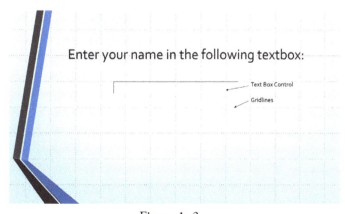

Figure 1–3

Switch to Slide Show view, go to slide 2, and click in the text box accepting the default *properties* for the control. In the case of the text box you just inserted, if the length of text you entered was longer than the width of the text box, the text will not wrap, so you would only see the portion of the text that fits into the size of the text box. Try it. Switch to Slide Show view and type a line of text longer than the width of the text box. Delete the text, and replace it with your name again.

On slide 3 you will enter a text box, height 3" and width 2" as shown in figure 1–4. We will adjust the *properties* of the text box control so that it fits our criteria. After you have inserted the text box object, make sure it is still selected and click the *Properties* button (Developer/Controls/Properties). The *properties* sheet is displayed. Properties enable you to change the appearance of the object. Figure 1–5 shows the *properties* sheet for the text box you inserted on slide 3.

Slide 3

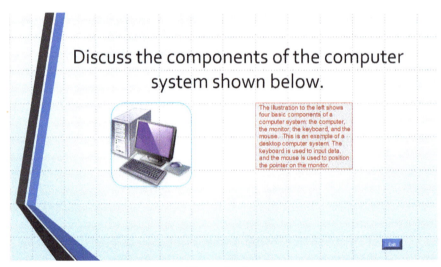

Figure 1–4

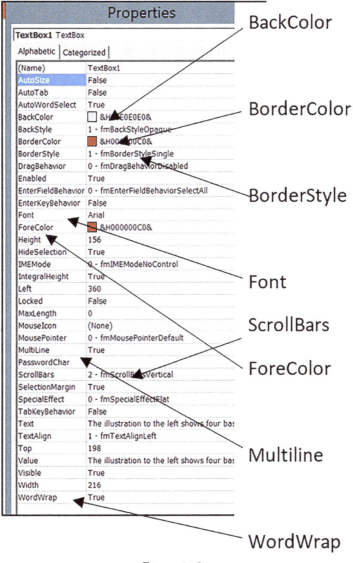

Figure 1–5

The BackColor was changed to *gray*, the BorderColor was changed to *dark red*, the BorderStyle was changed to *1*, the font was changed to *Arial*, the ForeColor was changed to *dark red*, MultiLine was changed to *True*, ScrollBars was changed to *2*, and WordWrap was changed to *True*. Making these adjustments will change the appearance of the text box object. Make the adjustments to the *properties* sheet as shown in figure 1–5. Switch to Slide Show view and enter the following information in the text box control.

> *The illustration to the left shows four basic components of a computer system: the computer, the monitor, the keyboard, and the mouse. This is an example of a desktop com-*

puter system. The keyboard is used to input data, and the mouse is used to position the pointer on the monitor. Information displayed on the monitor is one type of output.

The scroll bar will not be displayed until you fill up the text box. Note that word wrap is enabled and you have multiple lines of text. *Note: On the properties sheet you have an option to change the DragBehavior from a 0 to a 1, which would enable drag behavior, and you could drag text from one text box to another. You will use this property in an application at the end of this chapter.*

Action Buttons

Next we will add *action buttons* to navigate through the Slide Show. Action buttons are built-in button shapes that you can add to your presentation, and then assign an action to occur when you click or move over the button. Move to slide 1 and make sure your gridlines are displayed. To insert a forward or next button, click Insert/Illustrations/Shapes/Action Buttons/Forward or Next. The action buttons are at the bottom of the shapes displayed. Click and drag to draw the shape, height .3" and width .6", as shown in figure 1–6. Use the gridlines to assist in placement. Add an effect, Bevel Angle (Format/Shape Styles/Shape Effects/Bevel Angle). Note the action button appears in a color that complements the design and theme colors selected. Click on the action button and click the copy button. Move to slide 2 and click Paste. The action button should appear in the same location as it appeared on slide 1.

Figure 1–6

Move to slide 3. On slide 3 we want to insert an action button that will let us end the Slide Show. Follow the same steps for adding the next action button, but select the custom button. *Drag and draw* a button the same size as the next buttons you added to slides 1 and 2. From the Action Settings dialog box that is displayed, select hyperlink to End Show. Add the Bevel Angle effect. Enter the text *Exit* on the button and size the text as necessary.

Set Up Show

The final step is to set up the Slide Show. Click Slide Show/Set Up/Set Up Slide Show, and in the Set Up Show dialog box, click Browsed at a Kiosk. With this setting, only your controls, the action buttons, and ESC key work during Slide Show view.

Save Presentation

Click the Save button on the Quick Access Tool bar at the top left of your screen to save the file using the same file type, name, and location.

Making an Analog Clock

Many of the presentations, instructional materials, and gaming activities you develop will be enhanced by integrating analog and digital clocks and timers. In this job you will learn how to create an analog clock and timer in PowerPoint.

Open the data file ***Lesson 1 Analog Clock or Timer*** and add your name in the subtitle placeholder. Apply the Slide theme. Add a new slide, blank layout. Insert an oval, height 5" and width 5", and change the fill color to *dark blue, Accent 1, Lighter 80 percent*. Change the outline color to *dark blue*; and change the outline width to 10 pt. To change the weight, right-click on the shape, and in the Shape dialog box, click Line, and change the width to 10 pt. Change the effect for the oval shape to Bevel Angle (Format/Shape Styles/Shape Effects/Angle). Align the oval to the slide, middle, and center as shown in figure 1–7.

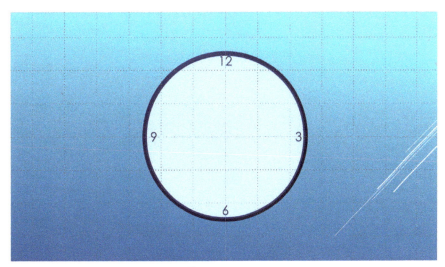

Figure 1–7

Adding Numbers to the Clock

Use WordArt to add numbers to the oval as shown in figure 1–7. Click Insert/Text/WordArt, dark blue, Accent 1, Shadow. Replace the text with the number 12, and change the font size to 28 pt. Center the number, and move it to the top of the oval as shown in figure 1–7. Repeat these steps for the number 6, but move it to the bottom of the oval. Repeat these steps for the number 3, but align middle and move it to the right of the oval. Repeat these steps for the number 9, but align middle and move it to the left of the oval.

Adding the Second Hand

Insert an oval shape, height .3" and width .3", and align to slide, center, and middle. The fill and outline colors should be *dark blue, Accent 1*, and the shape effect should be Bevel Angle. Add a block arrow up shape, height 4" and width .15", dark blue, Accent 1. Align at the center and move it up as in shown in figure 1–8. This block arrow will represent the second hand on the clock. Add a Shape Effect, Bevel Angle. Move the arrow behind the oval shape (Format/Arrange/Send Backward). We want the arrow to spin around the face of the timer in 60 seconds, but making it do that is a little tricky. Add the spin animation to the block arrow. Select the arrow and click Animation/Advanced Animation/Add animation/Emphasis/Spin. As you can see from the preview, it doesn't work. To preview it again, you can also click the Animation tab, and in the Advanced Animation group click Animation Pane. Click on the animation in the Animation pane at the right of your screen and click *Play From. Note that the block arrow has a superscript number tag indicating the order of the animation, and the animation in the Animation pane also has a number tag.* The colored star indicates the type of animation: *Entrance, Emphasis,* or *Exit*. Click on the animation in the animation pane, and press Delete to delete it.

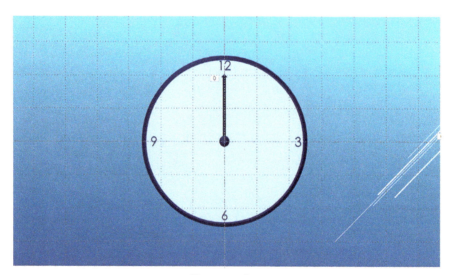

Figure 1–8

ADVANCED POWERPOINT: MORE THAN PRESENTATIONS!

Spinning on a Pivot

When you add a spin animation to a shape, it spins on its *pivot* or middle point. It spins in place. In order to work with the restrictions of the spin animation, we need to have the block arrow spin around the bottom of the arrow, a new pivot point.

To create a new pivot point for the arrow, follow these steps:
   a. Click on the up block arrow to select it and press Ctrl+D to duplicate it.
   b. Flip the copy of the arrow vertical. Click on the shape and click Format/Arrange/Rotate/Flip Vertical.
   c. Align the new arrow to the center and move it below the original arrow as shown in figure 1–9.

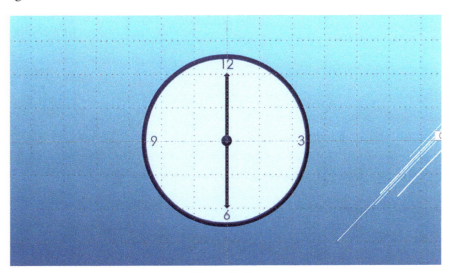

Figure 1–9

We want to make the bottom arrow transparent. Click on the shape to select it. Right-click and select format shape and change the shape fill to *100 percent transparent* and the line color to *no line*. The shape is still there, but you can't see it. A red outline is shown around the bottom arrow in figure 1–10 so that you can see what is happening. Your shape will not have the red outline. Click on the top arrow. Hold down the Shift key and click on the bottom transparent arrow. Click Format/Arrange/Group/Group. The original two arrows are now a single object as shown in figure 1–10.

We now want to animate the shape to spin. It will spin on its pivot or center point. The center of the shape is at the bottom of the top arrow now. Click on the shape, and click Animation/Advance Animation/Add Animation/Emphasis/Spin. The arrow now spins the way we want it to, but the timing is not accurate. The arrow, which represents a second hand of a clock, must spin 360° in 60 seconds or one (01:00) minute. Click the Animation tab, and in the Advanced Animation group, click Animation Pane. The animation will be numbered, and a colored star indicates an *Emphasis* animation.

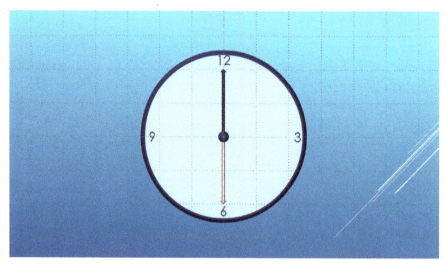

Figure 1–10

Click on the animation in the animation pane. Click the arrow to the right of the animation and change Start *With Previous*, Duration *60* (60 seconds will change to 1:00 seconds or 1 minute), repeat *5*. The second hand will now spin 360° in 60 seconds or 1 minute and will repeat 5 times. Once you have the animation working accurately, click on the arrow shape, and send the shape backward as shown in figure 1–11.

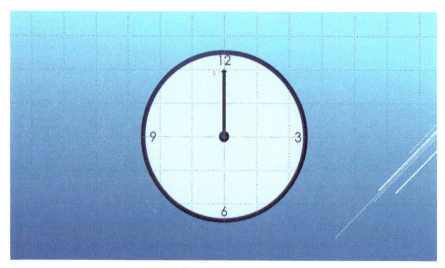

Figure 1–11

Timing and Rotation

The timing for different hands on a clock or timer is as follows:
    a. The second hand moves 360° in 60 seconds or 1:00 minute.
    b. The minute hand moves 6° in 60 seconds or 1:00 minute.
    c. The hour hand moves .5° in 60 seconds or 1:00 minute.

Adding the Minute Hand

To make the minute hand, figure 1–12, of the clock:
  a. Click on the arrow shape for the second hand and press *CTRL+D* to duplicate it.
  b. Size the shape to height 3.5" and width .15".
  c. Change the timing to with previous, 300 seconds or 5:00 minutes (60×5 for 5 minutes), repeat 0.
  d. Change the spin effect to 30° (6×5). Be sure to press Enter after you enter the effect amount.
  e. Align to center and on top of the first arrow.
  f. Send the new shape backward as needed.

Play the animation to make sure it is working properly.

Adding the Hour Hand

To make the hour hand, figure 1–12, of the clock:
  a. Click on the arrow shape for the minute hand and press *CTRL+D* to duplicate it.
  b. Size the shape to height 3" and width .15"
  c. Change the timing to with previous, 300 seconds (60×5 for 5 minutes), repeat 0.
  d. Change the spin effect to 2.5° (.5×5). Be sure to press Enter after you enter the effect amount.
  e. Align to center and on top of the first arrow.
  f. Send the new shape backward.

Play the animation to make sure it is working properly. Since all three animations are with previous, they play at the same time, and they have the same number tag.

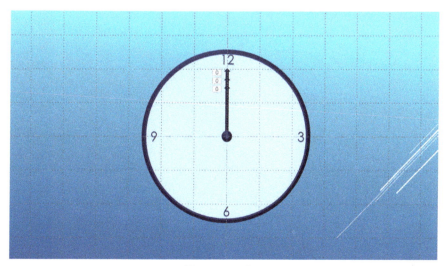

Figure 1–12

Adding Audio and WordArt

Once your clock is working accurately, we want to add WordArt to display the word *Stop* and a sound of a *bell* ringing at the end of five minutes since we designed the clock to run for a period of five minutes so that we could use it as a timer.

1. Add the word *Stop* in WordArt as shown on in figure 1–13.
    a. Use standard red for the text fill and outline.
    b. Animate the WordArt for (Entrance/Appear/After Previous).
2. To have a bell ring, click Insert/Audio/Online Audio/Bell/Insert to download a bell sound file.
    a. Click on the bell icon, and the contextual audio tools tab will be displayed.
    b. Click Playback/Start/Automatically.
    c. In the Animation pane, select With Previous.
    d. In the Slide pane, move the audio icon off the slide.

Note: An audio file has been inserted on slide 2 for your use if you are not able to download the bell sound.

Figure 1–13 shows the completed slide 2 along with the Animation pane. The objects in the Animation have been named so that they are easier to understand. You will learn to name objects in a later lesson.

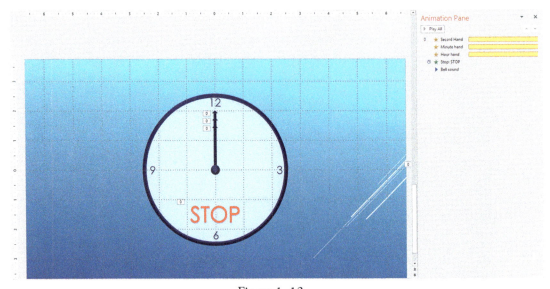

Figure 1–13

Lesson 1 Applications

Note: Many of the activities presented in this book can be used as interactive presentations, simulations, games, and apps.

Lesson 1 Application 1 Presentation Application

Open the data file **Lesson 1 Application 1 Presentation Application**, and add your name to replace the subtitle placeholder on the title slide. Use the *Facet* theme and *green* theme colors. Change the title color to *green, Accent 1*, or a similar color. Save the presentation to the folder where you save your work as **Lesson 1 Application 1 Presentation Application your name.**

On slide 2, add the title *Don't Be a Clock Watcher During Your Interview!* Align the Clip Art and title at the left. Move and size the Clip Art as needed. Add the Shape Effect, *green, 18 pt Glow, Accent color 1*.

In order to attract attention, add a working clock to the Clip Art as shown in figure 1–14. The clock should have an hour, minute, and second hand, and should run when the slide is displayed for one minute.

The size of the clock should be 2"×2". Add the Shape Effect Bevel Slope to the oval. Add other effects as desired.

Figure 1–14

Lesson 1 Application 2 Instructional Materials Application

Open the data file **Lesson 1 Application 2 Instructional Materials Application**, and add your name to replace the subtitle placeholder on the title slide. Change the title font size to 40 pt. Use the Vapor Trail theme and default theme colors. Save the presentation as a PowerPoint Macro-Enabled presentation to the folder where you save your work as **Lesson 1 Application 2 Instructional Materials Application your name.**

Figure 1–15 shows slide 2 of the presentation you will prepare. Display your gridlines to assist you in aligning the objects on the slide. The first step will be to insert eight text boxes in two columns. The text boxes in the first column are height .5" and width 5". Insert the first text box in the first column and adjust the size as necessary. While the text box is selected, click the *Properties* button and DragBehavior as shown in figure 1–16. You won't need to make any other property adjustments. Make three copies of the text box and align them as shown in figure 1–15. You will add the text later.

Insert the first text box in column 2. The text box should be height .5 and width 1.5". Enable drag behavior. Copy the text box as needed.

Run Slide Show view and add the text for each text box in the first column:

John was late for class.
Susan thought she made an A on the exam.
It is very difficult to learn to play football.
Some students study very hard to earn good grades.

Add a *60-second timer* on slide 2 that begins running when the slide is displayed. Add a *bell sound* that rings at the end of 60 seconds. Add *action buttons* to navigate through the Slide Show. Set up the show to be Browsed at a Kiosk.

Run Slide Show view, and double-click on the verb in each sentence to select it. Hold down the left mouse button and *drag and drop* (release the mouse button) it in the box to the right of the sentence. *Drag and drop* the verb back in the sentence.

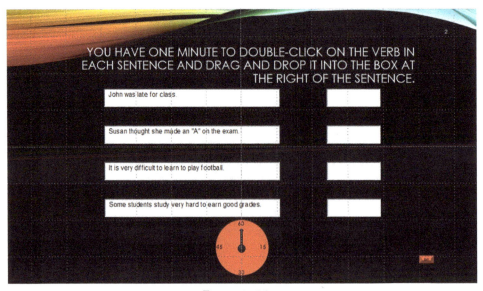

Figure 1–15

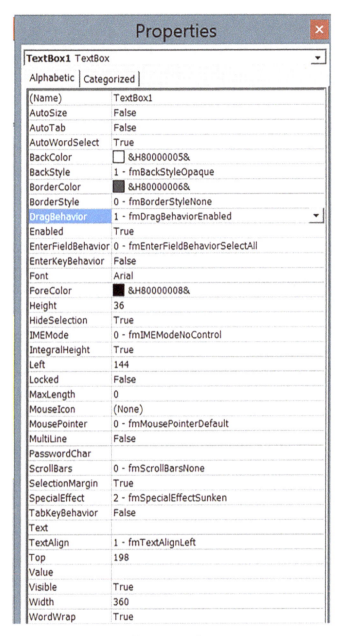

Figure 1–16

Lesson 1 Application 3 Gaming Application

Open the data file *Lesson 1 Application 3 Gaming Application*, and add your name in the second line in the subtitle on the title slide. The NewsPrint theme and NewsPrint theme colors have already been applied. Save the presentation as a PowerPoint Macro-Enabled presentation to the folder where you save your work as *Lesson 1 Application 3 Gaming Application your name*.

You need to complete slide 4 of the presentation. Add the two columns of text boxes as shown in figure 1–17. Change the BackColor of the text boxes in the left column to a *shade of red* and the text boxes in the right column to a *shade of gray*. Select *BorderStyle 1*. Add a timer that runs when the slide is displayed for 120 seconds. At the end of 120 seconds, a *bell* should ring, and after the bell, the *correct answers should appear* on the slide. Add *action buttons* to navigate through the Slide Show and to exit from slide 4. Set up the show to be *Browsed at a Kiosk*.

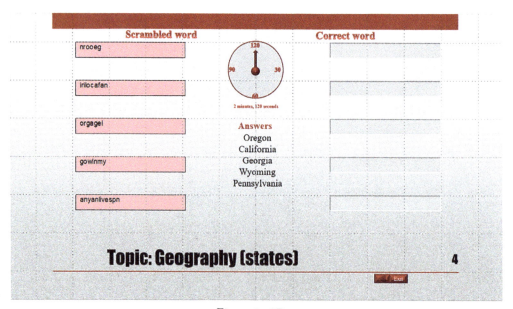

Figure 1–17

LESSON 2

Tracing and Image Mapping, Alternative Text, Custom Shows

Data Files

Lesson 2 Tracing, Image Mapping, Alternative Text, and Custom Shows
Eastern Division
Northern Division
Southern Division
Western Division
Lesson 2 Application 1 Presentation Application
Lesson 2 Application 2 Instructional Materials Application
Lesson 2 Application 3 Gaming Application

Overview

In this lesson, you will use a picture as the background for a slide, and then trace the picture so that you have only an outline. Being able to trace objects is a fundamental skill that will enable you to develop interactive presentations and apps for instruction and gaming applications. You will also learn to image map portions of slides and to display alternative text. Finally, you will learn to create Custom Shows.

Tracing

Open the data file *Lesson 2 Tracing, Image Mapping, Alternative Text, and Custom Shows*. Add your name to the subtitle, and save the file in the location where you save all your work as *Lesson 2 Tracing, Imaging Mapping, Alternate Text, and Custom Shows Your Name* as a PowerPoint Macro-Enabled presentation (the data file is already in that format). The Clarity theme has been applied.

Slide 2 of your data file is Blank Layout, and a map of California has been inserted as shown figure 2–1.

Figure 2–1

It will be easier to trace the state if we make the picture the background for the slide. Right-click on the picture, and from the menu displayed, click *Save as Picture*, and save it to the location where you save your work using the file name **California**. Use the default file type, .jpeg. Delete the picture from slide 2.

To make the picture the background for the slide, click the Design tab, and in the Customize group, select Format Background. Click *Picture or texture fill*. Navigate to your picture and click on it. Click Insert. The picture will now be the background of slide 2 as shown in figure 2–2. You can use the *Offset buttons* if you need to adjust the size of the background image.

Figure 2–2

It is easy to trace if you use the *Curve* tool in the Line group (Insert/Illustrations/Shapes/Lines/Curve). Once you select the Curve drawing tool, click at the point where you want to begin tracing. Click and drag the mouse. Every time you click the mouse, the line will reorient so that you can accurately trace the object. If you hold down the *Ctrl key* and click, the line will remain straight. Click again and you will be back to normal tracing. If the beginning and end point of tracing meet, the shape will be filled with color as shown in figure 2–3. To remove the color, right-click on the shape then click Format Shape/No fill. Copy the image to slide 3 as shown in figure 2–4. The line color was changed to standard red, 3 pt. Follow the instruction in this paragraph to trace the map on slide 2. Remove the fill color and change the outline to standard red, 3 pt. Paste the outline of the California map on slide 3.

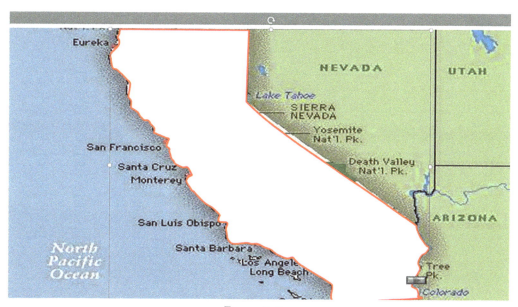

Figure 2–3

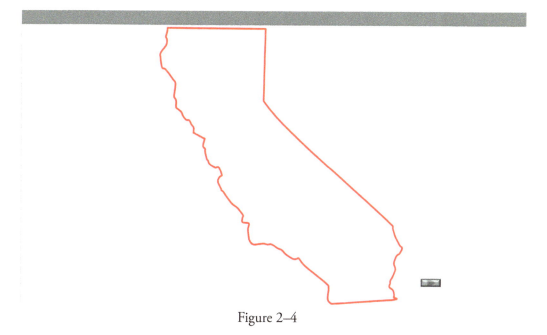

Figure 2–4

Slide 4 shows an image of a map of the United State as shown in figure 2–5. Save the Image as *US Map* as a picture. Delete the image from slide 4, and use the image you saved as the background of the slide as shown in figure 2–5. Trace the states of Washington, Oregon, and California. Change the outline color to red, and the width to 3 pt as shown on figure 2–6, and blue fill color. The tracing does not have to be perfect since you will make the object transparent later in this lesson.

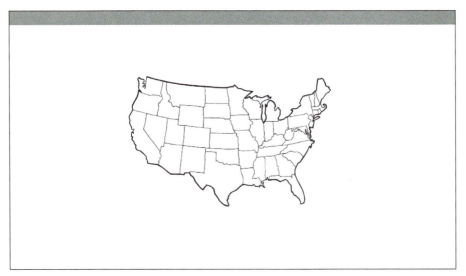

Figure 2–5

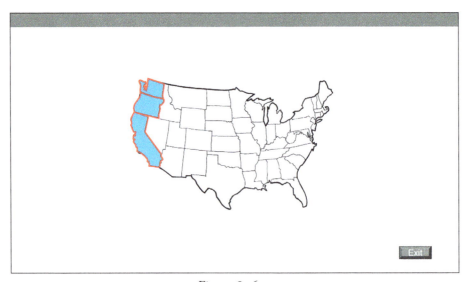

Figure 2–6

Image Mapping

The ability to trace images can be the source for training/instructional materials. For example, primary school students could be asked to point to a state and name the state and its capital city, or a doctoral student could be asked to point to and name the parts of the human heart.

Image mapping means identifying a section of an image that you can move the mouse over or click and some action will happen. For example, a question will pop up. If you are playing a game, it might cause an obstacle to appear. In this job you are going to develop a slide where primary school students practice learning the US states and their capital cities.

Step 1

In our example we are going to image map three states: Washington, Oregon, and California. When you move the mouse over one of the states, a question will appear asking the user to name the capital city. Clicking the mouse will display an image of the state with the capital city circled. Pressing ESC will bring you back to the US map.

Image map California, Oregon and Washington.

Right-click on the images you traced and select format shape. Make the shapes 80 percent transparent and no line color. When we are done with image mapping, we will make the shapes 100 percent transparent so that the user won't see them. Your slide should look like figure 2–7.

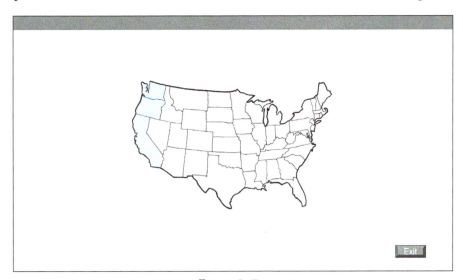

Figure 2–7

Step 2

Insert a rounded rectangle height 1" and width 3", and add an effect, Bevel Hard Edge, and center the rectangle as shown in figure 2–8. Send the new rounded rectangle shape to the back.

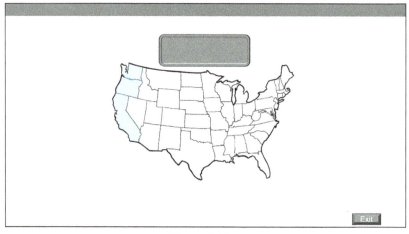

Figure 2–8

Alternative Text

Alternative text is text that appears when the pointer is moved over or clicked on an object or used by accessibility screen readers. Right-click on the traced image of California, select *Format Shape* and select *Size and Properties*, and then select *Alt Text*. See figure 2–9. Type the desired text in the description box. In the description box for Alt Text type: *This state is California. What is the capital city of California?* Repeat this procedure for Oregon and Washington.

Figure 2–9

Add Alt Text Button to the QAT

The Quick Access Toolbar, QAT, is located in the upper left corner above the ribbon. Click the QAT arrow at the right of the tool bar, and click More Commands. In the Customize Quick Access Toolbar dialog box, choose Commands not in Ribbon. Locate the command Alt Text. Click on the command. Click *Add*, and click *OK*. The command will be added to the QAT. Click on any of images covering the three states, and click Alt Text button on the QAT. The Alt Text for that state is displayed in the Format Shape pane at the right of the screen. The QAT is available when you are in normal view. We want to display the Alt Text when in Slide Show view when the user moves the pointer over one of the states.

Run a Macro

As you learned in Lesson 1, a macro is a saved sequence of commands or keyboard strokes that can be stored and then recalled with a single command or keyboard stroke. In later lessons, you will learn how to write macros using Visual Basic Applications (VBA). In this lesson, a macro is already written for you to assign to an object and to use to display Alt Text. Make sure your Developer tab is displayed. Refer to Lesson 1 if necessary. Make sure the security level is lowered to allow you to run macros. See Lesson 1 if necessary.

Click on the image covering the state of California on slide 4 to select it. Click the Insert tab, and in the Links group, click Action. Make these selections in the Action Settings dialog box that is displayed. Click the *Mouse Over* tab. Click the *Run macro* option button and select the macro *Alt_Text*. Place a check in *Play sound* check box and select *chime*. Place a check in the *Highlight when mouse over*. Click *OK*. See figure 2–10. Repeat this process for the images covering Oregon and Washington.

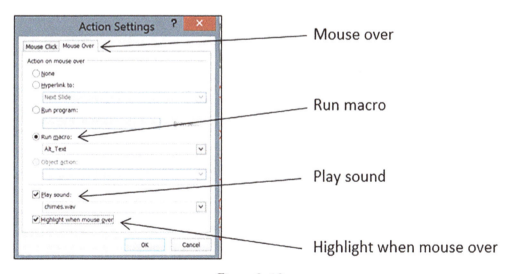

Figure 2–10

View slide 4 in Slide Show view. Move your mouse over the various states and the Alternative text you entered for each image will be displayed in the rounded rectangle shape. If the text is not displayed, make sure that you have sent the rounded rectangle to the back of all other images. Figure

2–11 shows the slide when the pointer is moved over Oregon. Size the rounded rectangle to height 1" and width 4" to fit all text, and center the shape. Change the font size to 14 pt. Make adjustments to the images and background as needed.

Figure 2–11

Custom Shows

Slides 5, 6, and 7 are in Title Only Layout, and include illustrations of the three states: California, Oregon, and Washington. Apply the picture style *Relaxed Perspective White* (Picture Tools/Format/Picture Styles) to each illustration. Add the title shown for each slide in figure 2–12. Draw an oval over the capital city for each state and change the shape fill to no fill and change the outline color to red, 3 pt. Align the images to the center and middle.

Figure 2–12

A *basic Custom Show* is a separate presentation that includes one or more slides from an existing presentation. When you create a basic Custom Show, the original presentation still contains all the slides. There are a number of reasons to create Custom Shows. One is to have the animation play each time you display a slide with animation on it. For example, if you animate a shape to bounce on to the screen when a slide is displayed, the animation will play when you display the slide for the first time, but if you click the previous button, it won't play. Another example is the ability to jump to a Custom Show and by pressing ESC return to the slide linked to the Custom Show. Custom shows are very important when developing games.

ADVANCED POWERPOINT: MORE THAN PRESENTATIONS!

In our example, we are going to create a Custom Show for each of the state slides in our presentation. To create a Custom Show, click the *Slide Show tab*, and in the *Start Slide Show group* click *Custom Slide Show, Custom Shows*. In the Custom Shows dialog box, click *New*. The Define Custom Show dialog box will be displayed as shown in figure 2–13. Name the show *California*, *check slide 5* (the slide with the state map of California) and click *Add*, click *OK, Close*. Repeat this process to create a Custom Show for the Oregon and Washington slide.

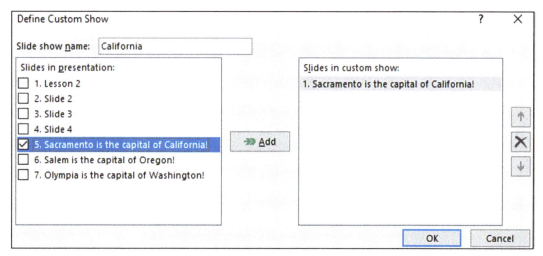

Figure 2–13

Linking to State Slides

Go the slide 4, and on the map, click on the image over California and click Insert/Links/Action. From the Action Settings dialog box displayed as shown in figure 2–14, click the *Mouse click* tab, and click the radio button *Hyperlink to* and select *Custom Show*. The Link to Custom Show dialog box as shown in figure 2–14 is displayed. Click on *California*, Check *Show and return*, and click *OK*. Repeat these steps for Oregon and Washington. Set up the presentation to be Browsed at a Kiosk. Display slide 4 in Slide Show view. You should be able to move the mouse over any one of the three states and see the Alt Text in the rounded rectangle.

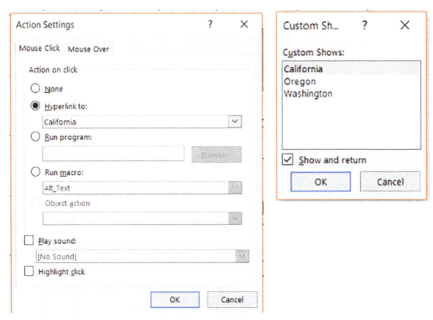

Figure 2–14

If you click any of the states when in Slide Show view, you should go to the slide with the map of that state. If you press the ESC key, you will go back to slide 4. Make sure that all links work.

Make Images Transparent

Once you have everything working properly from slide 4, you can make the images covering the three states transparent. Click on each of the three images and make them 100 percent transparent. You will no longer see the images over each state, but all the actions will still work because the image is still there. See figure 2–15.

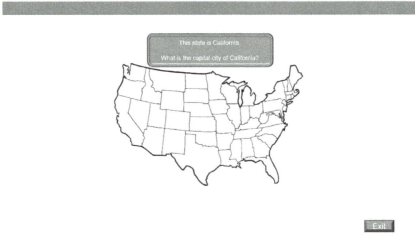

Figure 2–15

Display No Alt Text

When the pointer is not over any location on the map other than the areas you image mapped—California, Oregon, and Washington—you don't want any Alt Text displayed. Make sure you are on slide 4, which displays the outline of the continental United States. Draw a shape to cover the states you have not used in this lesson as shown in figure 2–16.

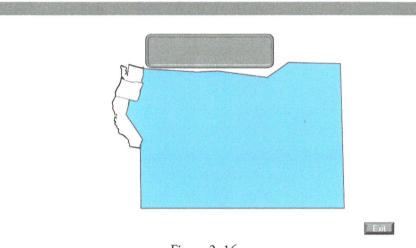

Figure 2–16

Right-click on the shape and make the fill 100 percent transparent with no outline. While the rectangle is still there, but not visible, click Insert/Links/Action. From the Action Settings dialog box that is displayed, click the Mouse Over tab, select the Run macro option button and select Alt_Text and then click OK.

We now need the rounded rectangle sent to the back since the Alt_Text macro displays the Alt Text in object 1, the first object on the slide. Objects are stacked on the slide in the order you insert them and are numbered 1, 2, etc. Making the text display in object 1 is just a choice made when writing the macro; any object could have been selected. Because we didn't enter any Alt Text for the large transparent object that you just added, when you move the pointer over it no text will be displayed.

Action Buttons

Add a Next action button to slides 1–3. Add a Custom action button to slide 4 to exit the presentation. Set up the Slide Show to be Browsed at a Kiosk. Test your presentation to make sure it is accurate, then save it again.

Lesson 2 Applications

Lesson 2 Application 1 Presentation Application

Open the data file ***Lesson 2 Application 1 Presentation Application***. Add your name to the file name and save it where you save your work. The Sketchbook theme and action buttons have already been added. Add your name in the subtitle placeholder on the title slide.

Slide 2 is in two content format. Add the following bullet list to the left content placeholder:

- *Eastern Division*
- *Northern Division*
- *Southern Division*
- *Western Division*

Animate the text for an *Entrance Effect, Float Up, With Previous, as one object* (Animation/Advanced Animation/Add Animation). Draw a separate oval to cover each item in the list. Make each oval 100 percent transparent with no outline. We are going to use the four transparent ovals to trigger an individual chart for each division that summarizes the financial performance of that division to be displayed. Each chart will *fade in, remain visible for 5 seconds, and fade out*. The four charts will be stacked on top of one another in the location of the right content place holder but will not appear until you click one of the transparent ovals that covers a division name in the bullet list. Delete the left content placeholder.

Insert the data file, ***Eastern Division***, from your data files folder. Animate the image for an *Entrance animation, Fade In, on Click*. Make sure the image is still selected, and add an *Exit animation, fade Out, After Previous, delay 5 seconds* as shown in figure 2–17. If you don't delay the exit animation, the object would appear and disappear at the same time and you would see nothing. Repeat these steps for the images of the other three divisions: ***Northern Division***, ***Southern Division***, and ***Western Division***. Move each of the images on the slide so that you can see at least part of each image. You will stack them on top of one another later.

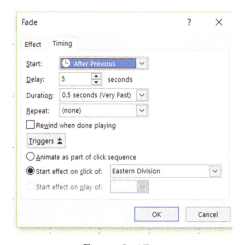

Figure 2–17

ADVANCED POWERPOINT: MORE THAN PRESENTATIONS!

The transparent ovals on top of each of the divisions in the bullet list image mapped four areas of the slide that can be used for a variety of actions such as displaying Alt Text, hyperlinking to other slides or objects, or to trigger actions. In this lesson, we will use the image map technique to trigger the images you inserted to appear when you click on one of the ovals. Click on the transparent image covering the Eastern Division. That object will be selected in the Animation Pane so that you can identify its number such as Oval 5. Be sure to remember the number of the oval. In the Animation Pane, click on the Entrance animation for the Eastern Division chart. Click the down arrow at the right of the animation, and click Timing. The Fade dialog box will be displayed as shown in figure 2–17. Click the button under *Triggers* in front of *Start effect on click of:* and select the oval you noted above covering the Eastern Division. In the illustration, Oval 5 was named Eastern Division so that it was easier to identify. You will learn to name objects in a later lesson. Display slide 2 in Slide Show view. The image for the Eastern Division should not be displayed. Click on the transparent oval covering Eastern Division, and the image should fade in, remain visible for 5 seconds, and fade out. Repeat the steps for the other three divisions.

Once the animations are working properly to display the images for the four divisions in any order, we need to stack the four images on top of one another and move them to the desired location on the slide. Select the four images of the charts. Align the object to the top and left. They should stack on one another. Move the images so that the top is aligned with the top of the bullet list and in the right placeholder. The order in which you stack the four images does not matter since each chart will only appear when you click the appropriate transparent oval to display it. Figure 2–18 shows slides 1 and 2 of the completed lesson.

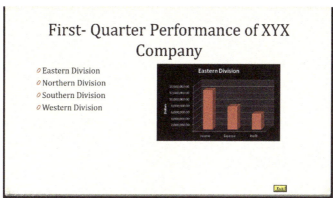

Figure 2–18

Lesson 2 Application 2 Instructional Materials Application

Open the data file ***Lesson 2 Application 2 Instructional Materials Application*** and add your name in the subtitle placeholder on the Title slide. Save the presentation where you save your work as a PowerPoint Macro-Enabled presentation type file. It should already be in that file type. Apply the *Urban Pop* Design and a color variant of your choosing.

Slide 2 includes seven different shapes. The rounded rectangle will be used to display Alt_Text. You need to add Alt Text for each of the other six shapes. For the first shape, add the following text for the description: *This is a red oval.* Repeat this process for each of the shapes other than the rounded rectangle. Name the color and shape.

Select all the shapes except the rounded rectangle, and align the shapes to the top and distribute them horizontally. While still selected, move the shapes down about one inch below the rounded rectangle.

Select the oval shape and click Insert/Links/Action. In the Actions Settings dialog box, click Mouse Click and make the selections shown in figure 2–19. Repeat this step for the other five shapes that you aligned. View slide 2 in Slide Show view. You should be able to click on any of the shapes, and its name and color will be displayed in the rounded rectangle. Add a rectangle to cover the entire slide and change the fill color to 100 percent transparent and no outline. Use a Mouse over action and Assign the Alt_Text macro to this shape. Send the rectangle to the back. Send the rounded rectangle that displays text to the back. Display slide 2 in Slide Show view. When you move about the slide, no text should be displayed in the rounded rectangle. When you click on a shape, its name and color should be displayed.

Figure 2–19

ADVANCED POWERPOINT: MORE THAN PRESENTATIONS!

Prepare slide 3 so that when the user clicks on one of the computer parts, the name of the part is displayed. Moving anywhere else on the screen will keep the rounded rectangle blank. Add a next action button on slides 1 and 2 and an exit action button on slide 3. Set up the Slide Show to be Browsed at a Kiosk. Save the presentation. Your completed slides will look like Figure 2–20.

 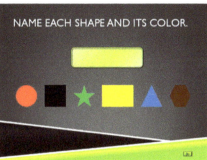 

Figure 2–20

Lesson 2 Application 3 Gaming Application

In this application, you will be creating a game called Minefield. The premise of the game is that your plane crashed and you managed to swim to a disserted island that was used during the war, but there are still many land mines and ocean mines. There also are scorpions roaming around. You must move your mouse pointer over the island. If you touch a mine, you lose. If you touch a scorpion, you lose. You can only win the game by touching your pointer to the rope (the rope will be moving) hanging from the rescue helicopter or the rescue boat (the boat will be moving). The shaded ovals in figure 2–21 represent areas image mapped and represent land mines. You will make these mines completely transparent when you have completed construction of the game.

Figure 2–21

Open the data file **Lesson 2 Application 3 Gaming Application**. Add your name in the subtitle place holder on the title slide and save the presentation. The presentation consists of six slides. All the slides have been completed except for the slide that will be the game. Add the *Honeycomb* Transition to slides 1 to 3 only, and set the duration for 2.5 seconds.

Create a Custom Show just consisting of slide 5. Name the Custom Show *Lost*. During the game, touching any of the mines or scorpions will take you to this losing slide. Create a Custom Show just consisting of slide 6. Name the Custom Show *Won*. During the game, touching the rope from the helicopter or touching the rescue boat will take you to this winning slide.

All the objects you need to complete the game are shown on slide 4 as shown in figure 2–22.

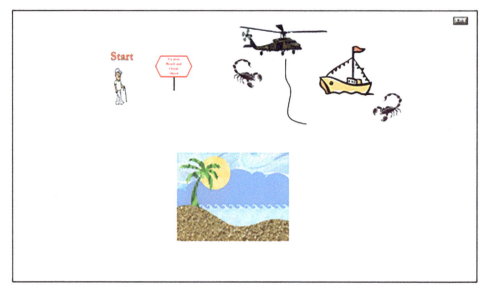

Figure 2–22

Completing the Game Slide
Step 1

Save the illustration of the beach as a picture to the folder where you save your work. Name the file **Beach**. Delete the image from slide 4. Format the background of slide 4 to use the *beach* picture as the background. Move the man, Start, caution sign, helicopter, rope, rescue boat, and scorpions to the positions shown in figure 2–21.

Step 2

Add the mines represented by ovals height .5" and width .5". Make the fill 80 percent transparent and no outline. You can make one mine and copy and paste the others. Move the mines to approximately the same positions as shown in figure 2–21.

ADVANCED POWERPOINT: MORE THAN PRESENTATIONS!

Step 3

Create mouse over hyperlink to the *Lost* Custom Show from each mine and the two scorpions. Be sure to click *Show and Return*. Add an *Explosion* sound. Create a mouse over hyperlink to the *Won* Custom Show from the rescue rope and the rescue boat. Be sure to click *Show and Return*. Add an *Applause* sound.

Step 4

Click on the scorpion on the left of the slide and move it off the slide to the left. Add a Custom Motion Path to the scorpion (Animation/Advanced Animations/Add Animation). In the Motion Paths group, select Custom Path as shown in figure 2–23.

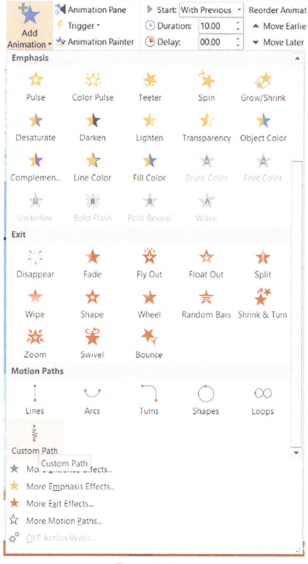

Figure 2–23

Drag and draw a path across the slide to the center and off the bottom of the screen. Double-click the mouse to end the path. The green arrow shows the beginning of the path, and the red arrow indicates the end of the path. Click on Animation Tab and in the advanced animation group click animation pane. The Custom Motion Path you just created should be the only animation listed. Click the arrow to the right of the animation and click With Previous. Click timing and change the duration to ten seconds, and repeat until end of slide. Click the Effects Tab and make a Smooth Start (0 seconds) and Smooth End (0 seconds). View slide 4 in Slide Show view to see the animation. Repeat this process with the scorpion at the right of the slide, but make the custom path stretch from right to left and off the screen at the center bottom. Change the speed to five seconds.

Click on the rescue boat. Add a Custom Motion Path to the beach area to the right of the palm tree. Change Start to With Previous, change the timing to 12 seconds, and repeat to the end of the slide with a smooth start and end.

Click on the rescue rope hanging from the helicopter. Add an Emphasis animation, Teeter, Medium, With Previous, Repeat Until End of Slide.

Click on slide 4 and click Slide Show view. All your animations should be working: the scorpions are moving, the rescue rope is moving, and the boat is moving. Touch any of the objects, and you should go to one of the Custom Shows. Pressing ESC will take you back to the game board from the losing or winning slide.

Step 5

Click on the mines and make them 100 percent transparent. Go to slide 3 and switch to Slide Show view. You are now in Slide Show and should click on the arrow that says *Move pointer here to start*. Clicking at that location puts you into position to play the game. You can now move the pointer around the slide to try and touch the rescue rope or rescue boat to win the game. If you touch one of the mines or scorpions, you will lose. Whether you win or lose, you can return to the start location from the win or lose slide.

Step 6

To prevent a player from just moving the pointer up and clicking on the rope or boat, add some additional mines in the water as shown in figure 2–24. Make the new mines transparent.

ADVANCED POWERPOINT: MORE THAN PRESENTATIONS!

Figure 2–24

Step 7

Set up the show to be Browsed at a Kiosk. Move the Exit button on the game board to the upper right corner of slide 4. Save your presentation. Figure 2–25 shows the slides in the presentation.

Figure 2–25

LESSON 3

Randomization, Triggers, ActiveX Option Button Control, Slide Masters

Data Files

Lesson 3 Option Button and Check Box
Lesson 3 Random Wheel
Lesson 3 Triggers
Lesson 3 Application 1 Presentation Application
Lesson 3 Application 2 Instructional Materials Application
Lesson 3 Application 3 Gaming Application

Overview

In Lesson 3 you will learn to randomize and its application to instructional materials, presentations, and gaming. You learn how to randomize a selection process where every option has an equal chance of being selected. You will do this without writing any VBA code. In later lessons, you will learn how to randomize by writing a short macro. You will also learn how to use triggers and logic to create interactive presentations and apps. You will also learn to use triggers to start an effect or action such as making something appear or disappear or starting a video.

Randomization

Randomization is a basic skill used in many games. Which player will go first? How many spaces can you move on a game board? It is important in education too for selecting random questions for an exam or determining who will go first in making a class presentation. In this job you will learn how to randomly select questions when reviewing for an exam. Of course, this same process will have many other applications.

Creating the Wheel

Open the data file **Lesson 3 Random Wheel**. The *Mylar* theme has already been applied to the presentation. Add your name to the title slide and save the presentation. Slide 2 contains a pie chart created by using the Chart option in the Illustrations group under the Insert tab (Insert/Illustrations/

Chart). The number of pieces needed was entered in column A, and the value of each piece was entered in column B in the default spreadsheet that was displayed. So that all pieces would be the same size, the number 1 was entered as the value of each piece. Figure 3–1 shows the worksheet that is the basis for the pie chart displayed.

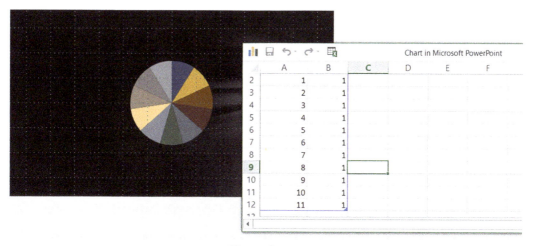

Figure 3–1

Save the chart on slide 2 as a picture, and then make the picture the background for the slide. Delete the pie chart from slide 2 so that you only have the chart as the background for the slide as shown in figure 3–2. Use the offset buttons in the Format Background pane to adjust the size of the picture as needed.

Figure 3–2

Use the curve tool and trace one piece of the pie chart. Change the line color to red 3 pt and change the fill color to 100 percent transparent. Copy the shape ten times and arrange the pieces as shown in figure 3–3. Use the rotation handle and direction arrows to arrange the pieces.

Figure 3–3

Remove the picture as the background (Design/Format Background/Reset Background). Your slide should look like figure 3–4 with the *Mylar* theme and the shapes you created.

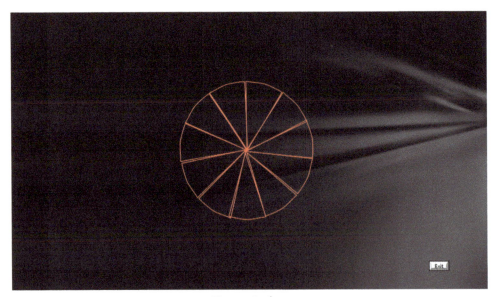

Figure 3–4

ADVANCED POWERPOINT: MORE THAN PRESENTATIONS!

Creating Questions

Add eleven slides, Title and Content Layout. Each slide will have a question, the answer, and a fifteen-second timer as shown in figure 3–5 for slide 3. This slide is displayed in the widescreen size available in Office 2013 and 2016. The topic for the questions is Data Networks.

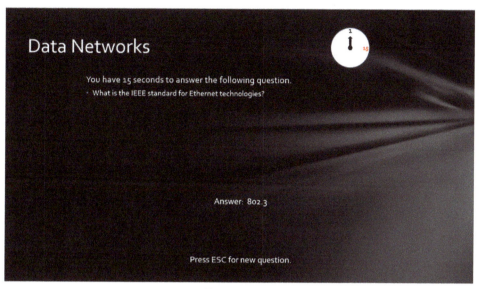

Figure 3–5

Add the title *Data Networks* in the title placeholder. Add the first two items for the bulleted list as shown. Add the answer in a text box at the bottom of the slide, and center the text box. Add another text box with the message *Press ESC for new question,* and center the text box. Create the timer as shown. Size the oval to 1.1"×1.1", and add the number 1 and 15 as shown. Have the second hand spin 90° in fifteen seconds. Have a computer beep sound play after fifteen seconds, and have the answer appear after the computer beep sound. You can substitute another sound if you can't locate the computer beep sound. You will repeat this process for the next ten slides. The question and answer for each of the slides is shown in table 3–1.

Number	Question	Answer
1	What is the IEEE standard for Ethernet technologies?	802.3
2	What is the name of the math system used for encoding computer information that only uses the numbers 0 and 1?	Binary
3	In a digital signaling system, how many bits does it take to equal one byte?	8
4	An IP addressing and subnetting method in which network and host information is manipulated without adhering to the limitations imposed by traditional network class distinctions is called?	CIDR, Classless Interdomain Routing

5	The process of using an algorithm to scramble data into a format that can be read only by reversing the algorithm to keep the information private is called?	Encryption
6	A package for data that includes the payload, addressing information, and control information is called a/an?	Frame
7	A measure of frequency equivalent to the number of amplitude cycles per second is called a/an?	Hertz
8	A term used to describe each trip a unit of data takes from one connectivity device to another is called a/an?	Hop
9	A connectivity device that retransmits incoming data signals to its multiple ports is called a/an?	Hub
10	IPv4 addresses are ? bit addresses.	32
11	A 12-character string that uniquely identifies a network node is called the ? address.	MAC (Media Access Control)

Table 3–1

Custom Shows

Make each of the slides containing questions a separate Custom Show. The first Custom Show should be named *one*, then *two*, etc. Refer to Lesson 2 if you need to review the steps for creating Custom Shows. You will have eleven Custom Shows.

Go back to slide 2 where you have the eleven pie-shaped pieces. Starting at the top, click on one of the pie pieces (make sure you have selected only one piece) and click Insert/Links/Action/Hyperlink/Custom Show/One/Show and Return/OK. Moving clockwise on the pie chart, follow this procedure to link each piece of the pie chart to a different Custom Show. Once you have completed this process, view slide 2 in Slide Show view and test your link to each of the Custom Shows. Make sure you can press ESC to return to slide 2. If you can't, check your link to the Custom Show and make sure you placed a check mark in the box *Show and Return*.

Randomize the Selection of the Question

Insert a round rectangle height 2" × width 4". Add an effect, Bevel Hard Edge, and the text *Click for random question*. Position the rectangle behind the wheel as shown in figure 3–6.

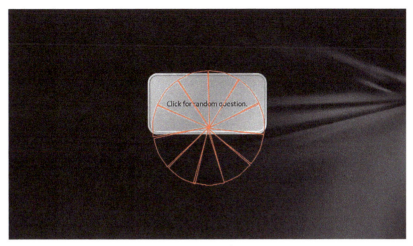

Figure 3–6

Group all the pieces of the wheel. Add an animation, Spin, to the wheel, With Previous, Slow, Repeat Until End of Slide. If you go into Slide Show view, the wheel should be spinning on top of the rounded rectangle. Next, format the wheel shape so that the fill for each shape is 100 percent transparent and select *no line*. The wheel is now transparent so that the user doesn't know what piece is being clicked since the wheel is spinning, and it is transparent. The selection now is random. Your slide 2 should now look like figure 3–7.

Figure 3–7

Browse at a Kiosk

Once you are sure that your random wheel on slide 2 is working properly and that you can randomly link to any of the eleven questions, set up the Slide Show to be *Browsed at a Kiosk*. When you do this, you won't be able to use any of the keys on the keyboard except the ESC key. If you start viewing the Slide Show from slide 1, you won't be able to move to slide 2. You need to add an action button on slide 1 to navigate to slide 2, and you need to add an action button to slide 2 to end the presentation. Save your presentation.

Custom Slide Background

Open the data file ***Lesson 3 Triggers***. Add your name as the subtitle. Save the presentation as ***Lesson 3 Triggers Your Name***. We are going to create our own background for the first slide. Click the Design tab, and in the Custom group, click Format Background. Click Pattern fill and then click on the first 50 percent pattern (row 2 and first column), and make the foreground white and the background black.

We are going to create an animation on the title slide to attract attention. However, remember *a little goes a long way*. You want your presentation viewed as a group of slides that complement one another, so settle on a few effects and use them consistently throughout the presentation. You don't want objects flying onto the screen from all directions.

On slide 1, the title slide, draw a rectangle height 1" and width 13" that stretches from the left edge of the slide to the right edge of the slide in Widescreen view. If you are using Standard view, the rectangle would be width 10". Move the rectangle on top of the title. Make the fill color Standard red, 50 percent Transparency, and No Line. Place the rectangle over the title.

Draw a rectangle 1"×6" and center it on top of the title. Make the fill color black, Background 1, 50 percent Transparency, No Line. Animate the rectangle for a Motion Path Right, With Previous, timing 3 seconds, Repeat Until End of Slide, Smooth start and Smooth end, Auto-reverse. Drag the green handle of the animation to the left edge of the slide and the red handle to the right edge of the slide. Hold down the Shift key to keep the line straight.

Make sure the rectangle you just created is selected, and press *CTRL+D* to duplicate it. Change the color to standard yellow, width 5", and place it on top of the copied rectangle. Change the animation to a Motion Path Left, With Previous, timing 3.5 seconds, Repeat Until End of Slide, Smooth start and Smooth end, Auto-reverse. Drag the green handle of the animation to the right edge of the slide and the red handle to the left edge of the slide. Hold down the Shift key to keep the line straight.

Duplicate the last rectangle you created and change the color to Standard Light blue, width 4", and place it on top of the other rectangles. Change the animation to a Motion Path Right, With Previous, timing 4 seconds, Repeat Until End of Slide, Smooth start and Smooth end, Auto-reverse. Drag the green handle of the animation to the left edge of the slide and the red handle to the right edge of the slide. Hold down the Shift key to keep the line straight.

Duplicate the last rectangle you created and change the color to white, Background 1, the width 3", and place it on top of the other rectangles. Change the animation to a Motion path left, With Previous, timing 4.5 seconds, Repeat Until End of Slide, Smooth start and Smooth end, Auto-reverse. Drag the green handle of the animation to the right edge of the slide and the red handle to the left edge of the slide. Hold down the Shift key to keep the line straight.

Select the four rectangles you animated and align them at the center and top. Move the rectangles on top of the first rectangle that you created that stretched across the entire screen. Make sure all the green and red handles for the animations are on top of one another. View the slide in Slide Show and save the presentation.

Triggers

Triggers are used to start an effect such as making an object appear or disappear, start a video, or play a sound. Before you can use a trigger, you first need to create the effect. Triggers can be very simple such as just making a shape appear, or they can be very complex involving logic and conditions. We will use more complex triggers later in this book when you learn to create simulations.

Stop Sign

Slide 2, in addition to the title, contains three objects, two Hexagon shapes with text, and a Line shape. Click on the red shape and add the effect, Bevel Angle. Repeat for the green shape. Add the effect, Bevel Circle to the line shape.

Create an oval height .2"and width .2". Add Standard red fill, No Line. Add the effect, Bevel Circle. Duplicate the oval and change the color to green.

Animate the Red or Green Sign to Appear

Click on the red hexagon shape and add an Entrance effect, Appear (Animation/Advanced Animation/Add animation/Entrance/Appear). The animation appears in the animation pane to the right of the screen. Click the down arrow at the right of the animation and select timing. In the Appear dialog box that displays, under Triggers, click Start effect on the click of, and select the first, red oval you created. The animation is numbered in the animation pane, and a mark appears next to the object in the slide pane. View slide 2 in Slide Show view. The red hexagon shape does not appear. If you click on the red oval, the trigger, it will appear.

We want the green shape to disappear when we display the red shape. Click on the green hexagon shape and add an Exit effect, Disappear, With Previous. Move the Exit effect so that it follows the Entrance effect in the animation pane as shown in figure 3–8.

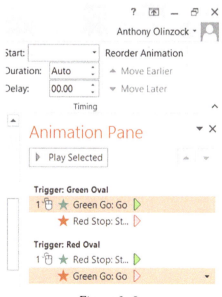

Figure 3–8

Click on the green hexagon shape and add an Entrance effect, Appear. Add a trigger for the shape to appear when you click on the second green oval you created. We want the red shape to disappear when we display the green shape. Click on the red hexagon shape and add an Exit effect, Disappear, With Previous. Move the Exit effect so that it follows the Entrance effect in the animation pane.

Create a Stop Sign

Align the green and red hexagon shapes to the center and at the top so that you can see only a single shape. Move the line shape to the bottom center of the hexagon shapes to create a stop sign. Move the green and red ovals below the bottom of the line. When you view the slide in Slide Show view, you will be able to click the red or green oval to change the sign. Add a gray background to the slide. Your working stop sign should look like figure 3–9.

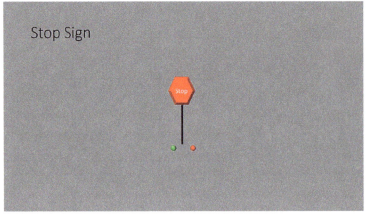

Figure 3–9

Puzzle

Slide 3 already contains a slide title, *Topic: Historical Place*. The answer to the puzzle, *Lincoln Monument,* is shown in the notes pane. A picture of the Lincoln Monument has been inserted on the slide. The gridlines are displayed to assist in sizing objects. The size of the puzzle is height 4" and width 3" or 12, 1" squares. The directions for playing the game are displayed at the bottom of the slide.

We are going to cover the puzzle with 1" squares that can be removed by clicking on them in any order. Insert a rectangle height 1" and width 1" and move it into the upper left square of the puzzle as shown in figure 3–10. Add an appropriate color to the rectangle, while the square is selected, type the number 1. Apply an effect, Bevel Angle. Add an Exit animation to square 1, Disappear. Add the trigger. Use the rectangle as the trigger for itself as shown in the animation pane. *Note: In this example, rectangle 4 with the number 1 on it is the trigger*. Duplicate the rectangle with a 1 on it and change the number to 2. Move the second shape to the right of the first rectangle. Because you copied the rectangle, the trigger is also copied, so you won't have to set it again. The trigger for rectangle 2 is rectangle 2. Add additional squares as shown in figure 3–11. Add a black background to the slide. Change the font color to white.

ADVANCED POWERPOINT: MORE THAN PRESENTATIONS!

Figure 3–10

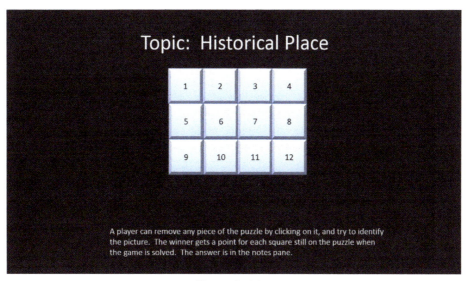

Figure 3–11

Switch to Slide Show view. You should be able to click on any piece of the puzzle to remove it.

Stop Light

Slide 4 contains a slide title, *Stop Sign*, and a *round rectangle* height 3" and width 1". Align the shape to the center and middle of the slide. Apply an effect, Bevel Hard Edge. Make three ovals, height .5" and width .5" for the lights, and color the ovals standard red, yellow, and green. Format each of the ovals for 60 percent transparent and move them onto the rounded rectangle to make the stop light as shown in figure 3–12. Align the ovals at the center and distribute vertically.

Figure 3–12

Create another oval height .5" and width .5" with Standard red fill and no outline. Apply the effect Bevel Circle, and move it on top of the first red oval. Repeat this process for the yellow and green ovals. Each of the partially transparent ovals represents the light off. The ovals with full color represent the lights on.

Below the stop light, insert four text boxes. Change light: R, Y G. *Note: Use a separate text box for Change light,* and for each of the letters *R, Y* and *G*. Align the text boxes at the top and distribute them horizontally.

Adding Triggers to Change the Light

We are going to use the letters you entered in the text boxes—*R, Y,* and *G*—to trigger the lights. Click on the red oval (full color) and add the animation Entrance Appear. Set the trigger for the animation the red R. When the red light is on, we want the yellow and green lights off. Click on the yellow oval (full color), and add an animation Exit, Disappear, With Previous. Move the animation in the animation pane below the first animation that made the red light appear. Click on the green oval (full color), and add an animation Exit, Disappear, With Previous. Move the animation in the animation pane below the last animation. Your animation pane should look like figure 3–13.

Figure 3–13

Repeat this process for the yellow light and the green light. When you have one of the lights appear, the other two have to disappear. Your completed slide and the animation pane should look similar to figure 3–14. View the slide in Slide Show view, and make sure you can use any of the letter

ADVANCED POWERPOINT: MORE THAN PRESENTATIONS!

to have any color light appear and the other two lights disappear. Add a black background with white text for the heading and the first text box.

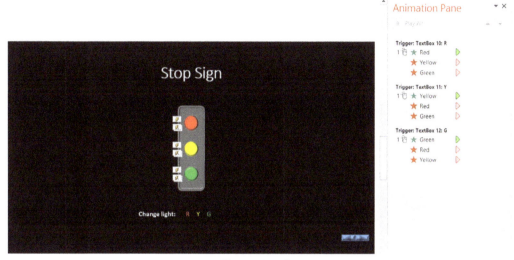

Figure 3–14

Wheel of Fortune Game

Slide 5 already has the name of the game, Wheel of Fortune; the topic for the game, Person: the game board made up of rounded rectangles height 1" and width 1", with no fill, and the letters of the alphabet as separate text boxes at the bottom of the game board.

Step 1

Enter each letter of the puzzle onto the game board. Use WordArt to enter the puzzle, *Supreme Court Judge,* as shown in figure 3–15. Notice the solution is in the notes pane at the bottom of the screen.

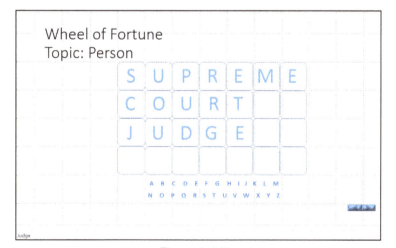

Figure 3–15

55

Step 2

Cover each letter in the puzzle with a rectangle height 1" and width 1". Select an appropriate color and effect for the square. Your slide should look similar to figure 3–16.

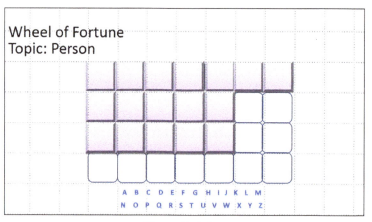

Figure 3–16

Step 3

Players will guess a letter, and that letter is clicked at the bottom of the game board. If the letter is in the puzzle, the letter will be the trigger to remove that puzzle piece or pieces.

Go through the letters of the puzzle in order:

SUPREME
COURT
JUDGE

The first letter is *S*. Click on the box covering the *S* position and add the effect Exit, Disappear. The animation will appear in the animation pane. Click the arrow next the animation and select Timing. In the Timing dialog box below, triggers select *Start effect on the click of,* and select the letter *S*. *Note: Be sure to select the letter S, not the WordArt S.* Go into Slide Show view and click on the letter *S* at the bottom of the puzzle. The box covering the letter *S* should disappear.

The next letter in the puzzle is *U*; however, there are three *U*s in the puzzle. Select each puzzle piece covering a *U* in the puzzle. There is one in each word. With the three puzzle pieces selected (hold down the *CTRL* key to select multiple pieces.), add the effect Exit, Disappear. In the animation pane all three animations are selected. Click the arrow next to the last animation. In the Timing dialog box below, triggers select *Start effect on the click of, and select the letter U*. Go into Slide Show view and click on the letter *U* at the bottom of the puzzle. The boxes covering the letters *U* should all disappear.

Repeat this process for the other letter in the puzzle. *If the player selects a letter that is not in the puzzle, when you click on that letter, nothing will happen once you set up the show to be Browsed at a Kiosk since the keyboard will be locked except for the ESC key. You will be able to click the mouse to select links activated by triggers.* Figure 3–17 shows the puzzle with the letters *S* and *U* removed.

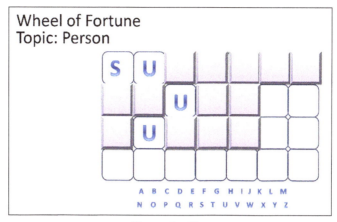

Figure 3–17

Tic Tac Toe

As you have probably realized, there are nine different *layouts* you can use for slides such as Title Slide, Title Only, or Picture with Caption. There is also a *Slide Master* for each of the layout templates, and an *Office Theme Slide Master* for all the slides in the presentation. In addition, you can create custom layouts and add additional slide masters if you want. The slide master's purpose is to let you make global changes such as replacing the font style or color or adding a picture and have those changes reflected on all the slides in the same layout, or all slides in the presentation if you use the Office Theme Slide Master. The placeholders on the slide master let you change the effects such as changing the size or color of the font for a title. You can also add objects to any of the slide masters, and those objects will appear on all slides using the same layout. The objects you add on the slide master are in the background of the slides of the same layout and can only be edited on the slide master. This feature is important for gaming since you can place a game board on the slide master so that it can be used over and over again, and is not changed by playing the game.

Slide 6 in your presentation is in Blank Layout, and no content has been entered. The gridlines should be displayed.

Step 1

In step 1, you are going to create the game board for a Tic Tac Toe game on the slide master for Blank Layout. Change the background for the slide to black. Click the View tab, and in the Master Views group, click Slide Master. In the Navigation Pane, move down and click on the Blank Layout to select it as shown in figure 3–18. The slide pane shows the blank slide with the gridlines showing. Use the gridlines as guides and the line drawing tool to draw the game board. Each line is three inches long and 3 pt weight. Use WordArt and ActiveX text boxes to complete the information on the slide master as shown.

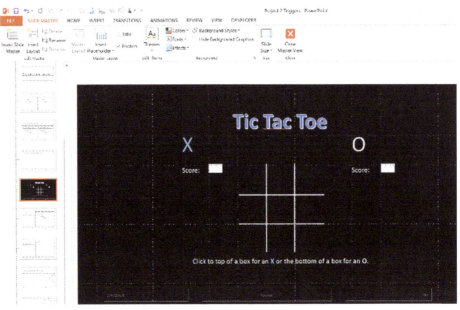

Figure 3–18

Step 2

Return to normal view, and insert WordArt to display **New Game** and position as shown in figure 3–19.

Figure 3–19

Step 3

Using WordArt, insert a capital *X* and change its color to blue. Move the letter to the center of the upper-left box in the Tic Tac Toe board (first row, first column). Draw a rectangle that covers the top one-third of letter *X* as shown in figure 3–20.

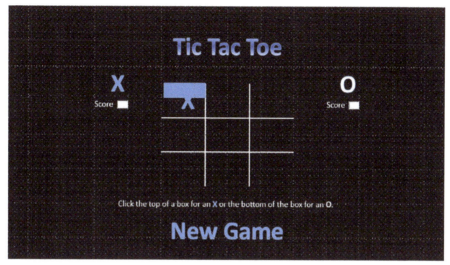

Figure 3–20

Step 4

In step 4 we are going to animate the letter *X* to appear when you click on the rectangle on top of the *X*. Click on the letter *X* to select it, and add an animation effect, Entrance, Appear. Click on the animation in the animation pane and use the rectangle as the trigger to activate the effect Appear. Run Slide Show view. The *X* should not be visible. Click on the rectangle, and the *X* should appear.

Once you have the animation working with the trigger, make the rectangle fill 100 percent Transparency with No Line. You will no longer see the rectangle. Go into Slide Show view. Click on the top portion of the box and the X will appear. Make any corrections necessary.

Once you have the animation for the *X* working in the first box, you can select the rectangle and the *X*. Hold down the Shift key and click on the rectangle and *X* as shown in figure 3–21. You can now copy and paste the *X* into each of the remaining eight places.

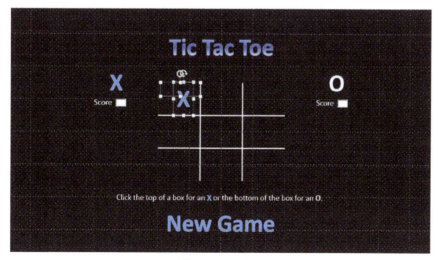

Figure 3–21

Once you have copied the *X* and rectangle to all boxes, your slide will look like figure 3–22. Each box has an *X* in it in normal view. View the presentation in Slide Show view. No *X*s are shown. You have to click the top one-third of any box to have the *X* appear. Make sure your triggers work to show *X*s in all boxes. Make any corrections needed.

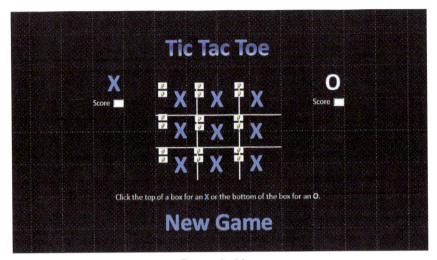

Figure 3–22

You will now repeat the process you used to enter *X*s into the squares to enter the *O*s. Use WordArt and insert a capital *O* in the first box on top of the *X* as shown in figure 3–23. You can use a white background, 1 font, color because your background is black. Cover the bottom one-third of the box with a rectangle. Click on the letter *O* to select it, and add the animation Entrance, Appear. Click on the animation in the animation pane and use the second rectangle as the trigger to activate the appear effect. Run Slide Show view. The *O* should not be visible. Click on the bottom rectangle, and the O should appear.

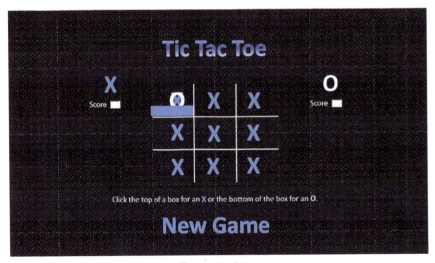

Figure 3–23

Once you have the animation for the letter *O* working properly in the first box, make the rectangle 100 percent Transparency with No Line. Copy the letter *O* and transparent rectangle to the other boxes. Your slide should look similar to figure 3–24.

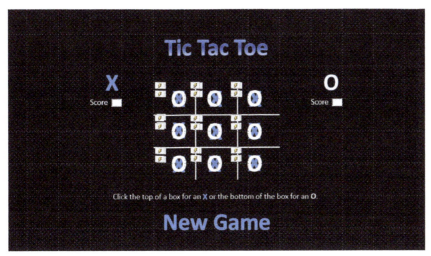

Figure 3–24

Step 5

At this point, the game can now be played in Slide Show view. You can click the top of any box to insert an *X* or the bottom of any box to enter an *O*. View slide 6 in Slide Show view and test playing the game. One limitation of the game; however, is that you can only play the game once. You could duplicate the slide to create additional game boards, but that would be a poor procedure. You need to create an animation to make all the *X*s and *O*s entered on the board disappear.

Step 6

In step 6 we are going to create a procedure to clear all the *X*s and *O*s from the game board so that it can be used over and over. Remember, anything we put on the slide master is in the background and will remain on the slide.

First, we need to select all the *X*s and *O*s. In order to do this, you might find it easier if you zoom in to make the game board larger and/or move the top transparent boxes in each square up about one-third inch. Hold down the CTRL key and click on the center of the first *X* and the right edge of the *O* in the first box to select both letters. Repeat this procedure until you have selected all the *X*s and *O*s on the game board. Once you have them all selected, apply the animation effect Exit Disappear. The animation will be applied to all the letters selected. Click the arrow next to the last animation in the animation pane for the new animation and set the trigger to be the text *New Game*. *Note: This is a difficult step, and it might take you a few tries*. If you moved the transparent rectangles, move them back into place when done. Figure 3–25 shows how the game board and animation pane look when you complete this step.

Once this step is completed, you can play the game in Slide Show view and clear the game board by clicking the *New Game* WordArt. You can keep score in the text boxes shown on the slide.

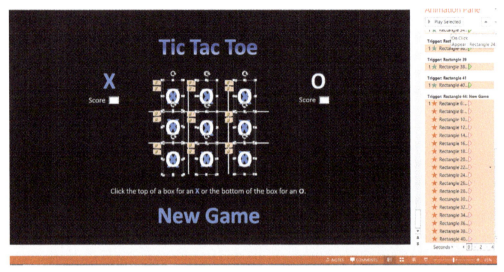

Figure 3–25

Complete the Presentation

Once you have completed all the slides, add action buttons to navigate from slide to slide using a next and previous button. Set up the Slide Show to be Browsed at a Kiosk.

Option Buttons and Check Boxes

Option buttons are used when you want the user to select only one item from a list of items. Option buttons are also called radio buttons. Once the user selects an option button, it can be changed but not removed. Figure 3–26 shows an example of the use of Option button.

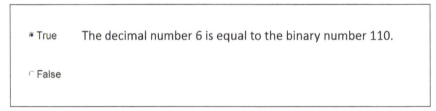

Figure 3–26

Check boxes are used when you want the user to be able to select more than one item from a list of items. You can click in the checkbox to mark it and click again to remove it. Figure 3–27 shows an example of the use of the check box.

ADVANCED POWERPOINT: MORE THAN PRESENTATIONS!

☐ Baseball   Check all sports you have participated in while in high school.

☐ Football

☐ Golf

☐ Gymnastics

☐ Tennis

☐ Track

☐ Basketball

Figure 3–27

Option Button

Open the data file ***Lesson 3 Option Button and Check Box***. Save the presentation. Add your name to the subtitle on the title slide. Slide 2 is in Title Only Layout and has a multiple-choice question in the title. You are going to use option buttons to supply four possible answers.

Display gridlines to make alignment easier. Click the Developer tab. (If it is not displayed, add it.) In the controls group, click on *Option button* and *drag and draw* the option button height .5" and width 2" as shown in figure 3–28. Make sure the Option button is still selected. Click on it if necessary to select and display the handles around it. Click the Properties tab in the Controls group to display the Property sheet as shown in figure 3–29.

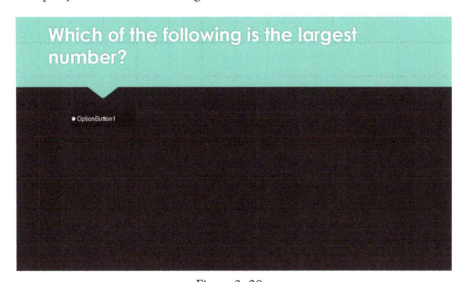

Figure 3–28

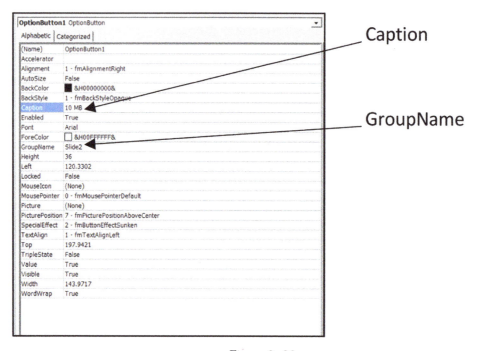

Figure 3–29

Change the *Caption* to *10 MB*, the first possible answer. Note that the *GroupName* is Slide2. For any group of option buttons with the same Group Name, you will only be able to select one button in Slide Show view.

Click on the Option button to select it and press *CTRL+D* to duplicate it. Change the caption to *50 KB*. Align it below the first option button. Add two more option buttons with the caption *2 GB* and *1 TB* as shown in figure 3–30. Use your gridlines to align the option buttons. View slide 2 in Slide Show view. You should only be able to select one Option button.

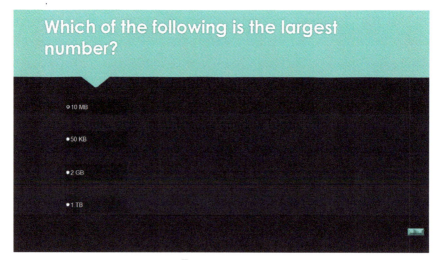

Figure 3–30

Check Box

Move to slide 3 in the presentation. Slide 3 is in title only format and has a statement in the title placeholder. In the controls group, click on *Check box* button and *drag and draw* the check box height .5" and width 2" as shown in figure 3–31. Make sure the check box button is still selected. Click on it if necessary to select it and display the handles around it. Click the *Properties* tab in the Controls group to display the Property sheet. Change the caption to the first problem in figure 3–31. There is no group name since the user can check multiple check boxes. Add three additional check boxes on shown in figure 3–31. View slide 3 in Slide Show view to make sure you can select multiple check boxes. You can remove a check by clicking on it a second time.

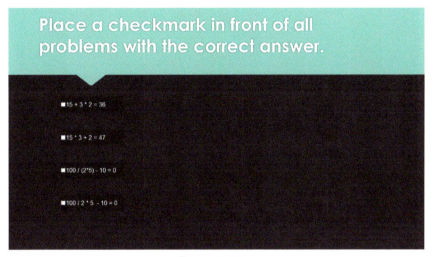

Figure 3–31

Add action buttons to navigate through the presentation. Add an Exit action button on slide 3. Add the *Cover* Transition to all slides. Setup the presentation to be Browsed at a Kiosk. Save the presentation.

Lesson 3 Applications

Lesson 3 Application 1 Presentation Application

A teacher has a computer literacy class of fifteen students. She wants to prepare a PowerPoint presentation that will be used as a review for a test on the first chapter of the computer literacy textbook. She has developed fifteen questions for the review and wants to randomly select students to answer the random questions. Open the data file ***Lesson 3 Application 1 Presentation Application***. Add your name at the end of the file name and save the file. Add your name in the subtitle on the title slide. The *Wisp* Design theme has been applied. Most of the work you will do will be to slide 2, which at this point looks like figure 3–32.

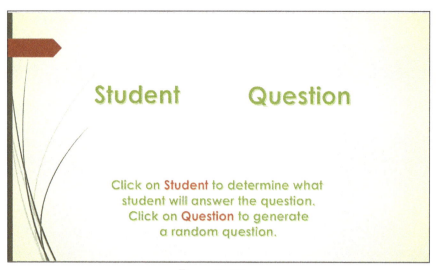

Figure 3–32

The names of the students in the class are each listed on a separate slide that is already completed, slides 3 to 17. WordArt with the message Press ESC to return is also on each slide. Make each of the slides with a student's name on it a separate Custom Show. Use the name of the student as the name of the Custom Show.

Fifteen review questions have already been prepared and are each listed on a separate slide that is already completed, slides 18 to 32, and the answer to each question is shown in the notes pane. Make each slide with a question on it a separate Custom Show. Name the Custom Show *one* for the first question, *two* for the second, etc.

You will have fifteen Custom Shows with a different student name, and you will have fifteen Custom Shows with a different question number.

Create Random Selection

On slide 2 create a wheel based on a pie chart with fifteen sections. Create a hyperlink from each section to a different Custom Show with a student's name. Be sure to check the *Show and Return* button. View slide 2 in Slide Show view and make sure each section of the wheel links to a different student's name and that pressing ESC returns you to slide 2. If you don't return to slide 2, make sure you put a check mark in the *Show and Return* box. Once you have the hyperlinks to the Custom Shows working, group the sections of the wheel. Apply an animation effect Emphasis, Spin, With Previous, Very Slow, Repeat Until End of Slide. Move the wheel so that the bottom is on top of the word *Student*. Make the wheel sections 100 percent Transparency with No Line. View slide 2 and make sure you can click on *Student* and randomly go to a student's name. Pressing ESC returns to slide 2. *Note: Your slide 2 will look like figure 3–33 before you make you wheels 100 percent Transparency with No Line.*

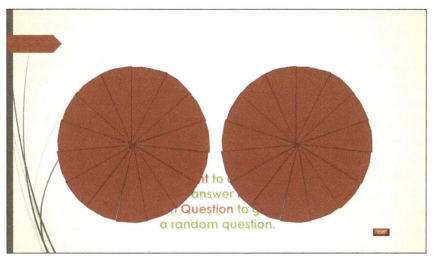

Figure 3–33

Repeat the steps you just completed to create a random selection for the fifteen questions. Move the top of the wheel over the word *Question*. Be sure to make the wheels transparent so that you can't see them.

Add an action button, Next, on slide 1. Add the effect Bevel Cool Slant to the button. Add a Custom action button to End Slide Show on slide 2. Add the word *Exit* to the button and the effect Bevel Cool Slant.

Set up the Slide Show to be Browsed at a Kiosk. Add the Transition *Fall Over* for a duration of 1.5 seconds for all slides. Substitute a different transition if you don't have the *Fall Over* Transition. Save your work. View the Slide Show from slide 1. You should only be able to use the action buttons, Links, and ESC key.

Lesson 3 Application 2 Instructional Materials Application

In this activity you will prepare a three-slide presentation as shown in figure 3–34.

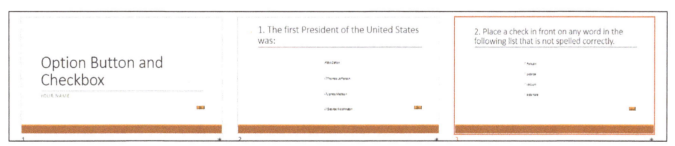

Figure 3–34

Open the data file ***Lesson 3 Application 2 Instructional Materials Application***. Add your name at the end of the file and save it again. Add an action button, Next, to the Title Slide and slide 2. Add the effect Bevel Circle. Add a Custom action button, Exit, to slide 3. Add the effect Bevel Circle. Add the *Curtain* Transition, 2 seconds duration to all slides. Set up the show to be Browsed at a Kiosk.

Go to slide 2. The question is already in the slide title. Create four option buttons for the possible answers as shown. Be sure to align the option buttons.

Go to slide 3. The statement is already in the title slide. Add the four check boxes with some words spelled correctly and others not.

Set up the presentation to be Browsed at a Kiosk. Save your presentation as a PowerPoint Macro-Enabled presentation.

Lesson 3 Application 3 Gaming Application

Games in which more than one player can play the game at the same time usually include some type of procedure to determine which person will go first. Also, board games usually include a procedure to determine how many spaces a player can move on the board. Two common random procedures are flipping a coin or rolling dice.

Flipping a Coin

Open the data file **Lesson 3 Application 3 Gaming Application**. Add your name to the file name and save the file. The *Organic* theme has been applied to the presentation. Replace the subtitle placeholder on the Title slide with your name.

In Normal view, use the Page Down key to view the slides in the presentation. Note that slide 2 is in Title and Content Layout. The bulleted items will be used as a menu. Slide 3 has a button to click to flip a coin, and slides 4 and 5 each have an illustration of a hand with a coin sitting on the thumb. On slide 4 the coin shows heads, and on slide 5 the coin shows tails.

Step 1 – Flipping a Coin

Make slide 4 a Custom Show with the name *heads*, and make slide 5 a Custom Show with the name *tails*.

Step 2 – Flip Coin Animation

Next, you need to animate the hand and coin on each of the slides. On slide 4, click on the hand and have it Appear, With Previous, Spin 30° Counterclockwise, Fast. Click on the coin and have it Appear With Previous, and add a Custom Motion Path Up to the center of the slide and Down to the lower, middle portion of the slide. Hold the left mouse button as you *drag and draw* the Motion Path. Double-click the mouse at the end of the path. Have the Motion Path start With Previous, Medium speed. Click on the coin again and add the Emphasis animation, Spin, Fast, With Previous, Repeat 3. Repeat these steps on slide 5. Figure 3–35 shows slide 4 including the Animation Pane.

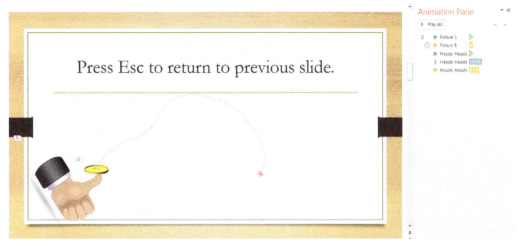

Figure 3–35

Step 3 – Random Wheel

Develop a random wheel on top of the rounded rectangle on slide 3. The wheel needs to have two sections. One section will hyperlink to the Custom Show Tails, and one will hyperlink to the Custom Show Heads. Be sure to click *Show and Return* for each hyperlink. Group the shapes. Add an Emphasis animation, Spin, With Previous, Repeat Until End of Slide. Make the shape fill 100 percent Transparency with No Line. View slide 3 in Slide Show view. You should be able to click on the rounded rectangle and randomly go to the Tails or Heads Custom Show. Pressing ESC should return you to slide 3.

Dice

Slide 6 has an image of dice already inserted on it. Slides 7 to 12 have a title inserted: *Press Esc to return to previous slide.* In addition, an image of a die is off the slide at the top left of the screen. These dice were made with a cube shape and ovals. Each of the die has a different number on the top portion of the slide ranging from 1 to 6.

Step 1 – Animate Throw of Dice

Go to slide 7. Click on the die at the top left of the screen. Animate the die for Motion Path Turn Down Right. Drag the red handle to the bottom center of the screen. The animation should be With Previous, Medium speed. Click on the die again, and add an Emphasis animation, Spin, With Previous, Very Fast, Repeat 3. View slide 7 in Slide Show view to make sure the animation is working properly.

Animate the die on slides 8 to 12 the same as slide 7. You can click on the die on slide 7 and; click on the Animation tab, and in the Advance Animation group, click Animation painter. Move to another slide and click on the die and the animation will be applied. See figure 3–36.

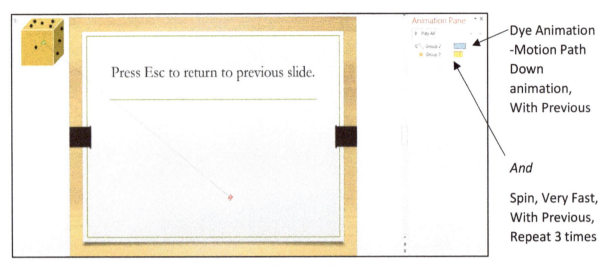

Figure 3–36

Step 2 – Make Each Slide with a Die a Separate Custom Show

Make each slide with a die on it a separate Custom Show, starting with slide 7. Name each Custom Show the number on top of the die on that slide. Slide 7 will be Custom Show Five, for example. When you are done, make sure you have Custom Shows 1 to 6.

Step 3 – Random Wheel

Create a wheel with six different sections and place it on top of the dice on slide 6. Create a hyperlink from each of the sections to one of the die slides, 1 to 6. Be sure to click Show and Return. Go into Slide Show view from slide 6 and make sure each section of the wheel takes you to a different die animation and that pressing ESC returns you to slide 6. Correct any errors. Group the shape. Add an Emphasis animation, Spin, With Previous, Repeat Until End of Slide. Make the shape fill 100 percent Transparency with No Line. View slide 6 in Slide Show view. You should be able to click on the dice image and randomly go to the one of the die animations. Pressing ESC should return you to slide 3.

Completing the Slide Show

Add an action button, Next slide to slide 1.

On slide 2, create a hyperlink from the Flip Coin text to slide 3. Create a hyperlink from Throw Dice text to slide 6. Create a hyperlink from Exit text to End Slide Show. On slide 3, create a Custom Button named *menu* that returns the user to the menu, slide 2; copy the *menu* button to slide 6.

Apply the *Peal Off* Transitions to all slides for a duration of one second. Substitute another Transition if you don't have that Transition.

Set up the presentation to be Browsed at a Kiosk. Save your presentation.

LESSON 4

3-D, Animating Static Objects, Game Boards, VBA

Data Files

Lesson 4 Creating an Animation from a Clip Art
Lesson 4 Introduction to 3-D
Lesson 4 Application 1 Presentation Application
Lesson 4 Application 2 Instructional Materials Application
Lesson 4 Application 3 Gaming Application

Overview

In Lesson 4 you will learn to create 3-D objects using 3-D format and 3-D rotation. You will also learn how to use various picture effects, 3-D rotation, 3-D format and animation to create an animation from Clip Art. Finally, you will begin to learn to create electronic game boards for apps and gaming.

Introduction to 3-D

Open the data file *Lesson 4 Introduction to 3-D*. Add your name at the end of the file name and save the file. Replace the text in the subtitle place holder on the title slide with your name. The Parallax Design theme has already been applied to the presentation.

Add Animation to Title Slide

There are times when you might want to add animation to the design theme to attract attention. We are going to add an animation to the title slide similar to the one you completed in the last lesson.

Slide 2 contains five rectangles of different lengths and color, height 1.6". Size the top rectangle to the width of your screen, either standard or wide screen. The width for the other rectangles is 6", 5", 4", and 3". Complementary colors to the design theme have already been selected. All rectangles are 50 percent Transparency with No Line. Copy the rectangles to slide 1 as shown. The longest rectangle is on the bottom and the shortest is on top. Select all the rectangles and align them to the center and to the top as shown in figure 4–1. Move them on top of the title and subtitle with equal space above and below the title. The title will be covered by the rectangles. Delete slide 2.

Figure 4–1

Click on the smallest rectangle that is width 3" and white, Background 1. Add an animation, Motion Path Right, With Previous, 12 seconds. Click the Effect tab and click Auto-reverse and Smooth Start and Smooth End. Drag red button or arrow to the right edge of the slide and the green button or arrow to the left edge of the slide as shown in figure 4–2. Hold the Shift key to keep the path straight.

Click on rectangle that is width 4" and Light blue color. Add a Motion Path, Left, With Previous, 10 seconds, Repeat Until End of Slide. Click the Effect tab and click Auto-reverse and Smooth Start and Smooth end. Drag the red button or arrow to the left edge of the side and the green button or arrow to the right edge of the slide as shown in figure 4–2.

Click on the rectangle that is width 5" and blue color. Add a Motion Path, Right, With Previous, 8 seconds, Repeat Until End of Slide. Click the effect tab and click Auto-reverse and Smooth Start and Smooth End. Drag the sizing adjustment handle, red button or arrow to the right edge of the side and the green button or arrow to the left edge of the slide as shown in figure 4–2.

Click on the rectangle that is width 6" and black, Text 1, Lighter 5 percent. Add a Motion Path, Left, With Previous, 6 seconds, Repeat Until End of Slide. Click the Effect tab and click Auto-reverse and Smooth Start and Smooth End. Drag red button or arrow to the left edge of the side and the green button or arrow to the right edge of the slide as shown in figure 4–2.

Add 3-D in a new text box (Insert/Text/Text Box/Draw Text Box), in 54 pt Corbel font. Format the text for a Perspective Relaxed rotation by selecting the text box and click the Format tab, and in the Shape Styles group, select 3-D rotation, Perspective Relaxed. Change the font color to red and drag the text in place after *Introduction to* in the title. Click on the new text box and copy and paste a new copy of the text, 3-D, on top of the original text box. Change the color of the font on top to dark blue. Add an Emphasis Animation, Blink, Very Slow, With Previous, Repeat Until End of Slide. Bring the two text boxes with 3-D to the front of the other objects on the slide.

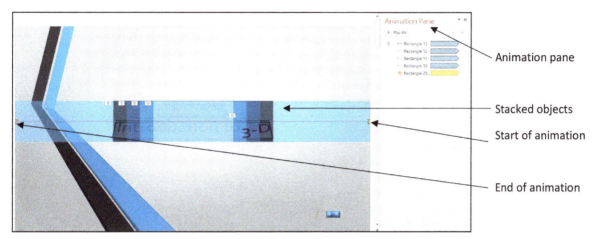

Figure 4–2

View the slide in Slide Show view to make sure it is working properly. All the rectangles except the bottom one are moving back and forth across the screen at different speeds.

Slide 2 – 3-D Cube

Your new slide 2 contains three images of fish, each sized height 3.5" and width 3.5". We are going to make a cube shape out of the three images. Click on the image of the shark. Right-click and select Format Picture. Click 3-D Rotation and from the Presets options and select Off Axis, 1 Top. Click the school of fish and apply the 3-D Rotation Off Axis, 1 Right. Click the image of the goldfish and apply the 3-D Rotation Off Axis, 1 Left. Move the three images to create a cube as shown in figure 4–3. Draw a rectangle 3.5"×3.5", add fill black, Text 1, No Line. Add the effect Soft Edge 25 pt. Apply a 3-D rotation, Off Axis 1 Top. Position the rectangle below the cube as shown in figure 4–3. Animate all four shapes on the slide for Entrance, Fade In, With Previous, Very Slow. View the slide in Slide Show view to see the effect.

Figure 4–3

Duplicate the three images that make up the cube. Change the rotation so that the goldfish is on top, the shark is in the front, and the school of fish is on the side. The animation also copied, so change the first of the three new animations in the animation pane to After Previous. View slide 2 in Slide Show view to see the effect.

Duplicate the three images again. Change the rotation so that the school of fish is on top, the goldfish is in the front, and the shark is on the side. Change the first of the three new animations to After Previous. View slide 2 in Slide Show view to see the effect.

Slide 3 – Steps

As you learn more about 3-D, you will see that you can create 3-D images by changing the rotation, format, and effects of objects. On slide 3 you are going to create three sets of steps: one set will face forward, one will face right, and one will face left.

To create a set of stairs facing right, follow these steps:

- Create a rectangle height 1.2" and width 2.5". Change the fill color black, Text 1, Lighter 50 percent and No Line.
- Right-click on the shape and apply 3-D rotation, Off Axis 1 Top.
- Set the 3-D format for Bevel, Circle, Top height 8 pt and width 8 pt; set the Depth to white, Background 1, 40 pt; set the Angle to 80°; set the Surface Material to Warm Matte; and set the Lighting to 2 pt.
- Duplicate the shape three times and arrange them as a set of stairs facing right as shown in figure 4–4.

To create a set of stairs facing left, follow these steps:
- Duplicate one of the steps facing right.
- Change the 3-D rotation to Off Axis 2 Top.

- Duplicate the shape three times and arrange them as a set of stairs facing left as shown in figure 4–4.

To create the stairs facing front, follow these steps.
- Duplicate one of the steps.
- Change the 3-D rotation to Perspective Front.
- Change the y Rotation to 290° and the Perspective to 45°.
- Duplicate the shape three times and arrange them as a set of stairs facing front as shown in figure 4–4.

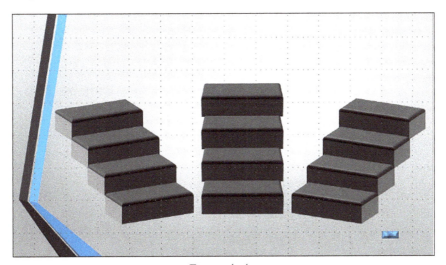

Figure 4–4

Slide 4 – Bookshelf

Copy the top step on the stairs facing the front from slide 3. Remember, 3-D rotation, 3-D Format, and effects all contribute to creating 3-D images. With just a few minor adjustments, we will create a bookshelf from the one step you copied.

Right-click on the shape. Go to 3-D rotation and change the rotation to 280°. Go to 3-D format and change the lighting to Contrasting, and change the material to Clear. Make three copies of the image and stack them to form a bookshelf as shown in figure 4–5. Insert a rectangle, gray, No Line, the size of the bookshelf, and send it to the back to represent the back of the bookshelf. Insert an illustration of books from online pictures or Clip Art. Ungroup the image and remove any unnecessary parts and then Regroup the image. Size and place the books in the bookshelf as shown in figure 4–5.

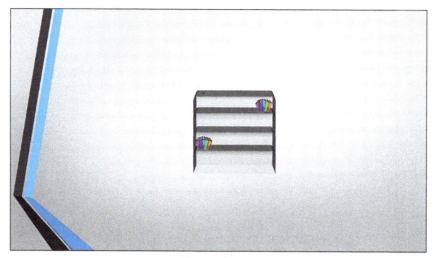

Figure 4–5

Slide 5 – Bouncing 3-D Balls into a Basket

Your data file, slide 5, has an image of a basket inserted. If you wanted to place balls in the basket, they would all be in front of the basket because objects are inserted on top of one another. To create the image that the balls are filling the basket, the basket must be cropped in two pieces with the back section layered behind the front section as show in figure 4–6.

Duplicate the basket image. Crop (Format/Size/Crop) the basket as shown in figure 4–6. Bring Forward the Front section of the basket (Format/Arrange/Bring Forward/Bring to Front), and Send Backward the back section of the basket (Format/Arrange/Send Backward/Sent to Back). Align the two sections of the basket at the left so that it looks like a single image. Move the images to the lower right corner of the screen.

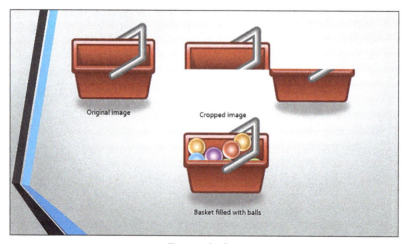

Figure 4–6

Creating 3-D Ball Images

To create the image of a ball, insert an oval height .6" and width .6". Right-click on the image and select Format Shape. Select Gradient fill, Radial, From Center. Set three gradient stops at 0 percent, 50 percent, and 100 percent. Using the Theme Colors, set the color positon 0 percent to blue, Accent 1, Lighter 80 percent; set the color for position 50 percent to blue, Accent 1, Darker 25 percent; and set the color for positon 100 percent to white, Background 1. Select No Line.

Add the 3-D Format, Bevel Circle, height 4 pt and width 10 pt. Set the Material to Powder and the Lighting to Flat. Add an Inside Center Shadow, black, Text 1, add an effect, Glow, black, Text 1, Lighter 50 percent, 85 percent Transparency.

Click on the ball shape, and press Ctrl+D to duplicate it four times. You can change the color of the four new balls by just changing the color of first two gradient positions, 0 percent and 50 percent to a different theme color such as the 0 stop to Lime, Accent 1, Light 80 percent and 50 stop to Lime Accent 1, Darker 25 percent. Make each of the new ball image a different color as shown in figure 4–7. Align the five ball images at the top and distribute them horizontally. Make copies of the balls and place them in the basket at various places, some in front of others. You might need to bring the balls forward or send backward so that they appear to be in the basket.

Next, we are going to animate the balls to bounce up and down twice at different speeds and different distances (Animation/Advanced Animation/Add Animation/More Motion Paths/Add Motion Path/Down). Click on the first ball shape at the top. Add a Motion Path Down, With Previous, 10 seconds, Smooth Start and Smooth End, Auto-reverse. Drag the red handle or arrow down to change the distance of the animation. Repeat this process for the other ball shapes, but select a different distance and time for each shape. All animations should be With Previous.

Finally, add a Custom Path to the first ball that moves it into the basket. Make the animation After Previous and the speed 2 seconds. If necessary, use the Bring Forward and/or Send Backward options in the arrange group. Repeat this process for the remaining 4 balls.

Figure 4–7

Slide 6 – Staircase

Slide 6 has a staircase facing right on it as shown in figure 4–8.

Figure 4–8

Step 1

To create the first step,
1. Use the Line Curve tool and draw a line, height .5"and width .5", as shown in figure 4–8. Hold down the Ctrl key to keep the line straight, click again to change the direction of the line. Double-click to end the line drawing.
2. Change the Line color to black Text 1, Lighter 50 percent.
3. Change the line weight to 3 pt.

Step 2

1. Format shape 3-D Rotation, Off Axis 2 Left.
2. Change the 3-D Format to Depth Size 100 pt, black, Text 1, Lighter 50 percent.
3. Change the Material to Soft Edge; Lighting, Harsh.
4. Change the Contour Color, to white, Background 1, Lighter 50 percent.
5. Duplicate the shape three times and arrange as shown in figure 4–8.

Step 3

1. Create a rectangle height 1" and width 4".
2. Format the rectangle for white, Background 1, Darker 50 percent, No Line.
3. Add a Shape Effect, Soft Edge, 25 pt.
4. Add a Shape Effect, Glow, 18 pt, white, Background 1, Darker 25 percent.
5. Apply a 3-D Rotation, Off Axis 2 Top. Use the rotation handle to adjust the rotation. Send the shape to back, position as shown in figure 4–8.
6. Copy two of the balls from slide 5. Delete the animations for the balls copied. Move the first ball off the screen to the top. Use a Custom Path, With Previous, 10 seconds, and have

the ball fall down from the top of the screen, bounce on the steps, and move off the screen to the right. Repeat these steps for the second ball, but make the animation After Previous and the time 12 seconds. *Note: If necessary, bring the ball objects to the front.*

Slide 7 – Animated 3-D Billboard

On slide 7 you are going to create an animated billboard as shown in figure 4–9. Size the city picture to height 10" and width 10" with a 50 pt Soft Edge. Align to Center and Middle. Insert a rounded rectangle height 2.5" and width 3.5" with Fill color and Line color of black, Text 1. Add a 3-D Rotation Off Axis 1 Right, and center it on top of the existing billboard in the illustration. Apply the 3-D Bevel Circle format to the Top Bevel, with a Depth of 10 pt.

Next, you will create of a light bulb that will be used to outline the entire billboard. Insert an oval shape .2"×.2", No Line. Add a gradient fill, Radial from center, 0 percent white, Background 1; 50 percent yellow; 100 percent black, Text 1. Add a Shadow, Inside Center, black, Lighter 50 percent. Add a Glow 12 percent, black, Lighter 50 percent. Add a format 3-D, Bevel Circle. Add the animation Emphasis, Pulse, .2 seconds, With Previous, Repeat Until End of Slide. Duplicate the shape as many times as necessary to outline the billboard as shown in figure 4–9.

Next, you will add text and animation to the billboard. The text will be three lines:

Deidra
Live
in concert!

Create the text using WordArt and rotate as necessary to align with the billboard. The first line of the text will be animated for Entrance, Zoom, Very Slow, With Previous, Delay 2 seconds. The same text will be animated to Exit, Disappear, After Previous, Delay 2 seconds.

Lines 2 and 3 of the text will be animated for Entrance, Zoom, Very Slow, After Previous, Delay 2 seconds, and animation Exit, Disappear, After Previous, Delay 2 seconds.

Use the Zoom animation to have the photo of *Deidra* zoom in to the billboard Very Slow, After Previous, Delay 2 seconds. Adjust the picture as necessary. Do not make the image disappear. Draw an oval around the picture with no fill and a yellow line and yellow glow, rotate as necessary. Add the animation Emphasis, Pulse, After Previous, .1 seconds, Repeat Until End of Slide. Add a slide Transition of your choice. Add action buttons to navigate the presentation. Your slide 7 will look like figure 4–9 when Browsed in Slide Show view.

Figure 4–9

Creating Animation from Clip Art

Open the data file *Lesson 4 Creating an Animation from Clip Art*. Add your name to the file name and save the presentation. Add your name in the subtitle placeholder on the title slide. The Main Event Design theme has already been applied to the presentation.

Slide 3 – Animation

On slide 3, we are going to use the Clip Art from slide 2 to create an animation where an athlete will perform an exercise on the trampoline and the judges will give her a score after the animation.

Creating the Background

To create the gym floor, draw a rectangle, height 5", across the width of the screen. Add a Texture Fill, Medium Wood, No Line. Draw a rectangle to cover the remainder top portion of the screen—light blue, No Line.

Creating the Judges' Table

Copy the judges' table from slide 2 and place it on slide 3 in the upper, left section. Ungroup the illustration (Format/Arrange/Group/Ungroup), delete the red number scores, and group the illustration again. Duplicate the illustration so that you have two illustrations. Use WordArt to create three separate scores, *9.0, 10* and *9.5*. Use red fill for the text color for the WordArt and size to 24 pt. Refer to figure 4–10.

Creating the Gymnast and Trampoline

Copy the gymnast and trampoline illustration from slide 2 to slide 3. Ungroup the illustration and delete the blue background. Select all the sections representing the gymnast and group them as a separate object. Select all the sections representing the trampoline and group them as a separate object as shown in figure 4–10. Size the two images as needed.

People Image

Copy the image of the people from slide 2 and paste it on to slide 3, placing it in the upper right corner as shown in figure 4–10.

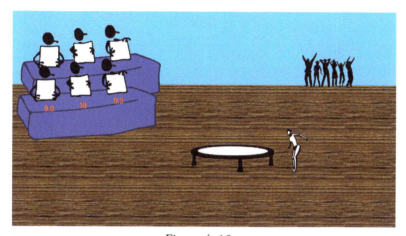

Figure 4–10

Dimming the lights

Draw a rectangle that covers the entire slide. Use black, Text 1 as the fill color, No Line. Make the fill 25 percent Transparency. Add an animation Entrance, Fade, With Previous, 10 seconds. View slide 3 in Slide Show view so that you can see how the dim effect works.

Create the Spotlight

Move the transparent black rectangle off the screen to the bottom and move the image of the trampoline to the bottom center of the screen, and position the gymnast on top of the trampoline. If necessary, bring the image of the trampoline to the front and the gymnast in front of the trampoline. Move the back rectangle back on top of the slide. The second set of judges, the numbers, the gymnast, and the trampoline need to be in front of the black rectangle.

Draw a Trapezoid shape (listed under basic shapes) that extends from above the top of the screen beyond the bottoms of the screen as shown in figure 4–11. Add a Gradient Fill, Linear, Top Right to Bottom Left; 0 percent yellow, 50 percent Transparency; 20 percent white, Background 1, 60 percent Transparency; and 100 percent white, Background 1, 70 percent Transparency. Add a 50 pt Soft Edge.

Animate the shape for Entrance, Appear, After Previous and Emphasis, Teeter, With Previous, .1 seconds, Repeat Until End of Slide. Your slide in Slide Show view will look like figure 4–11.

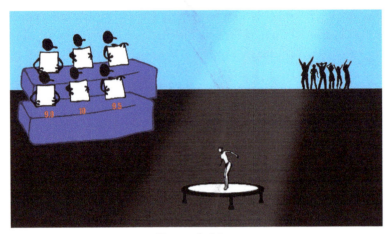

Figure 4–11

Animate the Gymnast

The gymnast and trampoline should be in front of the black rectangle used to create the image of lights dimming and the spotlight.

Animation 1 Motion Path Up and Down Twice

Click on the gymnast and add a Motion Path Up, After Previous, Medium, Repeat 2, Auto-reverse with Smooth Start and Smooth End. Adjust the starting point, green arrow, so that the gymnast starts the animation in the middle of the trampoline and adjust the red arrow so that it stretches up to the blue background.

Animation 2 Motion Path Up and Down with a Clockwise Spin

Click on the gymnast and add a Motion Path Up, After Previous, Medium, Auto-reverse with Smooth Start and Smooth End. Adjust the starting and ending point as necessary. Add an Emphasis, Spin, With Previous, Delay .5 seconds.

Animation 3 Motion Path Up and Down with Two Counterclockwise Spins

Click on the gymnast and add a Motion Path Up, After Previous, Medium, Auto-reverse. Adjust the starting and ending point as necessary. Add an Emphasis, Spin, Repeat 2, Counterclockwise, Fast, With Previous, Delay .5 seconds.

Animation 4 Custom Motion Path Off the Trampoline to the Left and onto the Floor

Click on the gymnast and draw a Custom Motion Path off the trampoline and onto the floor, 2 seconds, After Previous. Figure 4–12 shows slide 3 after you create the animation for the gymnast.

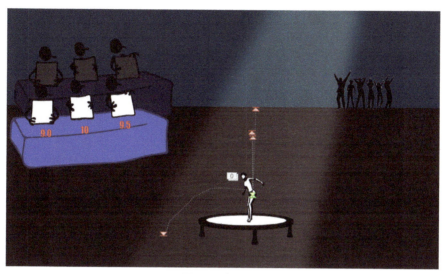

Figure 4–12

Move the Spotlight and Display Judges' Scores

Move the second image of the judges exactly on top of the first image. The first image should be behind the black rectangle, and second image of the judges should be on top of the black rectangle. Move each of the numbers, 9.0, 10, and 9.5 on top of one of the score boards held by the judges.

Click in the middle of the spotlight and draw a Custom Motion Path to the middle of the judges, After Previous.

Have the Second Image of the Judges and the Scores Appear

Click on the second image of the judges, it should be in front of the black rectangle. Add and animation Entrance, Appear, After Previous. Click on the score for the first judge, the right most score, and add an animation Entrance, Appear, After Previous, Delay, .5 seconds. Click on the score for the second judge, and add an animation Entrance, Appear, After Previous, Delay, .5 seconds. Click on the score for the third judge, and add an animation Entrance, Appear, After Previous, Delay, .5 seconds. Figure 4–13 shows slide 3 in Slide Show view at the end of all animations.

Figure 4–13

Slide 5 – Animation

Copy the Clip Art image on slide 4 to slide 5. Increase the size of the Clip Art and ungroup it. Group all parts of the man's head as a single object. Group all parts of the boy's head as a single object, and all other parts of the man and boy as a separate object as shown in figure 4–14.

Figure 4–14

Place the head of the man and boy back into the original position. Animate the man's head to Spin Clockwise 20°, With Previous, Slow, Auto-reverse. Animate the boy's head to Spin Clockwise 20°, After Previous, Slow, Auto-reverse. View slide 5 in Slide Show view, and save the presentation.

Use Visual Basic Applications (VBA) to Create a Macro in PowerPoint

We are going to write a simple macro that will display the text *Hello, my name is Your Name*. Open a new Blank PowerPoint presentation. On the title slide add the title, *VBA*, and *your name* as the subtitle.

Click the Developer tab, and in the Code group click Macros. In the Macro Name dialog box, enter the name *Hello*, and click the *create* button. A *module* is inserted, and part of the code for the macro is written as shown in figure 4–15. Although VBA stores codes in several ways, the most common way is to write the code in a module. You are now working in what is called the Integrated Development Environment or IDE. You can return to your PowerPoint presentation by clicking the PowerPoint button on the ribbon at the top of the screen. You can return back to the module by clicking Visual Basic in the Code group under the Developer tab.

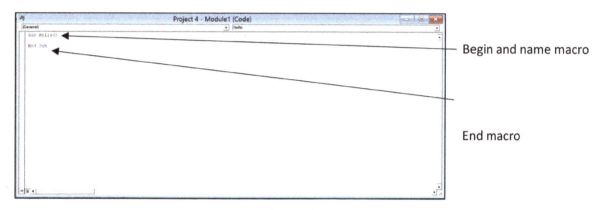

Figure 4–15

If you clicked on the Macros tab in the Code group, you would see the name of the macro you created, *Hello*. If you click on the name of the macro and click Run, the macro would run, but you wouldn't see anything because you didn't write any code between the line that started and named the macro, *Sub Hello()*, and the line that ends the macro, *End Sub*.

We are going to write one line of code between the two lines displayed that will display the message *Hello, my name is your name* when you run the macro. We will indent the line to make it easier to identify the code we write.

Place your cursor below the line *Sub Hello ()* and press tab. Type the line exactly as shown in the figure 4–16, *MsgBox ("Hello, my name is Your Name.")*, but replace *Your Name* with your *first name*.

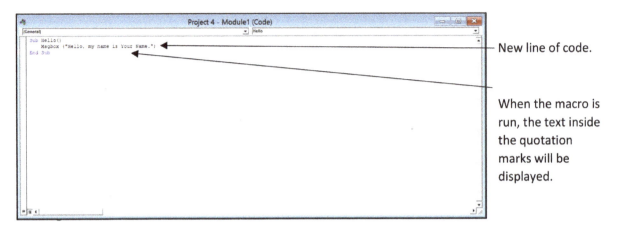

Figure 4–16

Run Macro

To run the macro you have written, return to PowerPoint and click Macros in the code group. Click on the name of the macro and click *run*. The message box shown in figure 4–17 will be displayed. Click OK to close the box.

Figure 4–17

Create a new macro named *Correct* that displays the word *Correct* when the macro is run. Create a new macro named *Incorrect* that displays the word *Incorrect* when the macro is run.

The code for the three macros you have written is shown in figure 4–18.

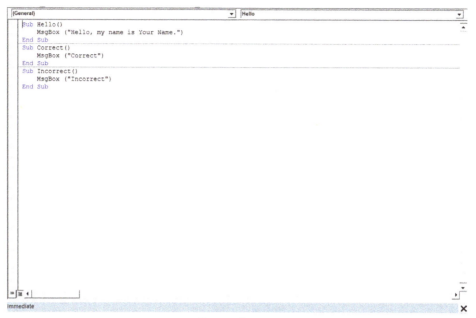

Figure 4–18

Save the Presentation

Remember, you must save a presentation with a macro as a PowerPoint Macro-Enabled presentation. Save your presentation as ***Lesson 4 VBA 1 Your Name***, a PowerPoint Macro-Enabled Presentation.

Lesson 4 Applications

Lesson 4 Application 1 Presentation Application

Open the data file ***Lesson 4 Application 1 Presentation Application***. Add your name to the file name and save the file again. Add your name to replace the subtitle placeholder.

Creating the Basket

Slide 2 has an image of a basketball net and basketball player. The *Retrospect* Design has already been applied. You are going to create a ball and place it in the player's hand and add a Custom animation so that the ball moves from his hand up and down through the net with an ending bounce. Make a copy of the basketball net so that you have two images. Ungroup the first image of the basketball net and delete as much of the Gold color objects as you can, then group the image again. Ungroup the second image of the basketball net and delete as much of the blue- and gray-colored objects as you can; then group the image again. See figure 4–19. *Note: If you use the zoom slider on the task bar to increase the size of the objects displayed, it will be easier to complete this step.* Move the blue image to the back and the gold image to the front to form one basket again.

Figure 4–19

Creating the Ball

Draw an oval shape, height .6" width .6". Add a Gradient Fill, Radial, From Center, No Line. Use four gradient positions and apply the following colors to each position:

0 percent white, Background 1
30 percent orange Accent 2, lighter 40 percent
85 percent orange Accent 2, darker 25 percent
100 percent orange Accent 2, darker 50 percent

Apply a 3-D format, Top Bevel Circle, height 10 pt and width 10 pt, Material, Warm Matte, Lighting 3 pt. Add a Shadow, Inner Center, black, Text 1. See figure 4–19.

Arrange the objects on the slide as shown in figure 4–20. The blue part of the basket should be sent to the back and the gold part of the basket should be brought to the front. The ball should be in front of the blue part of the basket, but behind the gold part of the basket.

Click on the center of the ball and draw Custom Path up and down through the bottom of the basket, With Previous, Slow, Repeat Until End of Slide, Smooth Start and Smooth End, Bounce End .75 seconds.

Add appropriate action buttons to navigate through the presentation and set up the presentation to be Browsed at a Kiosk. Save your file.

Figure 4–20

Lesson 4 Application 2 Instructional Materials Application

Open the data file ***Lesson 4 Application 2 Instructional Materials Application*** and add your name in the subtitle placeholder. Save the file. The *Banded* Design theme has already been applied. Instructions for completing this lesson are shown on slide 2 of the presentation. In this lesson, you will create and run two macros. Add necessary action buttons to navigate through the presentation and set it up to be Browsed at a Kiosk.

Lesson 4 Application 3 Gaming Application

In the activity, you will prepare game pieces, a random wheel, and a simple game board. In this job the game pieces won't move, and the game board will not be active. The goal is to learn how to create game pieces and a sample game board. In a future lesson, we will use macros so that you can click on a game piece to move it, and click on any space on the game board to move the game piece to that location.

Open the data file ***Lesson 4 Application 3 Gaming Application***. Add your name to replace the subtitle placeholder on the title slide and save the presentation again. The *Ion Boardroom* theme Design has been applied, and action buttons have been integrated into the design to navigate the presentation.

Slide 2 – Game Pieces

On slide 2 we are going to create three game pieces as shown in figure 4–21. We will create the first game piece and then duplicate it and change the font color and shape fill.

Draw an oval height 1.5" and width 1.5" with a White Marble Texture Fill and No Line. Make sure the object is selected and type the number *1*. Size the number to 100 pt, and change the color to black, Text 1, Lighter 50 percent. Add a Shadow, Inner Diagonal Bottom Left to the text. Add a 3-D Format Bevel Angle to the top and Bevel Circle to the bottom of the shape. Change the Depth to 5 pt. Select Warm Matte for the Material and Soft for the Lighting. Change the Angle to 110 percent. Change the 3-D Rotation to Off Axis 1 Top.

Duplicate the first game piece, and change the number to 2, the text color to dark purple, Text 2, Lighter 40 percent. Change the texture fill to Blue Tissue Paper.

Duplicate the second game piece, and change the number to 3, the text color to orange, Accent 4, lighter 40 percent. Change the texture fill to Pink Tissue Paper.

Figure 4–21

Slide 3 – Game Wheel
Step 1

Slide three contains all the objects that you will need to create the wheel that will look like figure 4–22 when completed.

Figure 4–22

Move the red oval that is divided into six equal pieces to the center of the slide. One of the pieces was traced from a pie chart and then duplicated five times. The six pieces were then arranged into an oval shape.

Move the gold donut shape on top of the oval so that it serves as the border.

Move the gold oval to the center of the red oval.

Select the three shapes, red oval, gold donut shape, and gold oval and align them at the center. Group these three pieces.

Move the arrow shape and the rectangle shape with text as shown in figure 4–22. Select the grouped shape, the arrow, and the rectangle with text and align them at the center so that your slide looks like figure 4–22.

Step 2

In step 2 we will add the animation to start and stop the wheel. Click on the oval shape that makes up the wheel, and add an animation, Emphasis spin, Very Fast, Until Next Click. Display the Animation Pane and click on the animation. Click the arrow at the right, click Timing, and under Triggers select *Start effect on click of:* and select the rectangle with the text: *Click to start and stop*.

Click on the oval shape again and add an animation Emphasis, Spin, *Quarter Spin*, Very Fast. Display the animation pane and click on the animation. Click the arrow at the right, click timing, and under triggers click *Start effect on click of:* and select the rectangle with the text: *Click to start and top*. Your Animation Pane should look like figure 4–23. The last animation you added must be the last animation in the animation pane.

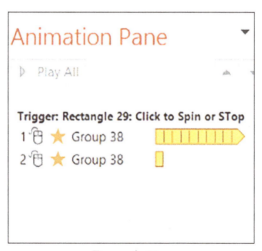

Figure 4–23

In Slide Show view, you should now be able to click the rectangle box to start the wheel spinning and to click it again to stop the spinning.

Slide 4 – Simple Game Board, Part 1

Create a rectangle shape height 1" and width 1". Add a Gradient Fill, Rectangular from Center, Bevel Slope, height 20 pt and width 6 pt. Gradient colors are white, background 1 at position 0 percent and Lavender Accent 5, Lighter 40 percent at position 100 percent. Duplicate the shape to create the game board shown in figure 4–24. Be sure that all the shapes are aligned properly.

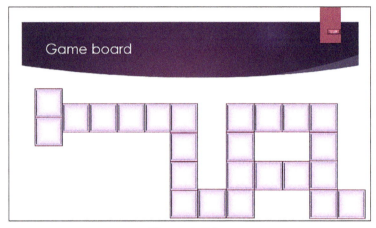

Figure 4–24

Since we will be creating electronic games, it is easy to add exciting features to the game board. As mentioned earlier, when we construct actual games, you will be able to click on a game piece and then click on the rectangle shape you want to move to, and the game piece will move automatically. Some game pieces will have special functions that are activated when you click on them such as display text or graphics, give the player a free spin, activate a bonus game, indicate the game is won, just to name a few. We are going to create examples of those special shapes now, but we won't be creating the text or graphics or bonus game that they link to at this time. The game board after these special shapes are created will look like figure 4–25. All these special shapes will be animated.

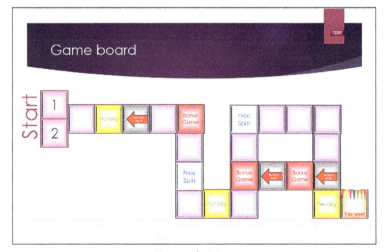

Figure 4–25

ADVANCED POWERPOINT: MORE THAN PRESENTATIONS!

Start

Create the word *Start* in WordArt, rotate the text and position it as shown in figure 4–25. Change the text color to Plumb, Accent 1. Add the numbers *1* and *2* in the two shapes shown to the right of the word *Start* to indicate player 1 and 2. Just click on the shape and enter the number. Change the gradient color of those two shapes at the 100 percent position to purple, Accent 6, Lighter 60 percent.

Penalty Shape

Click on the first shape that has the word *penalty* on it in figure 4–25. Change the gradient color at the 100 percent stop to standard yellow. Type the word *Penalty* in the box and change the font color to light green. Add the animation to the square Emphasis, Grow/Shrink, With Previous, Fast, Repeat Until End of Slide, and Size 105 percent and check Auto-reverse. View slide 4 in Slide Show view to see the new animation. Duplicate the penalty shape twice and replace the other two shapes in the game board with the penalty shape as shown.

Back to Start Shape

Click on the shape to the right of the first penalty shape. Change the gradient color at the 100 percent stop to gray-25 percent, Background 2, Darker 25 percent. Insert a block arrow left with red fill inside the shape. Add text, *Back to Start*, and font color white, Background 1. Add the animation to the Block Arrow, Emphasis, Wipe From Right, With Previous, 7 seconds, Repeat Until End of Slide. Duplicate the Back to Start shape twice and replace the other two shapes in the game board with the Back to Start shape as shown.

Bonus Game Shape

Click on the first Bonus Game shape. Change the gradient color at the 100 percent stop to standard red, 30 percent Transparency. Type the words *Bonus Game* in the shape, and change the font color to Standard red. Apply the animation to the shape, Emphasis, Teeter, With Previous, .3 seconds, Repeat Until End of Slide. Duplicate the Bonus Game shape twice and replace the other two shapes in the game board with the Bonus Game shape as shown.

Free Spin Shape

Click on the first Free Spin shape. Change the gradient color at the 100 percent stop to Sky blue. Type the words *Free Spin* in the shape, and change the font color to blue. Animate the shape to Emphasis, Spin, With Previous, 10 seconds, Delay 3 seconds, Smooth Start and Smooth End, Auto-reverse, Repeat Until End of Slide. Duplicate the Free Spin Shape once and replace the other shape in the game board with the Free Spin Shape. Change the rotation effect to Counterclockwise.

You Won Shape

Click on the You Won shape. Change the gradient color at the 100 percent stop to orange, Accent 4, Lighter 40 percent. Add the text shown and press Enter in front of the text to move it to the bottom of the shape. Add the text animation Emphasis, Wave, With Previous, 8 Seconds, Until the End of the Slide. Adjust the size of the Wave as needed to keep the text in the shape. Add the animation Emphasis, Complementary Color to the text, With Previous, Very Fast, Repeat Until End of Slide.

Banner

Move the banner motion clip on slide 4 to the top of the last shape as shown. Size as necessary.

Add action buttons to navigate through the presentation and set up the presentation to be Browsed at a Kiosk. Apply the *Wind* Transition, 2 seconds duration to all the slides. Save your presentation.

LESSON 5

VBA (Assign Macros to Objects), Drawing with Shapes, Shooting Moving Targets

Data Files

Lesson 5 Drawing with Shapes
Lesson 5 Moving Targets and Shooting Bottles
Lesson 5 VBA 2 Use Object to Launch Macro
Lesson 5 Application 1 Presentation Application
Lesson 5 Application 2 Instructional Materials Application
Lesson 5 Application 3 Gaming Application

Overview

In Lesson 5, you will begin to use simple VBA code to enhance your presentations, instructional materials, and to create games and apps. You will also learn additional drawing techniques.

Use an Object to Launch a Macro Action

Open the data file *Lesson 5 VBA 2 Use Object to Launch Macro*. Add your name to the file and save it again as a PowerPoint Macro-Enabled presentation. The *Facet* Design theme has been applied to the presentation. The presentation contains the macros you wrote in a previous lesson: *Correct* and *Incorrect*. Click Developer tab and in the code group click Macros to see and run each of the macros. In this lesson, you will use objects to cue or launch the run macro action.

Slides 2 to 4

Prepare slides 2 to 4 as shown in figure 5–1. Do not add the action buttons or slide numbers at this time. Slide 2 is in Title and Content Layout with three lines of text. Do not underline the words. Slides 3 and 4 contain the same group of shapes: L-shape, rectangle, right triangle, triangle, and left triangle. Use gridlines to assist you in creating the five shapes that make up the object. Add the colors shown. The size of the combined shape should be height 1" and width 2".

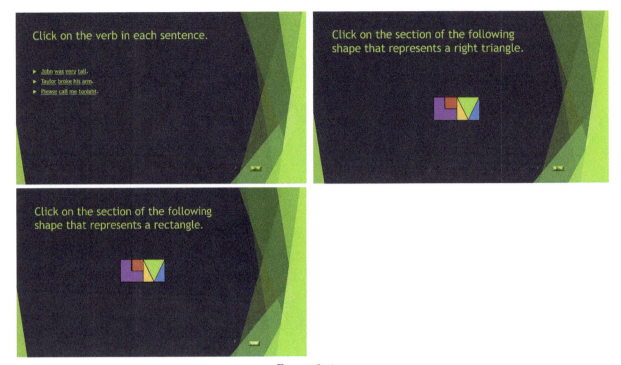

Figure 5–1

Slide 2

Select the first word in the first sentence, *John*. Note: *Only select the word and not the space before or after it. John* is not the verb, so we want to launch the macro *Incorrect*. Click Insert tab and in the Links group click Action. From the Action Settings dialog box, select Run Macro. Select the Incorrect macro and click OK. Click on the word *was*. *Was* is the verb in the sentence. Click the Insert tab, and in the Links group click Action. From the Action Settings dialog box, select Run Macro. Select the Correct macro and click OK. Repeat this process for each word in each of the sentences.

Change after Macro Color

Click the Design tab, and in the Variants group, click the More Button and Select Colors. Click Custom Colors and change the Follow Hyperlink color to standard red. View slide 2 in Slide Show view and click on each word in each sentence to make sure everything is accurate. Make any necessary changes.

Slides 3 and 4

Click on each shape and select an Action to run the appropriate macro, *Correct* or *Incorrect*. Select Highlight click from the Action Settings dialog box when the correct object is selected. View slides 3 and 4 in Slide Show view and click and all the shapes to make sure everything is accurate. Make any necessary changes.

Completing the Presentation

Add action buttons to navigate the presentation, and set up the presentation to be Browsed at a Kiosk. Add the *Peel Off* Transition to all slides for a duration of 1.25 seconds. Add the slide number to all slides except the title slide. Save the presentation.

Drawing with Shapes

Open the data file **Lesson 5 Drawing with Shapes**. Add your name to the subtitle placeholder on the title slide and save the presentation again adding your name to the file name. The *Crop* Design theme has been applied to the presentation.

Slide 2

Slide 2 is Blank Layout. Create the drawing shown in figure 5–3 on slide 2. This slide contains many objects such as pictures, lines, and shapes. It will be difficult to complete this slide unless you name the shapes on your screen as you add them. To name a shape click the Home tab and in the Edit group click Select then Selection Pane. Objects you add to the slide are listed from the last one at the top to the first one at the bottom. To name an object, click on it and it will be highlighted in the Selection Pane. Click on the current name and replace it with a name that identifies the object such as the sample shown in figure 5–2. The objects currently on your slide 2 have been named.

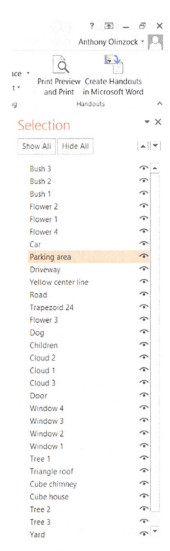

Figure 5–2

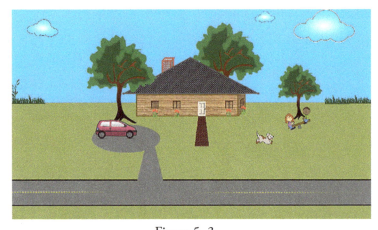

Figure 5–3

The house was created with a Cube shape. The roof is a Triangle, and the chimney is a Cube. Texture fill was added to the house and pattern fill was added to the roof and chimney. Online pictures were used to find images for the trees, flowers, bushes, clouds, car, children, dog, door, and windows. The pictures were sized, formatted, and cropped as needed. A blue rectangle was used to create the sky, and a green rectangle was used to create the lawn. Shapes were used to create the sidewalk, road, and parking area. Shapes were sent backward or forward as necessary to stack the objects properly on the screen. The side window was given a 3-D Rotation. You can use the shapes currently on slide 2 or locate other images. Delete the images on slide 2 if you do not want to use them.

Slide 3

Create the objects on slide 3 shown in figure 5–4.

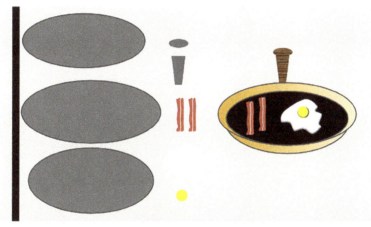

Figure 5–4

The oval at the top left is height 1.9" and width 4.4". The center oval is height 2.2" and width 5", and the bottom oval is height 2.3" and width 4.5". The small oval above the trapezoid shape is height .3" and width .7". The trapezoid shape is height 1" and width .5". The bacon was drawn using the Curve line tool, two dark red shapes and one white shape were drawn and then grouped and sized. The egg white was drawn with the Curve line tool, and the egg yolk is an oval shape .4"×.4" with a yellow fill. The effect Bevel Circle was added to the egg yolk and white.

Arrange the three oval shapes that make up the frying pan. Add a gradient fill to the two shapes that make up the frying pan, and a black fill to frying area of the pan. The handle was made by grouping the small oval and the trapezoid shape and adding a texture fill. The two shapes were grouped. Move the bacon onto the pan. Move the egg white onto the pan and add a Bevel Circle Effect. Add the egg yolk and add a Bevel Circle effect.

Slide 4

Copy the image already on your slide 4. This image was downloaded from online pictures. Ungroup the second image and recolor it as shown in figure 5–5. *Note: When you click Format/*

Arrange/Group/Ungroup, you see the message shown in figure 5–6. Click yes, and click Format/Arrange/ Group/Ungroup again and the image will be separated into the many shapes that make up the image as shown in figure 5–7.

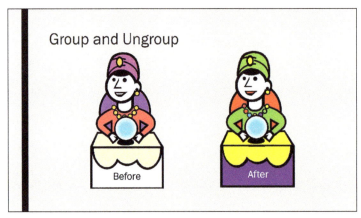

Figure 5–5

Figure 5–6

Figure 5–7

Once the image is ungrouped, you can select any shape and format it as desired. Change the color of the image as shown, and add the text shown in both images. Regroup both images.

Slide 5

The three shapes in the first column of figure 5–8 are already on your slide. Format the star for the effect 3-D Bevel Angle, height 6 pt and width 11 pt, and use a 75 percent Pattern fill, Foreground green and Background black, Text 1. To add the pattern, Right-click on the shape, select Format Shape, select Fill, select Pattern.

Save the picture on your slide that was downloaded from pictures online to your desktop, and use it for the fill of the Heart shape. Format the Heart shape for 3-D Bevel Circle, height 6 pt and width 11.5 pt. Add a dark red outline, 3 pt, to the Heart and an 8 pt dark red Glow. Format the Smiley Face for 3-D Bevel Hard Edge height 6 pt and width 15 pt. Add a blue outline, and use the yellow adjustment handle to change the Smile to a Frown. Delete the picture from the slide.

Copy the shapes in the first column and paste them to make the second column. Align the three objects at the center and distribute them vertically. Copy the second column to create column 3. In column 3 use the Bring Forward and Send Backward formatting options to layer the objects as shown in figure 5–8.

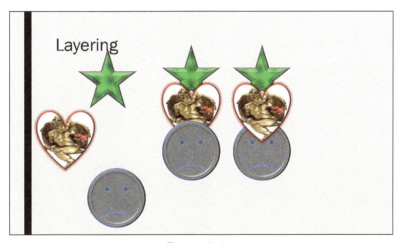

Figure 5–8

Slide 6

Your slide 6 already has an image of two trees, and motion clips of a flying saucer and a tank. All the shapes you need to create the robot (rectangles, ovals, line, and a block arc) have already been created, as shown in figure 5–9.

Figure 5-9

We are going to create an animated robot that moves in place. The trees and flying saucer will be moving behind the robot, and the tank will move onto the screen in front of the robot. It will appear that the robot is walking, but it will be moving in place. In future jobs we will make objects actually walk across the screen. Figure 5-10 shows the slide we will create.

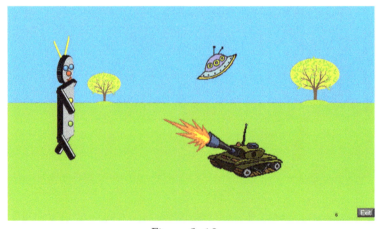

Figure 5-10

Step 1 – Create the Sky and Ground

Draw a rectangle that covers about one-third of the screen from the top down. Use Light blue fill color and No Line. Send the shape to the back. Draw a rectangle to cover the remaining bottom section of the screen. Use light green fill and No Line. Send the rectangle to the back. Make sure that you have covered the entire slide and that all objects are in front of the two rectangles.

Step 2 – Create the Robot

Click on the oval that represents the head and apply the effect 3-D Bevel Circle, height 6 pt and width 6 pt, Depth 10 pt. Apply a 3-D rotation Off Axis 2 Right. Apply the same effects to the body, arms, and legs. Position the head on the body of the robot. You might have to bring it to the front. Position the left arm and leg. Position the right arm and leg. You might have to send them backward or bring them forward to get them positioned accurately.

Place both yellow line shapes on the head of the robot to represent an antenna.

Format the ovals for the eyes and nose the same as the body shapes. Format the shape for the mouth the same as the body shapes, but make the Depth 2 pt. You might have to bring the ovals to the front. Copy one of the eye shapes four times. Change the colors of the ovals and place them on the body portion of the robot. Align at the left and distribute the four ovals vertically.

Step 3 – Animate the Robot

Click on one of the lines representing the antenna. Animate the line for Emphasis, Teeter, With Previous, Speed .1 seconds, Repeat Until End of Slide. View the slide in Slide Show view to see the animation. Click on the line and under the Animation tab in the Advanced Animation group, click Animation painter. Click the second line representing the antenna. The animation will be copied.

We are going to make the ovals on the front of the body blink at different speeds. Click on the first oval and animate it for Emphasis, Blink, With Previous, Repeat Until End of Slide, Duration 1 second. Use the Animation Painter to apply this animation to the other ovals, then change the speed for each oval so that they are all blinking at a different speed.

We want to animate the left arm and leg to move forward when the right arm and leg move backward. We will use the spin effect to do this, but as you learned in a previous lesson when you were making timers, objects spin at the pivot point, which is the center of the object. Apply the spin animation to the left arm and notice how it spins.

Click on the left arm and press Ctrl+D to duplicate it. Place the duplicated shape above the top of the original shape. Format the Fill for the top shape to 100 percent Transparency and No Line. Then group the two shapes. Add an animation Emphasis, Spin, Counterclockwise, 40°, With Previous, Auto-reverse, 2 seconds, Repeat Until End of Slide. Repeat this procedure to create the animation for the left leg.

Click on the right arm and press Ctrl+D to duplicate it. Place the duplicate shape above the top of the original shape. Format the Fill for the top shape to 100 percent Transparency and No Line, then group the two shapes. Add an animation Emphasis, Spin Clockwise, 40°, With Previous, Auto-reverse, 2 seconds, Repeat Until End of Slide. Repeat this procedure to create the animation for the right leg. View the slide in Slide Show view to see the motion effect for the robot.

Animate the Other Objects on the Slide

Drag the flying saucer, trees, and tank off the slide to the right. Click on the flying saucer and create a Custom Path to have the flying saucer move around the screen and back off to the right.

Have the animation start With Previous, 12 seconds, and Repeat Until End of Slide, Smooth Start and Smooth End. You can slow down the speed by using a higher number such as 15 or 20. Make sure the flying saucer is in front of the background and behind the robot.

Animate the large tree for a Motion Path Left and off the left side of the screen. Start With Previous, 12 seconds and Repeat Until End of Slide, Smooth Start and Smooth End. Animate the small tree for a Motion Path left and off the left side of the screen. Start With Previous, 16 seconds, Delay 3 seconds, and Repeat Until End of Slide. Make sure the tree objects are in front of the background and behind the robot.

Animate the tank for a Motion Path Left. Have it move to within approximately two inches of the robot. Start With Previous, 15 seconds, Smooth Start and Smooth End. Do not repeat this animation.

View the slide and make sure everything is working properly. Make any changes needed.

Finish the Presentation

Add slide numbers (Insert/Text/Slide Number) to all slides but the Title slide. Add action buttons to navigate and exit the Slide Show. Set up the show to be Browsed at a Kiosk. Apply the *Blinds* slide Transition to all slides for a duration of two seconds. Save the presentation.

Moving Targets and Shooting at Bottles

Open the data file **Lesson 5 Moving Targets and Shooting Bottles**. Replace the subtitle placeholder with your name and save the file again.

Slide 2

Your slide 2 already has the WordArt *Points,* the numbers (*10, 20, 30, 40, 50,* and *60*), and the large target already created. Create the small target using oval shapes with a black outline and the colors shown. Format the ovals that make up the small target to the sizes shown in figure 5–11.

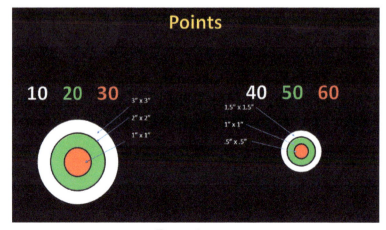

Figure 5–11

Name Shapes

Because so many of the shapes are the same, ovals or rectangles, for example, it will be difficult to tell them apart when you want to identify them for animation or triggers. To eliminate that problem, we are going to name the shapes. To display the Selection Pane: Home/Editing/Select/Selection Pane. Select the object (the large white oval) you want to name in the PowerPoint window, and it will be highlighted in the Selection Pane. Click on the default name in the Selection Pane, and name it *Large white oval*. The names used to name the objects on the screen are shown in figure 5–12. Name all objects. You will not have the action button shape yet.

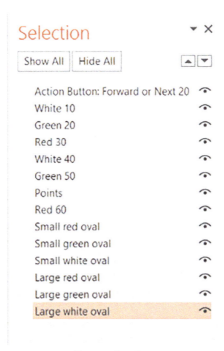

Figure 5–12

Trigger Points to Display

When the game is played and the user clicks on an oval, we want the points for that oval to be displayed. For example, if the user clicks on the large white oval, the number 10 in white should be displayed.

Click on the number named white 10 in the selection pane. The WordArt will be highlighted on the slide. Add the Animation Entrance Appear.

Display the animation pane. The animation for the white number 10 will be highlighted. Click the arrow to the right of the animation and click Timing. Under triggers, click *Start effect on click of* large white oval. View slide 2 in Slide Show view. Click on the large white oval. The number 10 should appear. We also want the White 10 to disappear after it is displayed. Click on the number named White 10 in the Selection Pane. Add the Animation Exit Disappear, With Previous, Delay 1.5 seconds. Move the animation after the Entrance animation. Your animation pane should show the animations shown in figure 5–13. Animate all the remaining numbers for both the large and small target to appear and disappear when you click on the appropriate oval.

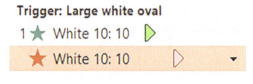

Figure 5–13

View slide 2 in Slide Show view. Make sure you can click on each oval and the appropriate number appears and then disappears after 1.5 seconds. Make any necessary corrections. Since the number only appears when you click on the appropriate oval, we are going to stack the number on top of one another under the word *Points*. Stack the numbers, align at top, and center.

Animate Targets

The difficulty of skill games such a shooting at a moving target depends on the size of the target, the speed at which the target moves, and the path of the movement. We are going to make the large target relatively easy to hit.

Select the three ovals together that make up the large target and move them off the screen to the left. While the three ovals are selected, add a Custom Motion Path Right, With Previous. Move the red arrow off right edge of the screen. Hold the Shift key to keep the line straight. You will have to do this for each of the three shapes. Make sure the green arrows indicating the start of the animations are all on top of one another and the red arrows indicating the end of the animations are on top of one another. The three animations will be selected in the animation pane. Set the speed to 10 seconds, Repeat Until End of Slide and select Smooth Start and Smooth End and Auto-reverse. You have created a moving target. View slide 2 in Slide Show view and use the mouse pointer to click on the target. The points should display when you click on an oval.

Repeat these steps for the small oval, but move the target off to the right and up toward the top section of the slide, and draw a Custom Motion Path Left with a slight up and down path, Start With Previous, Repeat Until End of Slide, Auto-reverse, Smooth Start and Smooth End, and set the speed to 8 seconds. It will be more difficult to hit the small target because it is smaller, the speed is faster, and the path is more difficult. View slide 2 in Slide Show view and try to hit the targets. Make any corrections needed.

Slide 3

Your slide 3 should look like figure 5–14. At this point three images of bottles have been inserted and named bottle 1, bottle 2, and bottle 3. A gun scope image has been created and filled with red color. The scope is made up of a donut shape and four lines. Two rectangular shapes have been added and sent behind the scope and are now colored blue.

ADVANCED POWERPOINT: MORE THAN PRESENTATIONS!

We are going to create a game where the scope moves across the screen and the bottles will only be visible when the scope moves over them. You can shoot each bottle by clicking the pointer inside the scope when it is over a bottle.

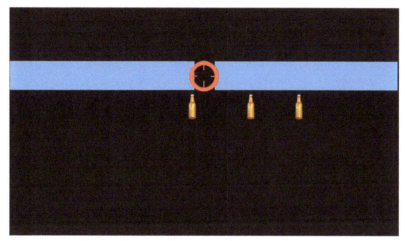

Figure 5–14

Step 1

Click on each of the blue rectangles and change the shape fill to black, Text 1, No Line. Move the scope shape down and over the first bottle as shown in figure 5–15. Use the directional left and right arrows to move across the bottles. They should only be visible when the scope is over them.

Figure 5–15

Step 2

Move the scope above the bottles. Click on bottle 1 and apply and Animation, Exit, Dissolve Out. Set the trigger the click of bottle 1. View slide 3 in Slide Show view, click on the bottle through the scope with your mouse, and it should dissolve out. Click on the animation in the animation pane, click Effects tab and add a Laser sound. Animate one of the breaking glass sounds already on the slide to play After Previous under the Exit animation. Move the icon off the slide. Move the scope over the first bottle. View slide 3 in Slide Show view. Click on the bottle through the scope and the bottle should dissolve out and you should hear the laser sound and glass breaking.

Because you are shooting at bottles through a scope, we want the scope to move too. Click on the scope object to select it. Add an Animation Emphasis, Grow/Shrink, With Previous, .1 second, Auto-reverse. Move the animation so that it is before the breaking glass sound. View slide 3 in Slide Show view and click on the first bottle through the scope. It should dissolve out, you should hear a laser sound and glass breaking, and scope should grow/shrink. Your animation in the animation pane should look like figure 5–16.

Figure 5–16

Move the scope object over bottle 2 and repeat step 2. Move the scope object over bottle 3 and repeat step 2.

Step 3

Make sure the scope is aligned so that when you move it left or right on the screen you can see the bottles through the scope. Move the scope to the left so that none of the bottles are visible. Select the scope object and animate it for a Motion Path Right, Smooth Start and Smooth End, Auto-reverse. Set the time for 15 seconds, With Previous, Repeat Until End of Slide. Move this animation to the top of the Animation Pane. View slide 3 in Slide Show view. When you click the mouse, the scope will move across the screen and you can click on the bottles through the scope. If you can't see all the bottles, adjust the length of the Motion Path.

We are going to create a trigger to start the game. Insert a rounded rectangle 1"×2". Type the words *Start Game* in the rectangle. Change the font and line color to red, and no fill color. Center the rectangle at the bottom section of the slide. Click on the Motion Path animation for the scope animation and set the trigger the *rounded rectangle* you just created with the words Start Game in it. When you click on Start Game in Slide Show view, the scope should move back and forth across the bottles, and you shoot them by clicking on them through the scope. Your slide should look like figure 5–17.

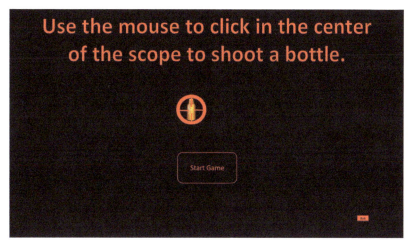

Figure 5–17

Complete the Presentation

Add action buttons to navigate the presentation. Set up the presentation to be Browsed at a Kiosk. Add a *Fall Over* Transition, 2 seconds, to all the slides. Save the presentation.

Lesson 5 Applications

Lesson 5 Application 1 Presentation Application

In this activity you are going to create a character by drawing, tracing, and formatting shapes and lines. Open the data file ***Lesson 5 Application 1 Presentation Application***. Add your name at the end of the file name and save it again. Figure 5–18 shows the slides that make up the presentation.

View slides 2 and 3 in Slide Show view. Slides 2 and 3 show the shapes used to draw a character and accessories in PowerPoint. Slide 4 shows how the character was put together. Finally, slide 5 shows the character in front of animated background as though she were walking a runway, and sound and flashing have been added to give the impression of pictures being taken and flash bulbs going off. Use slide 6 to create your own drawing.

All the parts needed to complete the drawing are on slides 2–3. You can trace and modify the shapes as desired, change colors and shading, and add different accessories. To use an appropriate skin tone, select the object, and click Format/Shape Styles/Shape Fill/More Colors. Once you complete the drawing, add a complementary background and action buttons to navigate through the presentation. Set up the presentation to be Browsed at a Kiosk. Apply the *Glitter* Transition to all slides for a duration of 3 seconds.

Figure 5–18

Lesson 5 Application 2 Instructional Materials Application

Open *Lesson 5 Application 2 Instructional Materials Application*. Add your name to the file name and save it again as a PowerPoint Macro-Enabled presentation. The *Berlin* Design theme has already been applied to the presentation. Add your name to replace the subtitle place holder on the title slide. Slides 2 and 3 are shown in figure 5–19.

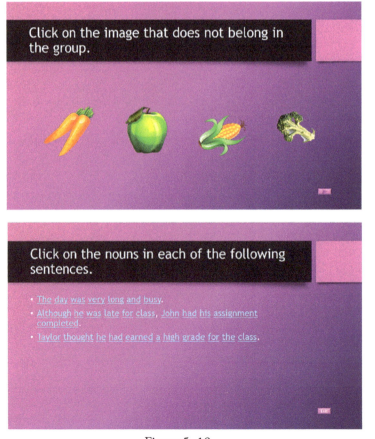

Figure 5–19

Create two macros. The first macro should just display the work *Correct*. The second macro should display the words *Incorrect. Try again.*

On slide 2, click on each of the four images and have clicking on the image launch the appropriate macro. On slide 3, select each word and have clicking on the word launch the appropriate macro.

Add appropriate action buttons to navigate the presentation. Set up the presentation to be Browsed at a Kiosk, and apply an appropriate Transition to all slides (Use the *Switch* Transition if available.).

Lesson 5 Application 3 Gaming Application

Open the data file ***Lesson 5 Application 3 Gaming Application***. Add your name to the file and save it again.

On slide 3, make four balloons, each a different size and color. The balloon is made up of a teardrop shape, a triangle, and a line. All parts of the balloon should be grouped. Add a gradient fill to each balloon.

Add a Custom Motion Path for each balloon to move around the screen when it is viewed in Slide Show view until end of slide. Add a different speed for each Motion Path in seconds: 16, 14, 12, and 10 seconds. Remember difficulty level involves size, speed, and Motion Path. The largest balloon should be the easiest to burst.

Add a trigger to each balloon so that it will dissolve out when clicked and play a whoosh sound. The point value for bursting each balloon should also be displayed: 10, 20, 40, and 60. Your slide 3 should look like figure 5–20.

Figure 5–20

Slide 5 contains a Clip Art image of a skier, and slide 6 shows a ski jump. Using the image from slide 6 to create an animation where the skier appears, slides down the jump, and off into the air completing two forward spins in the air and continues down and off the screen. *Hints: You will need to size the image. You will need to make the skier appear and disappear to adjust the angle for Motion Paths. You will need to adjust the effects for Motion Paths for a Smooth Start and End to avoid pauses in the animation.* Figure 5–21 shows the skier continuing down the hill after completing two spins.

Figure 5–21

Add appropriate action buttons to navigate through the Slide Show. Set up the presentation to be Browsed at a Kiosk, and an appropriate Transition to all slides.

LESSON 6

Game Boards Continued, Advanced Triggers, Logic and Simulations

Data Files

Lesson 6 Game Boards Continued
Lesson 6 Application 1 Presentation Application
Lesson 6 Application 2 Instructional Materials Application
Lesson 6 Application 3 Gaming Application

Overview

In this lesson, you will build on the concepts learned in Lesson 4. Specifically, you will learn how to move pieces on a game board and how to add a variety of dynamic features to an electronic board. In the sample problem, you will build the game board and bonus game shown in figure 6–1 along with many other features of electronic games. Some of the squares on the game board in figure 6–1 do not look aligned because they are animated and are moving.

Creating an Electronic Board Game

This sample game is used for as an educational game where two groups of students answer questions related to how computers calculate to review for a class test. The winning team gets five bonus points on the test. Clicking the help button explains the rules of the game and how the game is played.

Figure 6–1

Help

Steps for playing the game:

- Click *Spin Wheel* to determine whether Player 1 (Team 1) or Player 2 (Team 2) will start the game first. The highest number goes first.
- The player going first should click *Answer Question*.
    o The player will have 30 seconds to answer a random question that will be displayed. The instructor will have the answer in the *notes pane*.
    o If the answer is correct, the player clicks *Spin Wheel* to start the wheel spinning. Clicking *Spin Wheel* again stops the wheel.
    o The player clicks her/his game piece, and all or a portion of the game piece will show a red mark indicating it is active and then the player clicks the destination square.
    o The second player would then repeat this process.
    o If two players land on the same game square, the second player to land on that square moves to the *hold position* until her/his next spin.
    o If a player lands on a *Penalty square,* when the square is clicked, the penalty will be displayed. and the game piece does not move to the penalty square. The penalty is taken from the location of the game piece before the penalty square was clicked.
    o If a player lands on a *Back to start square*, the game piece will not move to that square. The player must click on the *Start square* to return to that position.
    o The *number* on the wheel indicates how many spaces the player can move forward on the board.
- When a *Bonus Game* square is clicked, your game piece won't move, and you are automatically taken to the bonus game.
    o The player clicks on any one of the sixteen squares to reveal a *bonus*. Not all squares have a bonus under them.
    o If a *bonus* is won, the player places a *check mark* next to the bonus prize won on the game board.
    o A player can use a *bonus* prize at any time during the game when he or she is the active player. The *check mark* is removed when a bonus prize is used.
- The first player to land on the *You Win* square wins the game and receives five bonus points for the next test, assuming the game is used for educational purposes.

Dynamic Squares

Penalty squares, bonus squares, back to start squares, free spin squares, and the *You Won square* are dynamic. They are animated in some way and/or launch an action. Clicking on the *penalty* square will cause the penalty to be displayed. Clicking on the *bonus* game square will take the player to the bonus game. Clicking on the *You Won* square will launch an action.

Game Wheel

You click on the *game wheel* to determine which player will go first or to determine how many spaces you move on the board if you answer your question accurately within 30 seconds.

Answer Question

Clicking on *Answer Question* will take the user to a random question. All slides with questions have a 30-second timer displayed.

Bonus

Clicking on the *bonus square* will open one of three bonus games. The user can click on one of sixteen squares to reveal a bonus. The bonus section on the game board provides check boxes for each player to keep track of any bonuses won in the *bonus game*. A player can choose to use a bonus at any time during her/his turn and then removes the check mark.

Macros

Two macros have already been written and are available for you to use.

MovePiece Macro/NewLocation Macro

The *MovePiece* macro is assigned to both game pieces.

The *NewLocation* macro is assigned to all the game squares except the *Penalty, Back to Start, Bonus Game, Free Spin, Help,* and *You Won* squares.

To assign the macro to a game piece or game square, you will click on the object and click the Insert tab, and in the Links group click Action and then in the Action Settings dialog box, click Run Macro. Select the macro you want to use and click OK. Once you assign the macros to the game pieces and game squares, you can click on a game piece, it will be highlighted with red color indicating it is the active player, and you can click on the square you want to move it to and the game piece will move to that square.

Building the Game Board

Open the data file **Lesson 6 Game Boards Continued** and add your name to the subtitle placeholder on the title slide. Save the file, again adding your name at the end of the file name. It should be saved as a PowerPoint Macro-Enabled presentation.

The presentation is composed of thirteen slides, the title slide, the game board slide, the help slides, the bonus slides, and the question slides. Much of the work has already been completed for you.

Step 1 – Help

Slides 3 to 6 are the help slides. Create a Custom Show named *Help* that is made up of slides 3 to 6. Refer to previous lessons if you need help creating a Custom Show.

Have the help square on the game board launch the Help Custom Show. Click on the help square, click Insert/Links/Action. In the Action dialog box click Hyperlink to Custom Show, Help, check *Show and Return*, and click OK, OK.

View slide 2 in Slide Show view and click on the Help square. Make sure it takes you to the help slides and that you can press ESC to return to slide 2. Correct any errors you find.

Step 2 – Create Check Boxes

On the game board to the left of the wheel is a list of the six bonus options that can be won when playing the bonus game. Create six *ActiveX Check Boxes* under number 1 and six under number 2. Do not include a caption. Refer to previous lessons if you need help. View slide 2 in Slide Show view and make sure you can insert and remove a check in each box.

Step 3 – Random Questions

Slides 10–13 have four questions created. You would, of course, use many more questions in an actual game. We are just learning the procedures here. Make each question a separate Custom Show named 1, 2, 3, and 4.

Each question slide has a timer created, the actual second hand is composed of two parts, the top part that you see, and the transparent section below it that you can't see so that you can animate it to spin on its pivot. You need to set the hand to move 180° in 30 seconds, With Previous, so that it starts as soon as the slide displays. Also, add a sound at the end of the animation such as a bell or a computer beep to play after the time has expired. A bell sound is already available on each of the slides, but you will need to animate it. Click on the Sound Icon, and a Contextual tab, Audio Tools, will be added to the ribbon. Click Playback/Audio Options/Start/ Automatically. Move the audio step after the clock spin in the Animation Pane to play After Previous. Repeat this for slides 10 to 13. Drag the Sound Icon off the slide. *Hint: You can use the Animation Painter to copy the clock animation to the clock hand on other slides.*

Step 4 – Select Question at Random

On slide 2, the game board slide, an oval object divided into four sections and grouped and partially transparent is on top of the prompt, Answer Question. Click on each individual section and link it to a different Custom Show, be sure to check the box *Show and Return*. Display slide 2 and click on each section and make sure a different question is displayed. Correct any errors you find.

Next, change the fill color to 100 percent transparent so that you can't see it. Animate the shape for an Emphasis, Spin, With Previous, 2 seconds, Repeat Until End of Slide. View slide 2 and test the wheel to make sure you are going to random questions.

Step 5 – Naming Objects on Slides

Click on the first Penalty square. Click the Home tab and in the Editing group click Select and then Selection Pane. The Selection Pane will be displayed at the right. Scroll down and you will see that this Penalty Square has already been named *Penalty 1*. The other Penalty Squares are also named. The Bonus Game squares have not been named. Click on the first Bonus Game square. Click on the name in the Selection Pane and name it *Bonus Game 1*. Name the other Bonus Games squares *Bonus Game 2* and *Bonus Game 3*. Click on the last square, You won. It should already be named Won. Name the other important objects on your slide.

Step 6 – Animate Penalty Squares

Click on the first Penalty square. Add an animation, Emphasis, Grow/Shrink, With Previous, Fast, Repeat Until End of Slide. Click the Effects tab and change size to 105 percent and Auto-reverse. View slide 2 in Slide Show view to see the animation. Make necessary corrections. Click on the first Penalty square again, click the Animation tab, and in the Advanced Animations group click the Animation Painter. Click on the next Penalty square and the animation will be copied. Repeat this procedure to animate the next Penalty square.

Step 7 – Animate Back to Start Squares

Apply the same animation you used for the Penalty squares to only the arrow on the Back to Start squares, but change the effect Size to 115 percent. You will have to animate the first arrow; then you can use the Animation Painter for the others.

Step 8 – Animate Bonus Game Squares

Click on the first Bonus square. Add an animation Emphasis, Teeter, With Previous, .1 seconds, Repeat Until End of Slide. Use the Animation Painter to apply it to the other Bonus Game squares.

Step 9 – Animate Free Spin Squares

Click on the first Free Spin square. And an animation Emphasis, Spin, Clockwise, With Previous, 8 seconds, Repeat Until End of Side, Delay 2 seconds. Use the Animation Painter to apply it to the other Free Spin square, then change the direction to Counterclockwise.

Step 10 – Animate You Won Square

Click on the You Won square. Add an animation Emphasis, Darken effect, With Previous, 5 seconds, Repeat Until End of Slide. Select the words *Your Won*. Animate the text for the animation Emphasis, Wave effect, 5 seconds, With Previous, Repeat Until End of Slide. Drag the banner animation from the top of the game board and place on the top of this square. Size as needed.

Step 11 – Launch Action from Penalty Squares

At the top of the game board on slide 2, the penalties are listed in red WordArt. Select the first penalty, *Go back 4 spaces*. Animate the text for an animation Entrance, Zoom, 2 seconds. Use Penalty 1 square as the trigger to launch the animation. View slide 2 in Slide Show view and click on the Penalty 1 square. It should launch the WordArt. Make any corrections necessary. Click on the WordArt again and apply an animation Exit, Disappear, After Previous, Delay 3 seconds. In the Animation Pane, move the Exit animation under the Entrance, Zoom animation. View slide 2 and make sure the Penalty 1 square launches the animation and that it disappears in 3 seconds. Move the WordArt to the blank area of the game board shown in figure 6–2. Repeat this process for the remaining two Penalty squares and WordArt. Stack the WordArt on top of one another since it will only be seen when launched and will then disappear after 3 seconds.

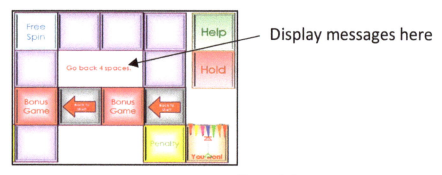

Figure 6–2

Step 12 – Animate Bonus Game

There are three versions of the Bonus game on slides 7, 8, and 9. Each of the games consists of twelve squares covering either a bonus or no bonus. Go to square 1 on slide 7 (the top, left square). Animate the square for an animation Emphasis, Spin, Fast, With Previous, Repeat 3 times. Click on the same square again and add an animation Exit, Collapse. Use the same square as the trigger to launch the Exit Collapse animation. If you don't have the Collapse animation, substitute another Exit animation. View slide 3 in Slide Show view to make sure the square spins and then collapses when you click on it. Once you have the first square working properly, you can click on it, click the Animation Painter in the Advanced Animation group, and click the other squares to copy the animation to those squares. Once you have all the squares animated, view the slide in Slide Show view to see how the Bonus game works. When a player wins a bonus game, he/she gets to click one of the sixteen squares to try and win a bonus. Repeat these procedures for slides 8 and 9. *Hint: You can use the animation painter to copy an animation from an object on one slide to an object on another slide.*

Create three new Custom Shows, one for each of the three Bonus Games on slides 7, 8, and 9. Name the Custom Shows *Bonus 1*, *Bonus 2*, and *Bonus 3*.

Go back to slide 2. In a previous step, you named each of the Bonus Game squares. Click on the Bonus Game 1 square and hyperlink to Bonus 1 Custom Show. Be sure to click *Show and Return*. Click on Bonus Game 2 square and hyperlink to Bonus 2 Custom Show. Click on Bonus Game 3 square and hyperlink to Bonus 3 Custom Show. View slide 2 in Slide Show view and test the link to the three Custom Shows. Correct any errors. *Hint: Be sure to use the square as the hyperlink, and not the text.*

Step 13 – Animate Won Object

Click on the red Winner object. Add an animation Entrance, Zoom, Slow. Make the trigger to launch this animation the Won square. Add an animation Exit, Disappear, After Previous, Delay 3 seconds. Move it after the Zoom Entrance animation. Move the object into the same area where you moved the WordArt. View slide 2 in Slide Show view to view the animation. Make any necessary corrections.

Step 14 – Animate Wheel

The wheel on the game board has already been created. You need to animate it so that you can click to *spin* and to *stop* the wheel. The wheel is in three pieces: the wheel, the arrow, and the rectangle with text. Click on the wheel and add an animation Emphasis, Spin, .1 seconds, Repeat Until Next Click. Set the trigger for the wheel to start spinning as the rectangle with the text *Click to start and stop*. Click on the wheel again and add an animation Emphasis, Spin .1 second, 90°. Make the trigger for this second animation also the rectangle with the text *Click to start and stop*. In the Animation Pane, make sure the second animation is listed after the first animation. If not, move it to follow the first animation. Test the wheel in Slide Show view. Click to *Start* and click again to *Stop*.

Step 15 – Launch MovePiece Macro from Game Piece

Click on the game piece at the top of the game board with number 1 on it. While it is selected click the Insert tab and in the Links group, click Action. From the Action Settings dialog box, click Run Macro and select the macro MovePiece and click OK. Repeat these steps for game piece with the number 2 on it.

Step 16 – Launch NewLocation Macro from Nondynamic Game Squares

Click on the first game square that is not a dynamic square (the dynamic squares are the *penalty* squares, *bonus game* squares, *free spin* squares, *you won* square and the *help* square), the square with the number 1 on it.

Make sure the square is selected and click the Insert tab, and in the Links group, click Action. From the Action Settings dialog box click Run Macro and select the macro NewLocation and click OK. This macro should be assigned to the squares with *number 1* and *number 2, all the boxes with purple shading*, and the *Hold* square. *Note: Be careful to select the square and not the text in any square.*

Testing the Game Board

View slide 2 in Slide Show view. Click on the game piece with the number 1 on it. It will be shaded in red. Click on the square with the number 1 on it. The game piece will move to that square.

Click on the game piece with the number 2 on it. It will be shaded in red. Click on the square with the number 2 on it. The game piece will move to that square.

Click on the game piece with number 1 on it. It will be shaded in red. Click on any square that is not a dynamic square, and it will move to that square. You can continue to move the game piece number 1 to any square that is not dynamic, even back to the start square with a number 1 on it or the Hold square.

Click on the game piece with a number 2 on it. It will be shaded red indicating that it is the active game piece. You can now move that game piece to any square that is not dynamic.

Click on the game piece with a number 1 on it. Move it to the Hold square.

Click on the Check Boxes to insert and remove a check marks.

Click on a Penalty square to see the penalty. Your game piece will not move because you take the penalty from the location where you started.

Click on a Back to Start square. Nothing will happen because you must move back to start.

Click on a Free Spin square. Your game piece will not move. You get to take another spin on the wheel and move from the Free Spin square.

Click on the You Won square. Your game piece will not move, but the Winner object will be displayed.

If everything is working, you are ready to play the game. You would follow these steps.

1. Spin the wheel to determine what player goes first.
2. The player going first would click on the Answer Question text, and a question is displayed and the 30-second timer starts. If the player answers the question accurately within 30 seconds (the answers are in the notes pane) then the player gets to spin the wheel. Otherwise, the other player gets to take her/his turn.
3. Any bonuses won are checked in the check boxes and can be used when the player is active (taking his or her turn).
4. The game goes on like this until one player reaches the You Won square.

Finish the Game

Set up the Slide Show to be Browsed at a Kiosk. Apply a slide transition of your choice. You should only be able to move in the Slide Show view by clicking one of the action buttons, the ESC key, or one of the hyperlinks.

Lesson 6 Applications

Lesson 6 Application 1 Presentation Application

Open the data file ***Lesson 6 Application 1 Presentation Application***. Add your name in the subtitle placeholder on the title slide and save the presentation again with your name added to the file name. Save the file as a PowerPoint Macro-Enable presentation. The *Facet* Design theme has been applied to the presentation. Slides 2 and 3 explain the purpose of the presentation: to lead a discussion on the advantages and disadvantages of home ownership.

On slide 4, as shown in figure 6–3, you will draw an animated scale. Ten ovals are available with the advantages and disadvantages of home ownership text displayed on them. A participant is asked to select one of the ovals and discuss why it is an advantage or disadvantage. The leader would then click on the oval, a red effect would appear. The leader then clicks on one side of the scale or the other (Advantage or Disadvantage) on an imaged mapped area, and the oval would move on that scale plate and the scale would move down slightly on that side, and the other side would move up an equal amount. The image mapped areas have the NewLocation macro assigned to each of them and well as serving as a trigger to move the scale down. All the ovals have the MovePiece macro assigned to them. Once an oval is dropped on one side of the scale, the red effect will disappear.

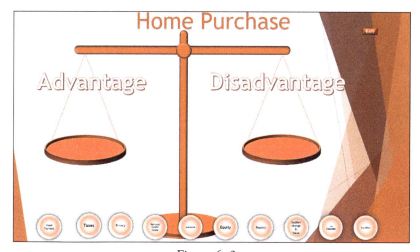

Figure 6–3

Steps for Completing Slide 4

Your slide 4 looks like figure 6–4.

Figure 6–4

Step 1

Refer to figure 6–5 as you begin to complete slide 4. Draw a rounded rectangle height 6.3" and width .25". Apply a 3-D Format Bevel Circle for the vertical bar. Use the yellow adjustment handle to make more of a round curve on the ends. Duplicate the rectangle and change the size to height 7.2" and width .25", and rotate it 90° for the horizontal bar. Create an oval .5"×.5". Format for Bevel Circle for the intersection of the vertical and horizontal bars.

Create an oval 2.7"×.2.7". Apply a 3-D Rotation Off Axis 2 Top, 3-D Format Top Bevel Slope, Depth 6 pt for the left scale tray. Duplicate the oval for the right tray. Duplicate the oval again and change the 3-D Format Top to none, and bottom to 3-D Format, Bottom Bevel Slope, Depth 6 pt. Use your gridlines as guides and make sure that the vertical and horizontal bars are aligned at the center and that both oval trays are placed accurately and aligned at the top. The bottom base might need to be brought to the front.

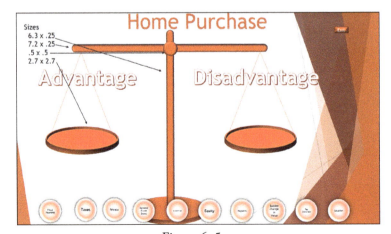

Figure 6–5

Refer to figure 6–6. Draw the lines shown to connect the scale trays to the horizontal bar. Change the width to 1 1/2 pt and use Dash type Rounded Dot, Cap type Round and Join type Round. Send the lines to the back. Group these objects: the left and right tray and dotted lines and the horizontal bar. Bring the oval covering the intersection of the vertical and horizontal bar to the front.

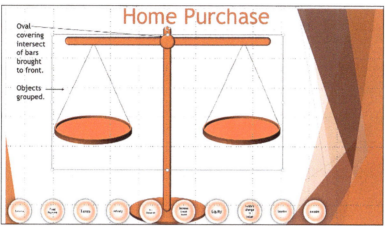

Figure 6–6

Step 2

The ovals at the bottom of the slide contain items that can be either an advantage or disadvantage of purchasing a home. In leading the discussion, we want participants to pick one of the ovals and give his or her reason why it is an advantage or disadvantage. The discussion leader would click on the item, a red effect will appear, and then click above one of the scale trays and the oval would move to that point. At the same time, that tray would move down slightly and the other tray would move up slightly.

MovePiece Macro

Click on the first oval at the bottom of the screen, then click the Insert tab, and in the Links group, click Action. From the Action dialog box, click Run Macro, MovePiece, OK. Repeat this procedure for each oval. Be sure to assign the macro to the oval and not the text inside the oval.

Image Map Drop Locations

Draw ovals height .8 and width .8 and place them on the scale plates as shown in figure 6–7. Name each shape beginning with one to eight on the left scale plate and nine to sixteen on the right scale plate. Select all the ovals at the bottom of the slide. Align them at the top and align distribute horizontally. While they are still selected, bring them all to the front.

Click on oval one on the right scale plate and click the Insert tab and in the Links group click Action. Click Run Macro, *NewLocation*, OK. Repeat this procedure for the remaining fifteen ovals on the slide scales. If you go into Slide Show view now, you can click on any oval at the bottom of the slide. A red effect will appear in the oval. You can click on any oval on either of the scale plates and it will move to that location. Exit Slide Show view and move the ovals back to the bottom of the slide and align them again. It doesn't matter what order they are in. Slide 4 will look like figure 6–7 at the end of this step.

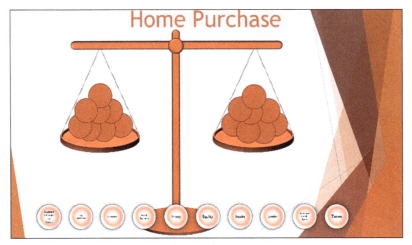

Figure 6–7

"You also want to be able to return any of the ovals with advantages and disadvantages to their original locations. When you move each of the ovals at the bottom to a new location on one of the scale plates, you will see that each is on top of a partially transparent oval. The NewLocation macro has already been assigned to each of these partially transparent ovals. You will now be able to move the ovals with advantages and disadvantages back to a location at the bottom of the screen."

Step 3

Animate the Scale

Select the scale object (the object you grouped). Click the Animation tab, and in the Advance animation group click Add animation, Emphasis, Spin. Display the Animation pane. It should only have one animation displayed, the Spin animation you just created. Click the arrow on the right side of the animation and click Effects. Change the rotation to 1°, Counterclockwise. Play the animation to make sure it is working. If it is working properly, click Timing again, and under Triggers select *Start animation on click of*, one (you named the ovals on the left scale plate one to eight). See figure 6–8. Repeat this process for objects two to eight.

Select the scale object again. Click the Animation tab and in the Advance animation group click Add animation, Emphasis, Spin. Display the animation pane, and click the arrow to the right side of the animation and click Effects. Change the rotation to 1° Clockwise. Click triggers and click start animation on click of Nine. Repeat this process for all the ovals on the left side scale plate, ten to sixteen.

View slide 4 in Slide Show view to make sure everything is working properly. *Note: Since we are only using a spin animation of 1° and it is likely that the number of items on each side of the scale will only* vary by two or three, we didn't animate the ovals on the plates to move or for the plates to tilt left or right. These additional animations would have to be added to a more complex example.

Step 4

Make the image mapped ovals on the scale transparent. Click on oval one on the right scale. Make the fill color 100 percent Transparency and No Line. Repeat this process for each oval on the scales. You can use the Format painter to speed up this process. You will no longer see the image mapped areas, but when you move your pointer over the location, a hand symbol lets you know you can click there to drop one of the ovals and move the scale.

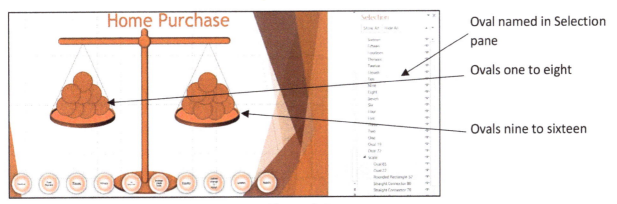

Figure 6–8

Complete the Presentation

Add the necessary action buttons to navigate the presentation. Add an appropriate slide transition. Set up the presentation to be Browsed at a Kiosk. Save the presentation. *Note: The gray ovals underneath the ovals indicating advantages and disadvantages of purchasing a home already have the new location macro assigned to them so that you can return the pieces to the original locations if necessary during Slide Show view.*

Lesson 6 Application 2 Instructional Materials Application

Open the data file ***Lesson 6 Application 2 Instructional Materials Application***. Save it again as a PowerPoint Macro-Enabled presentation, adding your name in the subtitle placeholder and at the end of the file name. The presentation contains three slides as shown in figure 6–9. The *Wood Type* Design theme has already been applied to the presentation.

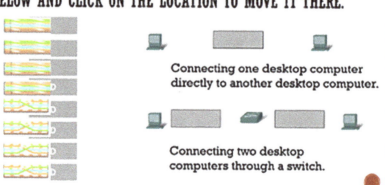

Figure 6–9

Slide 2 contains four examples of wiring standards used with unshielded twisted pair cabling used in computer networks. The examples have been moved to the right off the rectangles they are to sit on. There are also two boxes to the right of the cable standards. The macros *MovePiece* and *NewLocation* have already been added to this presentation. You will need to assign the *MovePiece* macro to each of the four examples of wiring standards, and you will need to assign the *NewLocation* macro to each of the six gray rectangles. When you are done, you should be able to click on any wiring standard and then click on either of the two gray rectangles in front of the name of a standard and move it there. You will also be able to move back to the original location. The answers are shown in the notes pane.

Slide 3 contains eight examples of wiring standards. The standards have been moved off the gray rectangles they will sit on. The left part of the screen shows two examples of situations where the user must select the appropriate wiring configuration. In the top section, the user needs to click on one of the eight wiring standards that could be used to connect two computers directly to each other. In the example at the bottom, the user needs to select appropriate wiring configuration to connect two different computers to a switch. Assign the *MovePiece* macro to each of the eight wiring configurations, and assign the *NewLocation* macro to each of the eleven gray rectangles. When you are done, you should be able to click on any wiring standard and then click on the rectangle between the two computers to move it there and you can also move any of the standards between the two gray rectangles between a computer and the switch, and move it there. You will also be able to move back to the original location. The answers are shown in the notes pane.

Add appropriate action buttons to navigate the presentation and set it up to be Browsed at a Kiosk. Add an appropriate slide transition to all the slides. Save the presentation.

Lesson 6 Application 3 Gaming Application

In this application, you will create a short, original board game. Open the data file **Lesson 6 Application 3 Gaming Application.** See figure 6–10. Replace the subtitle placeholder with your name and save the presentation again as a PowerPoint Macro-Enabled Presentation. The *Quotable* Design theme and *Drape* Transition have already been applied. The instructions for this assignment are shown on slides 2 and 3. You will make your game board on slide 4, and will add slides as needed for instructions and the bonus game. Add action buttons to navigate the presentation and set it up to be Browsed at a Kiosk. Save the presentation.

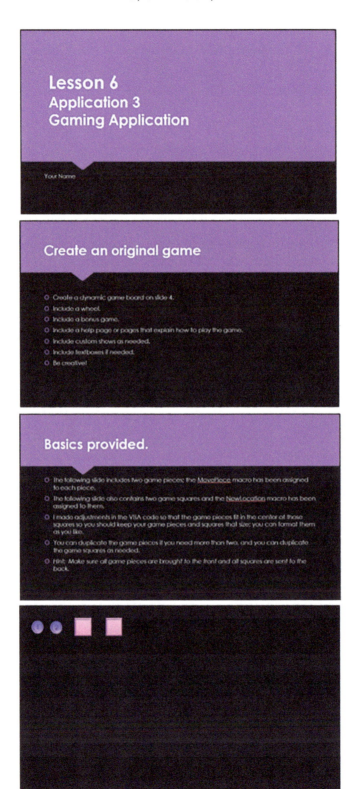

Figure 6–10

LESSON 7

VBA for Interactive Presentations, Teleporting, and Combining Animation Effects

Data Files

Lesson 7 Combining Animation Effects
Lesson 7 Teleporting
Lesson 7 VBA 3
Lesson 7 Application 1 Presentation Application
Lesson 7 Application 2 Instructional Materials Application
Lesson 7 Application 3 Gaming Application

Overview

In Lesson 7 you will continue to use VBA to expand the capabilities of PowerPoint. You will learn to use variables to store information for use in executing code, and you will learn how data is classified in VBA. You will also learn to teleport an object from one place on the screen to another. Finally, you will learn to combine animation effects to create complex animations.

VBA 3

In Lesson 7 you will continue working with VBA. A *variable* is a named storage location used to store temporary values or information for use in execution of the code in VBA. In this lesson, you will use a variable to store data that can be used or changed later while executing the code. You will be asking a user to enter her/his name so that the instructional materials you develop can be more interactive and user-friendly by using individual names when providing prompts and feedback.

In VBA, a *Dim* statement (Dim is short for dimension) is used for declaring a variable to hold an integer value. Defining the type of data in code assists in limiting the space used since some types of data require more space than other types of data. The Dim statement can be used anywhere in the code, but it should precede the first use of the variable, and all Dim statements are usually placed at the beginning of each *Sub procedure* (Sub and End sub enclose a series of VBA statements) or *Function procedure* (a Function can return a value). If you omit declaring a variable, it will default to *Variant* data type that can hold any type of data.

The type of data we are going to store in the code for this exercise will be a *string*—data that can include letters, symbols, and numbers and are enclosed in "".

Open the data file **Lesson 7 VBA 3**. The *Berlin* Design has already been applied to the presentation. Replace the subtitle with your name and save the presentation as a PowerPoint Macro-Enabled presentation.

Animating Objects on the Slide Masters

You were introduced to slide masters in Lesson 2. In this lesson, you will add animation on specific slide masters to attract attention. The four slides in the presentation are shown in figure 7–1. The four shapes—cross, oval, rectangle, and triangle—have already been added to the slide masters: the Title Slide master, the Title and Content slide master, and the Title Only slide master. There are slide masters for each of the nine standard layouts available for slides. In this job the only layouts you will use are the Title Slide Layout, Title and Content Layout, and Title Only Layout options.

To view the slide masters, you click View/Master Views/Slide Master. You then click on the slide master of the layout you want to use. The first one you will be using is the Title Slide Master. As you move the cursor over the various layouts, the name of the layout is displayed.

You need to add a circle Motion Path animation to each of the four shape objects (cross, oval, triangle, rectangle) already added to the title slide master (Animation/Advanced Animation/Add Animation/More Motion Paths/Circle), With Previous. You can select the four objects and animate all of them at the same time. Once you have animated them, align them at the Center and Top. Size the circle animations so that the object remains on top of the large rectangle when the animation is run. The timing for the first object, cross, should be 10 seconds and Repeat Until End of slide. The timing for the second object, oval, should be 12 seconds, Delay .5 seconds, Repeat Until End of Slide. The timing for the third object, triangle, should be 14 seconds, Delay 1 second, Repeat Until End of Slide. The timing for the fourth object, rectangle, should be 16 seconds, Delay 1.5 seconds, Repeat Until End of Slide. You will need to add these animations on the Title Slide master, the Title and Content slide master, and the Title Only slide master.

View each of the three layouts in Slide Show view and make sure none of the objects move outside of the rectangle background. Make any adjustments needed. Your animation on the title slide master will look like figure 7–2.

ADVANCED POWERPOINT: MORE THAN PRESENTATIONS!

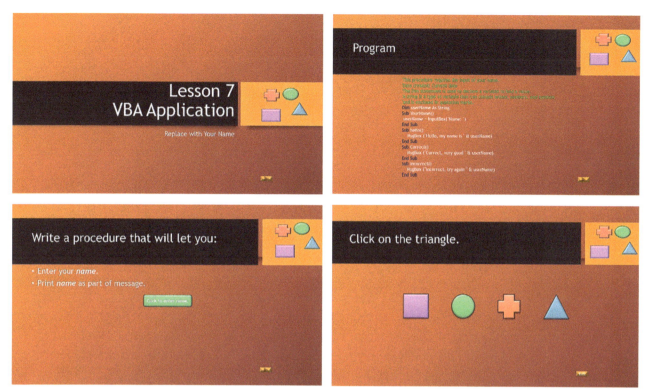

Figure 7–1

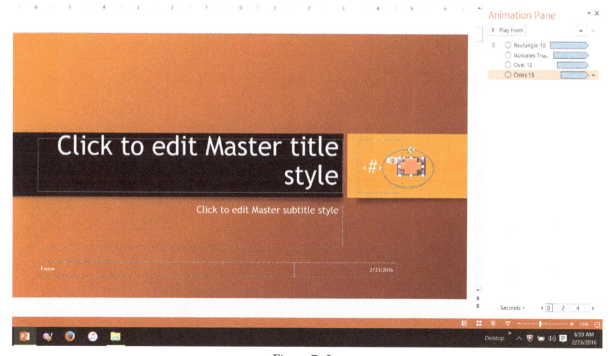

Figure 7–2

Writing the Macros

The code you will need to write is shown on slide 2. The color green indicates documentation that you write that is not part of the code and is ignored when running the macro. A single quotation mark identifies this type of documentation. The command Sub, in blue, starts a macro and End Sub in blue ends the macro. The only new code you will use in this lesson is:

```
Dim userName As String
Sub YourName()
        userName = InputBox("Name: ")
End Sub
```

This code uses Dim to indicate that the type of data stored in the userName variable will be *string*. When the macro YourName is run, the code UserName = InputBox("Name: ") will let the user type her/his name in the input box provided. Once a user enters her/his name, that variable, userName, can be printed as part of a MsgBox and displayed on the screen.

In previous lessons, when you wanted to create a macro, you clicked on the *Developer* tab and in the *Code* group clicked *Macro*. You entered the name of the macro you wanted to write, and clicked Create. You were automatically taken into the Visual Basic Editor where the initial code was already written in a module. In this lesson, we are not going to follow that procedure.

Microsoft Visual Basic for Applications

Click the Developer tab, and in the Code group, click Visual Basic. The Visual Basic editor will open. No module is displayed. Click the Insert tab and Click Module, a module will open named Module 1.

Type or copy and paste the code shown on slide 2 of your presentation into Module 1. Make sure there are no typing errors or if you used copy/paste that you didn't leave anything out.

Return to the PowerPoint Presentation

You can return to your PowerPoint presentation by clicking the close button at the top right corner of Microsoft Visual Basic for Application screen or click the View Microsoft PowerPoint button on the toolbar at the top of the screen.

View the Macros You Have Written

Once you are back to your PowerPoint presentation, click the Developer tab and in the Code group click Macros. The Macro dialog box shown in figure 7–3 will be displayed showing the four macros written from the code you entered. Run the macros in this order to make sure each of them works properly: YourName (type your name when prompted), Hello, Correct, and Incorrect. If your code is accurate, your name will have been added to the last three macros.

Figure 7–3

Assign Run Macro Action to Objects

Go to slide 3 and assign the *YourName* macro to the *Click to enter name object*.

Go to slide 4 and assign Incorrect macro to all the objects except the triangle. Assign Correct macro to the triangle.

View the Presentation in Slide Show View

View the presentation in Slide Show view. When you get to slide 3, click on the object *Click to enter name*, and enter your name. Go to slide 4 and click on each object. Your name should be added to each message displayed.

Finish the Presentation

Add the *Wind* Transition, duration 2 seconds, to all slides. Add appropriate action buttons to navigate the Slide Show. Set up the show to be Browsed at a Kiosk, and save the presentation.

Teleporting

In this job you will *teleport* an object from one location to another. It will instantly move from any location to its original position. You will not see the path of the movement. The advantage of teleporting rather than making an object just appear and disappear is that the object can be moved randomly to any position on the screen, and teleporting will have it appear in a position you set. It moves its location instantly, a useful technique for gaming applications.

Open the presentation **Lesson 7 Teleporting**. Add your name to the title placeholder and save the file again. The *Berlin* Design theme with a green variant has already been applied to the presentation. Your slide 2 shows the word *exotic* spelled out in WordArt inside rounded rectangles with no fill as shown in figure 7–4. We want to be able to mix up the letters and move them to a new location on the slide as shown in figure 7–5. When any of the letters is clicked, it will move to its place in the word. In this game the players try to guess the word with as few letters as possible placed in their proper positions in the word. When a player names the word, he/she receives as many points as there are blanks in the word. There would be multiple slides with different words on each of the slides. The first person to get twenty-five points wins.

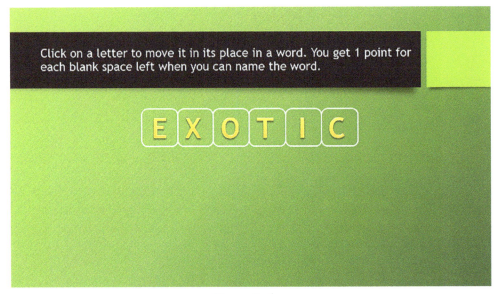

Figure 7–4

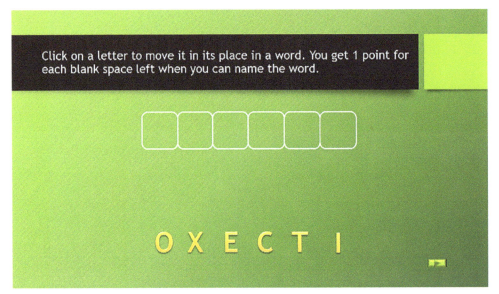

Figure 7–5

ADVANCED POWERPOINT: MORE THAN PRESENTATIONS!

Step 1

Move to slide 2 and click on the first letter in the word, *E*, and add a Motion Path down (you could use any direction, we just chose down). *Note: The green oval indicates the beginning of the animation, and the red oval indicates the end of the animation in Office 2013 or 2016, early versions will show an arrow.* See figure 7–6.

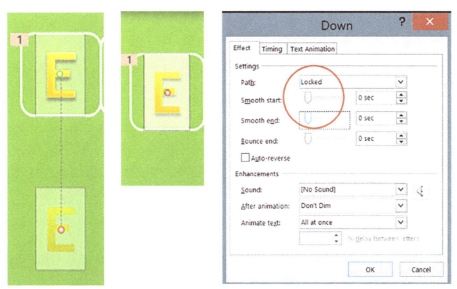

Figure 7–6

Step 2

Click on the red oval or arrow to select it, hold the Shift key to keep the direction straight, and move the red oval on top of the green oval. See figure 7–6.

Click the Animation tab, and in the Advance animation group, click Animation pane. The animation will be the only animation listed in the animation pane. Click the arrow to the right of the animation and click effect options. In the Down dialog box displayed, change the path to locked and Smooth Start and Smooth Stop to zero seconds. See figure 7–6. Click the arrow to the right of the animation again, and click timing. Set the letter, *E*, as the trigger to start the animation.

Step 3

Move the letter to the bottom portion of the slide. View the slide in Slide Show view, click the letter, *E*, and it should teleport to its original position. Exit Slide Show view, and move the letter back to the bottom of the slide.

Repeat steps 2 and 3 for each letter in the word. *Note: You could use the animation painter to speed up this process.* When you are done, drag the letters to the bottom of the slide and arrange them in random order. Align them at the top and distribute them horizontally as shown in figure 7–5. View slide 2 in Slide Show view to make sure it works properly.

Step 4

Move to slide 3 and add the teleport animation to the dog. Make the free-form shape that represents the grass the trigger the start the animation. Move the dog behind the dog house so that only his right ear and foot are visible. View slide 3 in Slide Show view to test the animation.

Finish the Presentation

Add the *Vortex* slide Transition, 3 seconds, to all slides. Add appropriate action buttons to navigate the Slide Show and set it up to be Browsed at a Kiosk.

Combining Animation Effects

Open the data file **Lesson 7 Combining Animation Effects**. The presentation contains eight slides with a dark blue background. Add your name in the subtitle placeholder and the file name and save your presentation.

Slide 2

Slide 2 contains a single star. Animate the star for a Spin animation, Medium, With Previous, and change the spin effect to 15° Clockwise as shown in the Spin animation dialog box shown in figure 7–7.

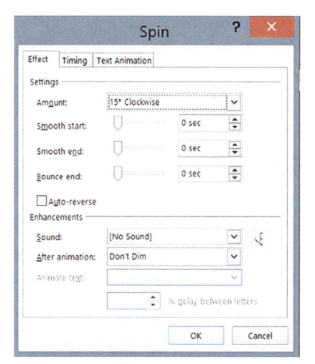

Figure 7–7

Make sure the star is selected and press Ctrl+D to duplicate it. The new star will move down and to the right. The animation was copied. Change the Amount of the animation to 30°. Repeat this process until you have created 12 stars, each rotating 15° more than the previous star. Your slide will look like figure 7–8, and the amount of animation will range from 15° for the first star to 180° for the last star.

Figure 7–8

Make sure that all the animations start With Previous. View slide 2 in Slide Show view to view the animation.

Slide 3

Drag your pointer and select all the stars on slide 2. Copy the stars and paste them on slide 3. While the stars are still selected, align them at the center and top and then move them to the center of the slide. It will look like only one star is there. When you copied the stars, you also copied the animation. View slide 3 in Slide Show view to view the new animation you have created.

Slide 4

Copy all the stars from slide 3 and paste them on slide 4. The animation is also copied. While all the stars are still selected, add an Exit Pinwheel animation. In the animation pane, change the first new Exit animation to After Previous, all the other Exit animations should be With Previous. View slide 4 in Slide Show view.

Slide 5

Copy and paste all the stars from slide 2 to slide 5. While the stars are still selected, add the Emphasis Complementary Color animation. The first new animation should be After Previous, and all the others should be With Previous. While the stars are still selected, add the Exit Basic Zoom animation. The first new animation should be After Previous, and all the others should be With Previous. View slide 5 in Slide Show view.

Slide 6

Copy all the stars from slide 3 and paste them on slide 6. While the stars are still selected, add an animation Emphasis, Spin, Counterclockwise. The first new animation should be After Previous and the rotation effect to 15°. All the other new animations should be With Previous, and each one should increase the rotation by 15°—that is, 15, 30, etc., to the last one which will be 180°. Make sure all the stars are selected and add an animation Exit, Swivel. The first new animation should be After Previous, and the others should be With Previous. View slide 6 in Slide Show view.

Slide 7

Copy all the stars from slide 3 and paste them on slide 7. While the stars are still selected, add an animation Emphasis, Grow/Shrink. The first new animation should be After Previous, and all others should be With Previous. While the stars are still selected, add an animation Exit, Stretchy. The first new animation should be After Previous, and all others should be With Previous. If necessary, substitute a different Exit animation. View slide 7 in Slide Show view.

Slide 8

On slide 8, replace the Your Name placeholder with your name. Select your name and animate it to spin clockwise on click, 15°, Auto-reverse. Duplicate your name and add 15° to the animation. Repeat until you have reached 180°. The first animation should be on click and all others should be With Previous. Select all the names and align them at the top and center and move them to the center of the slide. While all the names are still selected add an animation Exit, Pinwheel, the first new animation After Previous, and all others With Previous. View slide 8 in Slide Show view.

Finish the Presentation

Add action buttons to navigate the presentation and a transition of your choice. Save your presentation.

Lesson 7 Applications

Lesson 7 Application 1 Presentation Application

Open the data file *Lesson 7 Application 1 Presentation Application*. Add your name in the subtitle placeholder and save the file adding your name to the end of the file name. The *Damask* Design theme and *Doors* Transition has already been applied to the slides. Figure 7–9 shows the five slides in the presentation that you will prepare and animate.

Figure 7–9

Slide 1

Add an animation Entrance, Zoom, 8 seconds, With Previous to the title. Add an animation to the title Emphasis, Brush Color, After Previous. Add an animation to your name on the title slide Entrance, Zoom, 6 seconds, After Previous.

Slide 2

On slide 2 create 5 stars ranging in size from height 1" and width 1" to height 5" and width 5". Add a different fill pattern and color to each star, and arrange as shown in figure 7–9. Name each star object starting with *one* for the smallest star to *five* for the largest star.

Slide 3

Copy the stars from slide 2 on to slide 3. Arrange them so that the smallest star is on top and the largest is on the bottom. Align the stars to the center and middle.

Animating Slide 3

Select all the stars and add an animation Entrance, Zoom, Very Slow. The first animation should be With Previous and the others After Previous.

While all the stars are selected, add an animation Emphasis, Spin, Clockwise. The first animation should be After Previous and the others With Previous. The first animation, the large star, 1 second, the next star 2 seconds, the third star 3 seconds, the fourth star 4 seconds, and the fifth star 5 seconds.

While all the stars are selected, add an animation Emphasis, Grow/Shrink, Medium, Auto-reverse, 200 percent. The first animation should be After Previous and the others With Previous.

While all the stars are selected, add an animation Emphasis, Teeter .1 seconds, and repeat 50 times. The first animation should be After Previous and the other animations should be With Previous.

While all the stars are selected, add an animation Emphasis, Grow/Shrink, Medium, Auto-reverse, 150 percent. The first animation should be After Previous and the others With Previous.

While all the stars are selected, add an animation Emphasis, Spin, Very Fast, Counterclockwise, and repeat 20 times.

While all the stars are selected, add an animation Exit, Pinwheel, Medium speed, all After Previous.

Slide 4

Replace the WordArt placeholder with your name. Animate the WordArt for an animation Entrance, Bounce, Medium speed, the first animation With Previous, all others After Previous.

While the WordArt is still selected, animate it for Emphasis, Spin, Counterclockwise, Medium. The first animation should be After Previous and all others With Previous.

While the WordArt is still selected, animate it for Emphasis, Spin, Clockwise, Very Fast, and Repeat 3 times. The first animation should be After Previous and all others With Previous.

While the WordArt is still selected, animate it for an Emphasis, Wave, Very Fast. All animations should be After Previous.

Slide 5

Slide 5 contains 5 cogs. Animate the center cog to Spin Counterclockwise, Medium, With Previous, Repeat Until End of Slide. Animate the four other cogs to Spin Clockwise, Medium, With Previous, Repeat Until End of Slide.

Add an animation Motion Path Down, With Previous, Very Slow to the cog in the upper left corner. Move red arrow so that the cog interlocks with the center animation. View the animation in Slide Show view to see any adjustments needed. Repeat for the upper right cog.

Add an animation Motion Path Up, With Previous, Very Slow to the cog in the lower left corner. Move the red arrow so that the cog interlocks with the center animation. View the animation in Slide Show view to see any adjustments needed. Repeat for lower right cog.

Delay the first Motion Path for 5 seconds, the second for 10 seconds, the third for 15 seconds, and the fourth for 20 seconds. Figure 7–10 shows how the cogs will look after the Motion Path animations in both Normal and Slide Show view.

Select all 5 cogs and add an animation Emphasis Grow/Shrink, 170 percent, Very Slow, the first After Previous and the others With Previous.

Select all 5 cogs and add an animation Exit, Spinner, Slow, the first After Previous and the others With Previous.

Add WordArt *Teamwork builds success!* Change the font color to red and the size to 80 pt. Add an animation Entrance, Zoom, After Previous. Align the WordArt at the center and middle.

Complete the Presentation

Add action buttons to navigate the presentation and set it up to be Browsed at a Kiosk.

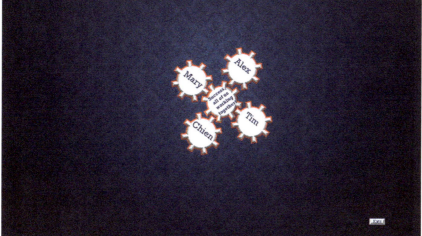

Figure 7–10

Lesson 7 Application 2 Instructional Materials Application

Open the data file ***Lesson 7 Application 2 Instructional Materials Application***. Add your name to the title placeholder and save the file as a PowerPoint Macro-Enabled presentation. The presentation contains six slides. The Ion *Boardroom* Design theme has been applied, and the *Switch* Transition. This presentation is a short review for a test. Figure 7–11 shows the slides of the presentation when this application is completed.

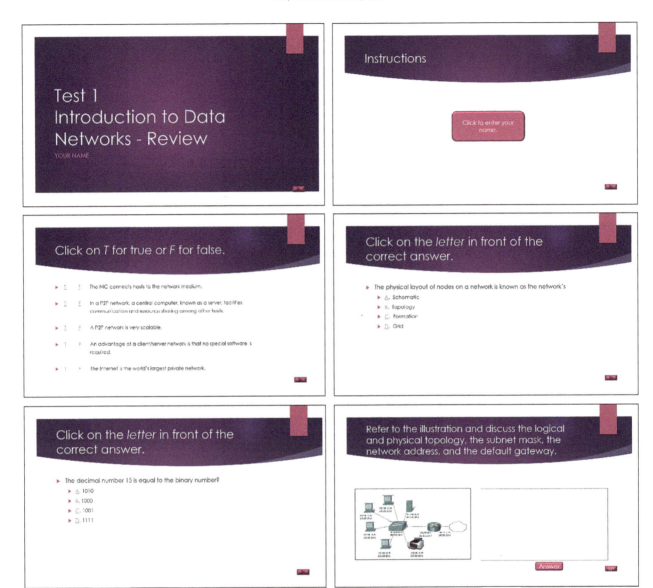

Figure 7–11

On slide 2, the user will be able to click the button to enter her/his name. The button will launch a macro.

On slide 3, the student will click *T* or *F*. Clicking a letter will launch a macro to display a *correct* or *incorrect* message.

Slides 4 and 5 contain multiple choice questions. Clicking any letter will launch a macro to display the *correct* or *incorrect* message.

Slide 6 contains an ActiveX Text Box Control where students can type their answers in Slide Show view. The *properties* have been adjusted to allow for word wrap, multiline, and scroll bars. Clicking the Answer box will launch the DisQues macro to display the correct answer.

ADVANCED POWERPOINT: MORE THAN PRESENTATIONS!

Step 1

You need to open the Visual Basic Editor and add a module. Type the following code for the four macros: YourName, Correct, Incorrect, and DisQues.

```
'This procedure requires the input of your name.
'Date created: Current date
'The Dim statement is used to declare a variable to hold a value.
'A string is a type of variable that can contain letters, numbers, and symbols
'and is enclosed in quotation marks.

Dim userName As String
Sub YourName()
    userName = InputBox("Name: ")
End Sub

Sub Correct()
    MsgBox ("Correct, very good " & userName)
End Sub

Sub Incorrect()
    MsgBox ("Incorrect, please review Chapter 1 of the textbook, " & userName)
End Sub

Sub DisQues()
    MsgBox ("Both the physical and logical topology of this network are the star topology. The subnet mask is 255.255.255 and the network address is 192.180.18.0. The default gateway is 192.180.18.1.")
End Sub
```

Step 2

Go to slide 2 and use the *Click to enter your name rounded rectangle* to launch the macro *YourName*.

Step 3

Go to slide 3 and use each *T* or *F* to launch the appropriate macro, *correct* or *incorrect*. The answers are in the Notes pane.

Step 4

Go to slides 4 and 5 and use each *letter* to launch the appropriate macro, *correct* or *incorrect*. The answers are in the Notes pane.

Step 5

Go to slide 6 and use the *Answer* rounded rectangle to launch the macro *DisQues*.

Step 6

View the presentation in Slide Show view and click on all possible choices to make sure the correct message box is displayed. Make any correction needed.

Step 7

Add necessary action buttons to navigate the presentation and set up the presentation to be Browsed at a Kiosk. Save the presentation.

Lesson 7 Application 3 Gaming Application

Open the data file **Lesson 7 Application 3 Gaming Application**. Replace the subtitle placeholder with your name. Add your name to the file name and save the file. Figure 7–12 shows the two slides in the completed presentation. The *Vapor Trail* Design has been applied and the *Drape* Transition has been applied.

Figure 7–12

On slide 2, in the center of the slide are five words. Some are not spelled correctly. The user clicks the *icon* under Yes if he/she thinks the word is spelled correctly or the *icon* under No if he/she thinks the word is not spelled correctly. The icon clicked will teleport down to the Island vacation if the user made the correct selection or it will teleport to jail if the user did not make the correct selection.

Step 1

On slide 2 use the rectangles and pictures provided to create the location for the island vacation and jail as shown in figure 7–12. You will need to apply appropriate 3-D Rotations and 3-D Formats.

Step 2

You will need to create the icon figure shown. All the shapes for the icon figure are all made from an oval except the mouth, which is a Block Arc Shape. The body was made by making an oval, placing a rectangle on top of the oval, and then clicking the oval first, hold down the shift key and click on the rectangle, and then click Subtract Shapes. If necessary, add the Subtract Shapes button to the *Quick Access Toolbar*. Figure 7–13 shows how the icon figure was made. Once you make the figure, duplicate it nine times so that you have ten icon figures. *Note: If you don't have Subtract Shapes, you can use the Flowchart Delay shape to create the body.*

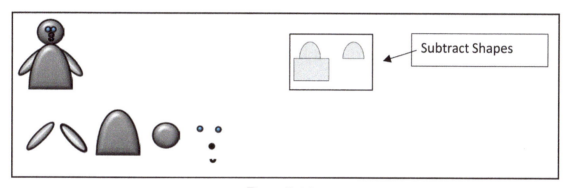

Figure 7–13

Step 3

Place five of the icon figures in the Island Vacation and five in Jail as shown in figure 7–14.

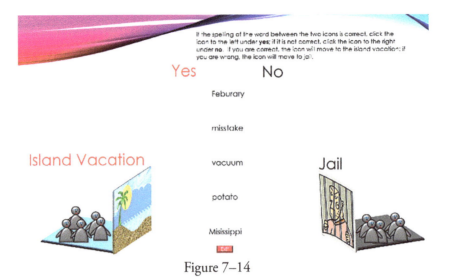

Figure 7–14

Animate each icon for a Motion Path Down. Drag the ending Motion Path arrow on top of the beginning Motion Path arrow and lock the path. Have the icon object serve as the trigger for the animation. Repeat this procedure for the remaining nine icon figures.

The answers for each word are shown in the Notes pane. The first word *February* is not spelled correctly. If the user clicked the icon under Yes, that would be the *wrong answer*. Therefore, drag one of the icons from the *jail location under Yes* to the left of the word. If the icon under Yes is clicked in Slide Show view, the icon will move to the Jail location. Drag one of the icons from *the Island Vacation* under the No to the right of the word. If the user clicked the icon under No, that is the *correct answer* so the icon will move to the Island Vacation if clicked in Slide Show view. Repeat this procedure for the other four words. Your slide will look like figure 7–15.

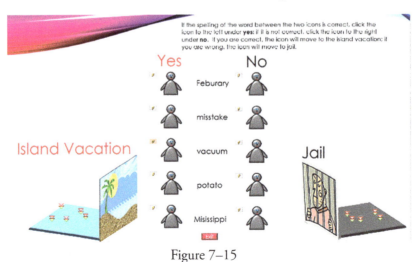

Figure 7–15

ADVANCED POWERPOINT: MORE THAN PRESENTATIONS!

Finish the Presentation

Add necessary action buttons to navigate the presentation and set it up to be Browsed at a Kiosk. Save the presentation.

In Slide Show view, if the user got all the words correct, the slide would look like figure 7–16.

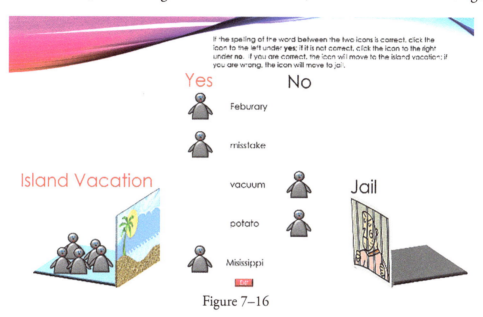

Figure 7–16

LESSON 8

Interactive Instructional Materials, VBA (Modifying Code), Traditional Board Games

Data Files

Lesson 8 Interactive Instructional Materials
Lesson 8 VBA 4 Drop-Down Menu and Math Problems
Lesson 8 Application 1 Presentation Application
Lesson 8 Application 2 Instructional Materials Application
Lesson 8 Application 3 Gaming Application

Overview

In this lesson, you will learn to create interactive instructional materials. The user will be able to add data and interact with the computer in Slide Show view. You will continue learning more VBA code for randomizing the selection of data. Finally, you will learn to create an electronic checkers game.

Interactive Instructional Materials

Interactive instructional materials facilitate learning through visualizing and manipulating one's own data in real time. Electronic technology makes it easy to develop original interactive instructional materials that can be used in a variety of situations at various educational levels.

Step 1

Open the data file *Lesson 8 Interactive Instructional Materials*. The *Children Happy* Design and *Peel off* Transition have already been applied to the presentation. Replace the subtitle place holder with your name and save the file again. The slides in the presentation are shown in figure 8–1. Action buttons have also been added to the presentation. You will need to do three things to each slide to make them interactive.

1. Add a sound representing the animal on each slide.

ADVANCED POWERPOINT: MORE THAN PRESENTATIONS!

2. Black out everything on the screen when a picture is clicked except the picture, the callout, and the action button.
3. Display a callout with text that answers the question posed at the right bottom of slides 2 to 5. To add the callout, click Insert/Illustrations/Shapes/Oval Callout.

Figure 8–1

Step 2

Go to slide 2 and set the playback for the elephant sound already on the slide to automatic as shown in figure 8–2. Move the sound icon off the screen to the right. Repeat this step on slides 3 – 5.

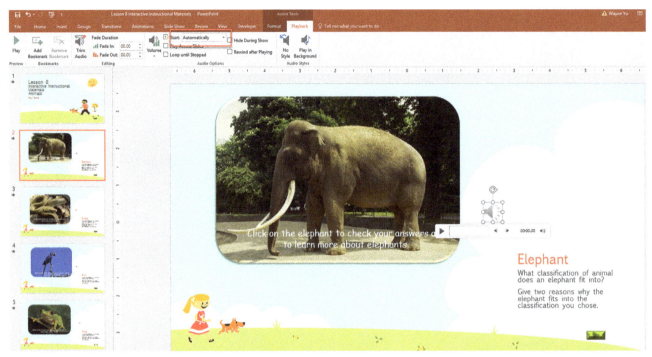

Figure 8–2

Step 3

Go to slide 2. We want to have the screen turn black when the picture is clicked and for a callout to be displayed providing the answers to the questions posed under the name of the animal.

Draw a rectangle the size of the screen with a black fill and No Line. Animate the rectangle for an Entrance, Fade, 10 seconds when the picture of the elephant is clicked. Animate the text on the elephant picture to Exit, Disappear at the same time.

Step 4

Animate the callout for an Entrance, Fade in, 10 seconds with the black rectangle. Arrange the objects on the slide so that only the picture of the elephant, the callout, and the action button are visible after the elephant is clicked. Your slide 2 should look like figure 8–3 after you have clicked on the elephant picture in Slide Show view.

Figure 8–3

Repeat this procedure for slides 3 to 5. The callout information for slides 2 to 5 is as follows:

Slide 2: *Elephants are classified as mammals because they are warm-blooded, have fur or hair, give birth to their babies, and nurse their babies with milk.*

Slide 3: *Snakes are classified as reptiles because they are cold-blooded, have scales, usually lay eggs, and have dry skin.*

Slide 4*: Bird is the classification, and birds have feathers and wings, are warm-blooded, and lay eggs.*

Slide 5: *The frog is an amphibian. Frogs live on land and in water. They lay eggs, and have moist skin and webbed feet.*

Complete the Presentation

View your presentation in Slide Show view to make sure everything is working properly. Set up the Slide Show to be Browsed at a Kiosk. Save the presentation.

Modify VBA Code

Open the data file **Lesson 8 VBA 4 Drop-Down Menu and Math Problems**. Replace the subtitle placeholder with your name and save the file again. The design for this presentation was created on the slide masters, and *Wind* Transition has already been applied to the presentation. Action buttons have also been added to navigate the presentation. The presentation contains seven slides, but we will only prepare the first four slides in this job. You will complete this job in the application activity at the end of this lesson.

Drop-Down Menu

Figure 8–4 shows slide 2 of the presentation. All slides but the Title slide are in Title Only Layout. On slide 2, the word *Menu* has been entered as the title, and WordArt has been used to indicate the various options under the menu. We are going to create a menu that floats down when you click on *Menu* in the title and floats up when you click on the word *Menu* again. We will then create hyperlinks for each menu option.

Figure 8–4

Step 1

Select all the words under the title Menu. Add an animation Entrance, Float Down to the objects. Display the animation pane. All the animations are still selected. Click the arrow to the right of the last animation and click Timing and under Triggers click start effect on click of Title 3: Menu.

View slide 2 in Slide Show view. The options under the menu are no longer visible. Click the word *Menu* and the menu will float down.

Step 2

Select all the words under the title, *Menu*. Add an animation Exit, Float Up to the objects. Display the Animation pane. All the animations are still selected. Click the arrow to the right of the last animation and click Timing and under Triggers click start effect on click of Title 3: Menu.

View slide 2 in Slide Show view. Click the word *Menu* and the menu options should float down. Click the word *Menu* again and the options will float up and out of view.

Creating Random Addition Problems

Go to slide 3. Slide 3 shows the code you will enter to create a macro that randomly generates addition problems, asks the user for the answer, and generates a correct or incorrect message. The code that you will need to enter is shown in figure 8–5.

'Date written.
'Dim is used to define variables.
'First and second are names of variables.
'10 * Rnd means select a number from the first ten integers, 0, 1, 2, 3, 4, 5, 6, 7, 8. and 9.
'Increase difficulty level by increasing the range for random numbers selected. For example, 20 * Rnd or 100 * Rnd.
'Change the operator to change the type of problem. For example, instead of + use -, *, or /.

```
Sub RandomQuestionAdd()
Randomize
Dim first As Integer
Dim second As Integer
first = Int(10 * Rnd)
second = Int(10 * Rnd)
answer = InputBox ("What is " & first & " + " & second & "?" )
If answer = first + second Then
    Correct
Else
    Incorrect
End If
End Sub

Sub Correct()
    MsgBox ("Correct. Good job.")
End Sub

Sub Incorrect()
MsgBox ("Incorrect. Take your time and try to do better.")
End Sub
```

Figure 8–5

The first six lines are in green and preceded by REM or ', and are documentation you will write to yourself indicating the date you created the code and some additional notes. They are ignored when the code is run.

The first macro begins with *Sub* and is named *RandomQuestionAdd*. The code following Sub uses *Randomize* to initialize the randomization process, *Dim* to indicate the type of data to be stored in the *first* and *second* variable. The *first* variable is a random number selected from the range 0 to 9, *Int (10 * Rnd)*. The *second* variable is a random number selected from the range 0 to 9, *Int (10 * Rnd)*. The variable *answer* is used to store the answer to the addition problem that asks *What is the first random number plus the second random number?*

If the answer the user enters equals the first variable + the second variable, the *Correct* macro is run. If the answer the user enters is not equal to the first variable + the second variable, then (Else) the *Incorrect* macro is run.

Open the Visual Basic Editor, and add a Module. Type or copy and paste the code shown on slide 3 into the module. Once you have entered the code, view and run the RandomQuestonAdd macro several times to see the problems generated and the request for an answer. Enter a correct and incorrect answer to see the message displayed. Correct any errors you might have made.

Launch Macro from an Object

Go to slide 4, and create a hyperlink from the Level 1 problems object to run the macro RandomQuestionAdd. Make sure you use the object and not the text to create the link. View slide 4 in Slide Show view and click on the Level 1 problems button to generate random questions.

Create a Link from the Menu to Addition Problems

Go to slide 2 and create a hyperlink from the WordArt object, *Addition*, to slide 4. Make sure you link the object and not the text. Click on the WordArt and then click on the border around it so that it changes to a solid line before you create the link. Display slide 2 in Slide Show view, click *Menu* to display the menu and then click on the WordArt object, *Addition*. You should be taken to slide 4. Click on the menu button at the bottom of slide 4 and you should be returned to menu. Click the *Menu* button to make the menu option float up.

Generating Addition Problems at Different Difficulty Levels

Display the Visual Basic Editor and copy all the code below the documentation (green text), and paste it after the last End Sub. Change the name of the macro from RandomQuestionAdd to *RandomQuestionAddLevel2*. The difficulty level of the questions is determined by the range of random numbers you select. In the first macro you used macros from 0–9. For the level 2 problems we will use numbers from 0–49. Go to the line for the *first* and *second* variables and change 10 to 50. You have changed the difficulty level of the problems.

Go to slide 4, and create a hyperlink from the Level 2 Problems object to run the macro RandomQuestionAddLevel2. Make sure you use the object and not the text to create the link. View slide 4 in Slide Show view and click on the Level 2 problems button to generate random questions.

Copy all the code you used for the *RandomQuestonAddLevel2* macro and paste it after the last End Sub. Change the name of the macro from RandomQuestionAddLevel2 to *RandomQuestionAddLevel3*. Go to the line for the *first* and *second* variables and change 50 to 100.

Go to slide 4, and create a hyperlink from the Level 3 Problems object to run the macro RandomQuestionAddLevel3. Make sure you use the object and not the text to create the link. View slide 4 in Slide Show view and click on the Level 3 problems button to generate random questions.

Test all the links from the menu on slide 2 to each level of addition problems. Save your presentation. You will be completing the presentation when you complete the applications at the end of this lesson.

Lesson 8 Applications

Lesson 8 Application 1 Presentation Application

Open the data file ***Lesson 8 Application 1 Presentation Application***. Add your name in the subtitle placeholder. Add your name to the end of the file name and save the file again. In this job you are going to develop a presentation to lead a class discussion related to birds.

Title Slide

Slide 1 contains a picture of a bird and the soft edge oval style has already been applied. The background theme for all slides is background style 11 (Design/Variants/More/Background Styles/11). The *Prestige* Transition has been applied to all slides. Duplicate the bird picture four times and arrange them horizontally across the screen as shown in figure 8–6. Format the artistic effect for the first picture by selecting the picture and then click Picture Tools/Format/Adjust/Artistic Effects for Pencil Grayscale. Format the second for Pencil Sketch. Format the third for Photocopy. Format the fourth for Crisscross Etching, and don't add any artistic effect for the original picture.

Figure 8–6

Animate the Pictures

Click on the first picture, the Pencil Grayscale artistic effect and animate it for an Entrance, Fade, With Previous, Very Slow. Animate the same picture for Exit, Fade, After Previous, Very Slow. Animation the second picture for Entrance, Fade, After Previous, Very Slow. Animate the same picture for Exit, Fade, After Previous, Very Slow. Animate pictures 3 and 4 the same as the second picture. Animate the last picture with no artistic effect for Entrance, Fade, After Previous, Very Slow.

Select all five pictures and then align them at the center and middle so that they are stacked on top of one another and you see only one picture as shown in figure 8–7. View the title slide in Slide Show view to see the animation.

Figure 8–7

Slide 2

Slide 2 contains a menu. The menu is in the title placeholder, and the words below the menu are in WordArt. Animate the menu options so that the menu options float down when you click on the menu object and float up when you click on menu object again. Later, you will create links from the menu options to specific slides.

Slides 3 to 6

Slides 3 to 6 will all be prepared the same way. Each slide contains a picture of a bird, a callout shape with information about the bird, and a text box with a message to click on the bird to see more information.

Click on the picture of the bird on slide 3. And a Motion Path diagonal down right as shown in figure 8–8. Use the picture as the trigger for the animation. Add an animation Emphasis, Grow/Shrink, With Previous, 150 percent. Select the text box and click on its border and add an animation Exit, Disappear, With Previous. Click on the callout and add an animation Entrance, Fade, With Previous, Very Slow. Draw a rectangle that covers the entire slide with dark blue fill and No Line. Animate the rectangle for Entrance, Fade In, With Previous, Medium. Add a text box with the message: Press ESC to return to menu as shown. The bird picture, the callout, and the text box you added should be in front of the large rectangle you added. Animate slides 4 to 6 the same as slide 3. Slide 3 after the bird picture is clicked in Slide Show view should look like figure 8–9.

ADVANCED POWERPOINT: MORE THAN PRESENTATIONS!

Figure 8–8

Figure 8–9

Custom Shows

View the slides in your presentation in Slide Show view and click on the bird on slides 3 to 6 to see the effect. Without exiting Slide Show view, click PgUp or back to move to a previous slide, the animation no longer works. Once you play the animation in PowerPoint and then go back to it, it doesn't play the second time. To avoid this, you need to create a Custom Show for slides 3 to 6. Name each separate Custom Show the name of the bird on the slide: *Flamingo, Penguin, Parrot,* and *Woodpecker.*

Menu Links

Go to slide 2 where you created a drop-down menu, and link each of the bird names in the menu to the appropriate Custom Show. Be sure to click *Show and Return* when you create the link. Create a hyperlink from Exit to *end the show*.

Finish the Presentation

Add an action button to move from slide 1 to slide 2. Set up the presentation to be Browsed at a Kiosk, and save the presentation.

Lesson 8 Application 2 Instructional Materials Application

Open the data file ***Lesson 8 Application 2 Instructional Materials Application***. Add your name to the title placeholder and after the file name. Save the file as a PowerPoint Macro-Enabled presentation. This is the file you began in this lesson. We are now going to add the sections for subtraction, multiplication, and division.

Figure 8–10 shows the minor code changes you will need to make to create subtraction, multiplication, and division questions

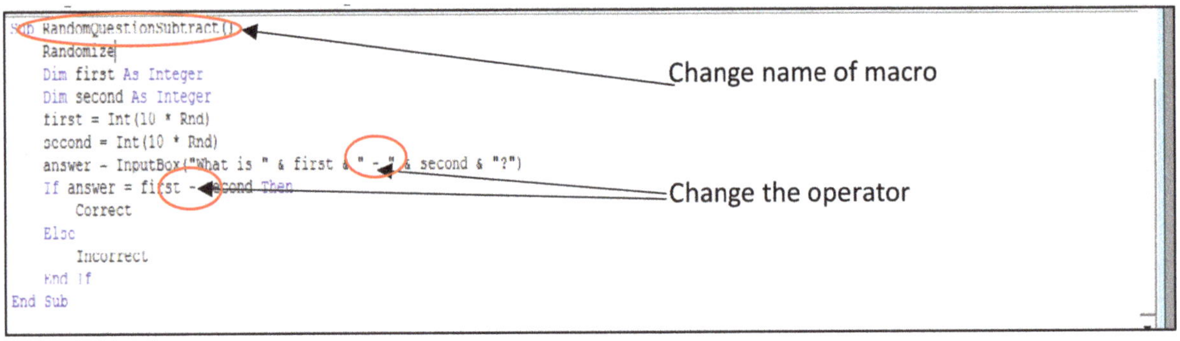

```
Sub RandomQuestionSubtract()
    Randomize
    Dim first As Integer
    Dim second As Integer
    first = Int(10 * Rnd)
    second = Int(10 * Rnd)
    answer = InputBox("What is " & first & " - " & second & "?")
    If answer = first - second Then
        Correct
    Else
        Incorrect
    End If
End Sub
```

— Change name of macro
— Change the operator

Figure 8–10

To create the first level of subtraction questions, follow these steps:

Step 1

Open the Visual Basic Applications editor and the first module. Select and copy the macro for the RandomQuestionAddLevel3 and paste it below the last line of code.

Step 2

Change the name of the macro to RandomQuestionSubtract.

Step 3

Adjust the number of random numbers as desired, leave it at 10 for the first level, 50 for the second level, and 100 for the third level.

Step 4

Change the operator symbols to either -, *, or /.

Repeat this process for the second and third level for subtraction, and repeat the process for multiplication and division. You will have a total of twelve different macros when you complete this job.

Create links from the menu to the subtraction, multiplication, division, code, and exit. Set up the show to be Browsed at a Kiosk and then save the file.

Lesson 8 Application 3 Gaming Application

In this job you will make an electronic checker game. The electronic game board will consist of eight rows and eight columns of squares height .75" and width .75", half black and half red. There are twelve checkers for each player height .5" and width .5". There are four king pieces for each player. There are sixteen placeholders for each player to hold the checkers and kings. These place holders are height .7" and width .7". The *movepiece* macro that you used in previous jobs will be assigned to each checker, and the *newlocation* macro will be assigned to the placeholders and to each black square. There are five slides with the rules for playing the game. The game board looks like figure 8–11.

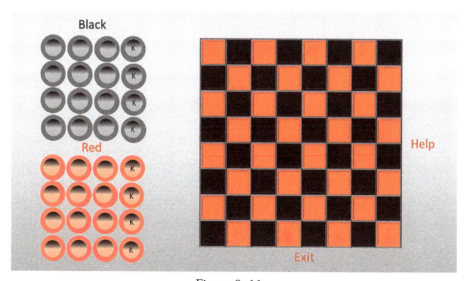

Figure 8–11

Step 1

Open the data file **Lesson 8 Application 3 Gaming Application** and replace the subtitle placeholder with your name on the title slide, and save the presentation again as a PowerPoint Macro-Enabled presentation. A picture of a checker board has been added to the title slide and its color washed out, and it was sent behind the titles. Design Style 10 was applied to all the slides, and the action button Next was added to the specific slides. The *Flip* Transition was applied to all the slides for a duration of 2 seconds. The Slide Show was set up to be Browsed at a Kiosk.

Create Custom Show

Slides 3 to 7 provide the rules for the game. Create a Custom Show named *Help* consisting of slides 3 to 7.

Hyperlink to Custom Show

Click on the object *Help* on slide 2. Make sure you select the entire object and not the individual letters. Create a hyperlink to the Custom Show Help. Be sure to click *Show and Return*. View all the help slides in Slide Show view and press ESC to return to slide 2. Make any necessary corrections. Add a hyperlink to exit the Slide Show view from slide 2. Use the word *Exit* at the bottom of slide 2 to launch the hyperlink.

Step 2

Assign the *movepiece* macro to all checkers, including the Kings. The macro has already been written and changed so that the game pieces will fit properly into the game squares.

Step 3

Assign the *newlocation* macro to all the black game board squares and to all the oval shapes to the left of the game board used as placeholders for the checkers, including the shapes to hold kings. Send all the black squares and oval placeholders to the back so that when you move a checker on top of it the checker does not move behind the oval or square. Move all checker pieces to the front.

Step 4

Go into Slide Show view and move all the checkers off the placeholders and onto the game board as shown in figure 8–12. Make any necessary adjustments.

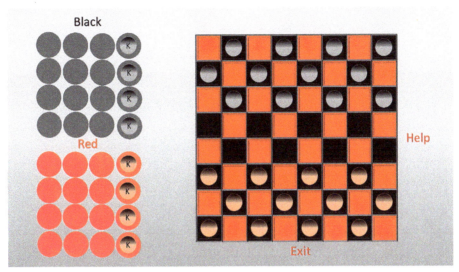

Figure 8–12

Step 5

Select any game piece and move back onto a placeholder. Click every other black square and the game piece should be able to move to each square. If the game piece disappears, exit Slide Show and move that black square to the back. Make sure all the king pieces can move onto the black squares. Go back into Slide Show view and troubleshoot to make sure that everything is working properly.

Step 6

Play a game of checkers with another person to make sure the game is working properly.

Step 7

Save the presentation as a PowerPoint Macro-Enabled presentation.

LESSON 9

Electronic Book, Animate Photos, Pivots, and Animation

Data Files

Lesson 9 Animated Photo
Lesson 9 Electronic Book
Lesson 9 Pivots and Animation
Lesson 9 Application 1 Presentation Application
Lesson 9 Application 2 Instructional Materials Application
Lesson 9 Application 3 Gaming Application

Overview

In this lesson, you will learn to create an electronic book. You will also learn to animate a static object such as a photo. Finally, you will begin to learn basic software features that will enable you to create realistic animations.

Electronic Book

Creating the Book Cover

Open the data file ***Lesson 9 Electronic Book***. The Book in Clouds academic presentation with video has already been applied. Add your name in the subtitle placeholder and at the end of the file name and save the file.

Slide 2 is in Blank Layout. Insert a rounded rectangle height 5" and width 3.8". Use the yellow adjustment handle to reduce the curve corners of the book cover. Add a Gradient fill, Linear right, blue Accent 1, Darker 50 percent at 0 percent position and blue Accent 1, Darker 25 percent at the 100 percent position. Duplicate the shape and reduce its width to .5" as shown in figure 9–1.

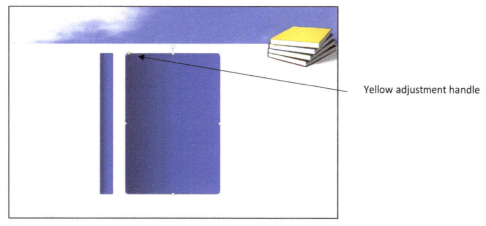

Figure 9–1

Drag the second shape to the left edge of the first shape and align the shapes at the top and left. Use WordArt and add the word *Title*, 40 pt Constantia, white, Background 1. Add the word *Author* in 28 pt Constantia, white Background 1 as shown in figure 9–2. Align the words at the center.

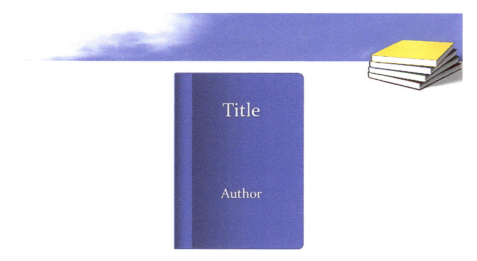

Figure 9–2

Select all the shapes that make up the book cover and group them. You will add an actual title and your name as author later.

Name the Book Cover Group

To name the group you created when you grouped all the shapes that make up the book cover, click the *Home* tab and in the *Editing* group click *Select* and then click *Selection pane* to display the Selection pane. Double-click on the group name and then change the name to *Book Cover* as shown in figure 9–3.

Figure 9–3

Add a slide 3, and make a copy of the book cover from slide 2 and ungroup the object and delete the binding and the two text boxes so that only the original rounded rectangle height 5" and width 3.8" is left as shown in figure 9–4.

Figure 9–4

Create the Inside Left Page

Draw a rectangle height 4.9" and width 3.7". Select Gradient fill, Linear Left and 5 positions: 0 percent, 5 percent, 20 percent, 40 percent, and 95 percent. Change the color at the 0 percent to white Background 1, Darker 35 percent. Change the color at 5 percent to white Background 1. Change color at 20 percent to white Background 1, Darker 5 percent, and positions at 40 percent and 95 percent to white Background 1. Select No Line. Add a shadow Outer Offset Right. Draw a vertical line height 4.9" and change the line color to white Background 1 darker 35 percent to represent the page edge and move it to the left edge of the page shape. Align the white page and the line at the top and left. Select the three objects that make up the inside left page and group them. Name the new shape *inside left page*. Your slide should look like figure 9–5.

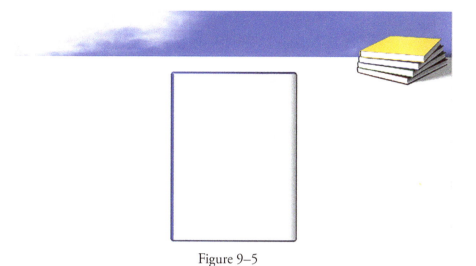

Figure 9–5

Inside Right Page

Select the inside left page shape and press Ctrl+D to duplicate it. Rotate the shape horizontally and align it with the inside left page as shown in figure 9–6. Align the two shapes at the top. Draw a vertical line 4.9" long, White, Background 1 darker 35 percent. Duplicate the shape five times and align all the new shapes at the top and group them as shown in figure 9–6. Once you have grouped the line shapes, change the width to .1" and move them to the right edge of the inside right page to represent page edges. Select all the shapes that make up the inside right page and group the shapes. Name the new shape *inside right page*.

Figure 9–6

Open and Close the Book Cover

Copy the inside left and right pages onto slide 2. Display the guidelines (View/Show/Guidelines). Drag the vertical guide to zero and make sure the left and right inside pages are aligned with that guide at the center as shown in figure 9–7. Make sure the inside left and right pages are aligned at the top.

Figure 9–7

Bring the book cover to the front so that it is on top of the right inside page. Make sure it is aligned at the center and top. Change the book title to *Halloween* and add *your name* as the author as shown in figure 9–8.

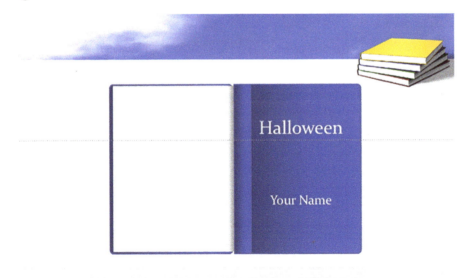

Figure 9–8

Arrange the Objects

View your Selection pane and make sure the book cover is the first named object followed by the inside left page and then the inside right page as shown in figure 9–9.

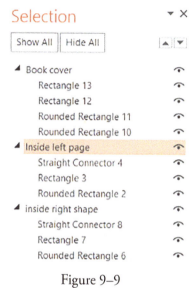

Figure 9–9

Animation to Open Book Cover

Click on the book cover and add an animation Exit, Wipe, From Right, Fast, On Click. Click on the inside left page and add an animation Entrance, Wipe, From Right, Fast, After Previous. Make sure that this animation follows the previous animation in the animation pane. View this slide in Slide Show view and click the mouse to begin the animation.

Animation to Close the Book Cover

Click on the inside left page and add an animation Exit, Wipe, From Left, Fast, On Click. Click on the book cover and add an animation Entrance, Wipe, From Left, Fast, After Previous. Make sure that this animation follows the previous animation in the animation pane. View this slide in Slide Show view and click the mouse once to open the book and a second time to close the book. Your animation pane should look like figure 9–10.

Figure 9–10

Create Pages 1 and 2

Add a new slide Blank Layout to the presentation. Copy the inside left and right pages from slide 3 onto the new slide. Ungroup the inside right page, and delete the portion that is the book cover. Ungroup the inside left page and delete the portion that is the book cover. Your slide should look like figure 9–11. When you create the pages of the book, left pages will be odd numbers and right pages will be even numbers. You will create pages 1 and 2 on this slide.

Figure 9–11

Standardize Format

All text within the book is in Cambria 12 pt font. Headings are Calibri 18 pt font, blue. And the first letter in each paragraph is Cambria 18 pt font, blue. Images have been added related to the text. Text boxes 3" wide were used for all text. The page numbers are in in Calibri 10 pt font, dark blue. The guide line was used to align the numbers. The completed pages 1 and 2 are shown in figure 9–12. Complete pages 1 and 2. You can use different images if necessary. Group all the objects that make up each page and name the two pages *Page 1* and *Page 2*. *Note: In figure 9–12, see how the guides were used to align objects on the slide.*

ADVANCED POWERPOINT: MORE THAN PRESENTATIONS!

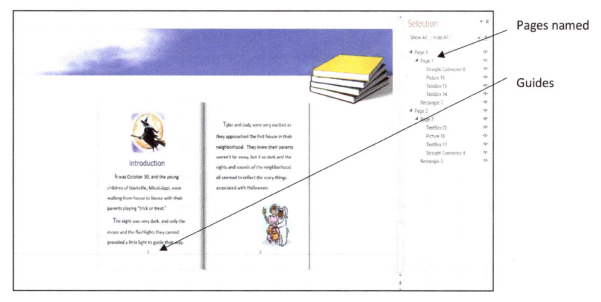

Figure 9–12

Create Pages 3 and 4

Pages 3 and 4 are shown in figure 9–13. Insert a new slide and complete the pages following the same procedures you used for pages 1 and 2. Group the objects on each page and name the pages *Page 3* and *Page 4*.

Figure 9–13

Animate Pages 1–2

Copy pages 1 and 2 on top of the inside left page and the book cover on slide 2. Animate page 2 for an Entrance, Wipe, From Right, Fast, On Click. Animate page 1 for an Entrance, Wipe, From Right, Fast, After Previous. Move the animation in the animation pane after the animation for page 2. Move the animations for pages 1 and 2 between the animations to open and close the book in the animation pane as shown in figure 9–14. View slide 2 in Slide Show view and click the mouse to open the book, and click the mouse again to turn pages 1 and 2. The animation to close the book will not work properly at this point.

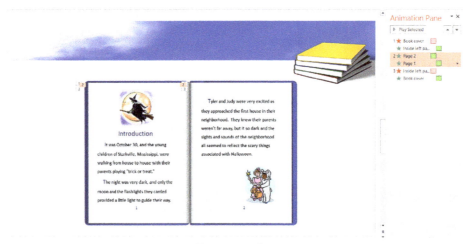

Figure 9–14

Animate Pages 3–4

Copy pages 3 and 4 on top of pages 1 and 2 on slide 2. Animate page 4 for Entrance, Wipe, From Right, Fast, On Click. Animate page 3 for Entrance, Wipe, From Right, Fast, After Previous. Move the animations in the Animation pane after the animation for pages 1 and 2 as shown in figure 9–15. View slide 2 in Slide Show view and click the mouse to open the book, turn pages 1 and 2, and turn pages 3 and 4. The animation to close the book will not work properly at this point.

Figure 9–15

ADVANCED POWERPOINT: MORE THAN PRESENTATIONS!

Because you are opening and essentially staking objects on top of one another, when you close the book, the pages will still be there. To avoid this problem, you need to have the previous two pages exit each time you display two new pages.

Click on the page 2 animation in the animation pane and add an animation Exit, Wipe, From Right, Fast, With Previous. Move the animation after the Entrance animation for page 4 in the animation pane. Click on the page 1 animation in the animation pane and add an animation Exit, Wipe, From Right, Fast, With Previous. Move the animation after the Entrance animation for page 3 in the animation pane. If you had additional pages in the book, you would repeat this process each time you displayed two new pages. View slide 2 and open the book, open pages 1 and 2, and open pages 3 and 4. The close book animation will not work properly at this point. Your animation pane will look like figure 9–16.

Figure 9–16

Modify Close Book Animation

Since there are no additional pages in our sample book, pages 3 and 4 are displayed when we close the book, so we need to have them exit. Click on page 3 in the animation pane and add an animation Exit, Wipe, From Left, With Previous, Fast. Move it after the Exit animation for the inside left page animation as part of the close book animation. Click on page 4 in the animation pane and add an animation Exit, Wipe, From Left, With Previous, Fast. Move it after the Entrance animation for the book cover in the close book animation. Your animation should work now. View slide 2 and open the book, open pages 1–2, open pages 3–4, and close the book. In order for your animations to work properly the animations in the animation page should look like figure 9–17. The objects in the selection pane should be in the order shown in figure 9–17.

Figure 9–17

Add Triggers to Animate the Book

Add the WordArt to the right of the book shown in figure 9–18. You should insert separate WordArt for *Open*, *1–2*, *3–4*, and *Close*. Use the WordArt as the trigger to open the book, turn pages 1–2, turn pages 3–4, and Close the book.

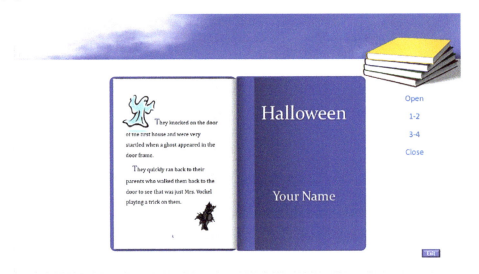

Figure 9–18

Finish the Presentation

Delete all slides except the title slide and the slide with your electronic book, slide 2. Add an appropriate transition and action buttons to navigate the Slide Show. Set up the show to be Browsed at a Kiosk.

ADVANCED POWERPOINT: MORE THAN PRESENTATIONS!

Animate Photo

Open the data file ***Lesson 9 Animated Photo***. Add your name in the subtitle placeholder and save the file again, adding your name to the file name. Background style 12 and the *Wind* Transition have been applied to the presentation. Two action buttons have also been inserted.

Go to slide 2. Slide 2 contains a picture of a winter scene. Click on the picture and click the Format tab. In the Adjust group, click Color. Click Set Transparent Color, and then click on the white background of the picture to remove it. While the picture is still selected, drag the corner sizing handles and size the picture so that it covers the entire slide. Your slide should look like figure 9–19.

Figure 9–19

We are going to animate this photo so that it will have a more dramatic effect when shown as part of a presentation. We will add these animations:

- Snow falling as long as the slide is displayed.
- The lake at the bottom of the photo will freeze over.
- The moon will appear in the sky over the house.
- The scene will change from daylight to darkness.

Adding Snow

To create a snow flake, insert an oval height .1" and width .1". Add a Gradient fill, Radial, From Center. At 0 percent position, white, Background 1, darker 15 percent; at the 50 percent position white, Background 1, darker 5 percent; and the 100 percent positon white, Background 1. Add a 1 pt Soft Edge effect. Make about ten snowflakes of varying sizes. Your snow flake will look similar to figure 9–20. Move the snowflakes off the slide at the top.

Figure 9–20

Animate Snow

For each of the ten snowflakes, add an animation Motion Path Down, With Previous, Repeat Until End of Slide. Set the time for each snowflake animation for varying times from 8 to 13 seconds. Also, delay the animation for various amounts of time such as .1 second or .2 seconds so that they don't all fall at the same time. Once you have the ten snowflakes done, copy them and move them to various position above the slide. Repeat this process again. Your slide will look similar to figure 9–21. You can see the green starting and red ending point. You can't see the snowflakes because the background above the slide is white. When you view the slide, the snowflakes will fall at various times and speeds as long as the slide is displayed. The slide screen has been darkened so that you can see the motion paths.

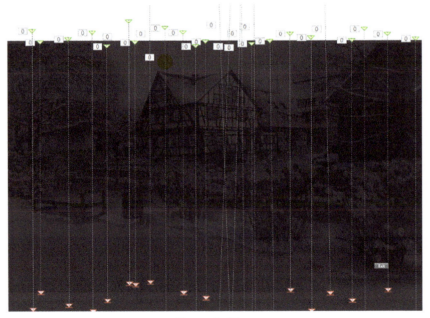

Figure 9–21

Create the Moon

Draw an oval height .5" and width .5" to represent the moon. Add a yellow fill color and No Line. Add a 1 pt Soft Edge. Move the shape above the top of the house in the picture. Animate the moon for Entrance, Fade effect, With Previous, 15 seconds.

Lake Freeze

Draw a free-form shape to cover the lake at the bottom of the slide as shown in figure 9–22. Roughly trace the lake edge and then you can just use a straight line at the bottom and left of the screen. Fill the shape with white Background 1, darker 15 percent, no outline. Animate the shape for Entrance, Wipe, From Top, With Previous, 15 seconds.

Figure 9–22

Darkness Effect

Draw a rectangle that covers the entire screen, and a black Background 1 Fill color with No Line. Make the fill color 25 percent Transparency. Animate the shape for Entrance, Fade effect, With Previous, 15 seconds. Move the rectangle shape behind the exit button as shown in figure 9–23.

Figure 9–23

View slide 2 in Slide Show view to make sure all the animations are working: snow falling, moon fades in, lake freezes, and the scene changes to night. If the animations are not working, make sure that they all are set to play With Previous.

Pivots and Animation

Open the data file **Lesson 9 Pivots and Animation**. Add your name to the subtitle placeholder, and add your name to the end of the file name and save the file. A gradient fill background has already been applied to the presentation, and the *Wind* Transition and action buttons have also been added.

Slide 2

Go to slide 2. Slide 2 consists of five plaque shapes with photos of dogs inserted into the shapes as shown in figure 9–24.

Figure 9–24

Center Dog Picture

Animate the center dog picture for an animation Entrance, Fade, With Previous, Slow. Add an animation Emphasis, Spin, After Previous, Counterclockwise, Very Slow, Repeat Until End of Slide.

Dog at Right

We want the dog at the right to Appear, After Previous. We want that photo to spin and to stay connected to the right edge of the center dog, so a simple spin emphasis will not work. We need to create a pivot so that it spins around from the center point of the dog at the center. Follow these steps:

- Click on the dog at the right and press Ctrl+D to duplicate it. Move the duplicate copy on top of the dog to the left of the center picture.

ADVANCED POWERPOINT: MORE THAN PRESENTATIONS!

- Format the duplicate picture so that the fill is 100 percent Transparency with No Line.
- Group the two shapes.
- Animate the grouped shape to Appear, After Previous.
- Animate the grouped shape for Emphasis, Spin, Counterclockwise, With Previous, Very Slow, Repeat Until End of Slide.

Dogs at Left, Top, and Bottom

Repeat the steps you completed for the dog at the right for the other dog pictures, but you will need to select each dog, duplicate it and move it directly on the other side of the center dog picture, make the shape 100 Transparency, group the two shapes, and then animate the grouped shape. For example, the dog at the bottom will be copied and the copied shape will be move to the other side at the top of the center dog. When you view slide 2 in Slide Show view, it will be spinning as shown in figure 9–25.

Figure 9–25

Slide 3

Copy the five dog shapes from slide 2 to slide 3. The animations will be copied. Click on the dog at the right and add an animation Motion Path Right, After Previous, Medium, Auto-reverse, Repeat Until End of Slide. Move the green start point to the middle of the center dog, and move the red end point approximately 1" from the right edge of the dog photo at the right as shown in figure 9–26.

Figure 9–26

Click on the dog at the bottom and add an animation Motion Path Down, With Previous, Medium, Auto-reverse, Repeat Until End of Slide. Move the green start point to the middle of the center dog, and move the red end point approximately 1" from the bottom edge of the dog photo at the bottom.

Click on the dog at the left and add an animation Motion Path Left, With Previous, Medium, Auto-reverse, Repeat Until End of Slide. Move the green start point to the middle of the center dog, and move the red end point approximately 1" from the left edge of the dog photo at the left.

Click on the dog at the top and add an animation Motion Path Up, With Previous, Medium, Auto-reverse, Repeat Until End of Slide. Move the green start point to the middle of the center dog, and move the red end point approximately 1" from the top edge of the dog photo at the top.

View slide 3 in Slide Show view and watch the animation. Display the slide long enough so that you can see the extent of the animation you created.

Slide 4

Slide 4 contains five pictures of planes, similar to slide 2, which contained five pictures of dogs. Follow the procedures you used for slide 2 to animate each of the five planes.

For each of the planes, beginning with the center and then working clockwise, add an animation Motion Path Up or Down, Medium, After Previous, to move each plane off the screen. You will need to adjust the length of the motion path to make sure the plane moves all the way off the screen.

View slide 4 in Slide Show view. Your slide should look similar to figure 9–27. Save your presentation.

Figure 9–27

Lesson 9 Applications

Lesson 9 Application 1 Presentation Application

Open the data file *Lesson 9 Application 1 Presentation Application*. Add your name to the file name and save the file. Add your name in the subtitle placeholder.

The presentation consists of three slides—the title slide, slide 2, and slide 3. On slide 2 there are five photos. Select one of the photos from slide 2 or select a photo of your own, and use slide 3 to animate the photo. You must add a minimum of six effects or actions. For example, you might have a plane flying across the screen, you could have a fish jumping from the water, you could transition from daylight to night, etc.

Add an appropriate slide transition and action buttons to navigate the presentation. Save your file.

Lesson 9 Application 2 Instructional Materials Application

Open the data file *Lesson 9 Application 2 Instructional Materials Application*. Add your name to the replace the subtitle placeholder and save the file.

On slide 2 create an electronic book following the instructions presented in this lesson. Your book can be on a topic of your choice but must include the following:

- Six to 10 pages in length
- A book cover
- An inside left and inside right page

- Pages 1 to 6 or more
- The book cover, inside left page, inside right page, and each additional page must be grouped and named
- A trigger to be clicked to open the book
- A trigger to be clicked to open each two pages—that is, 1–2, 3–4, 5–6, etc. Odd pages must be on the left side of the book and even pages must be on the right side of the book
- A trigger to be click to close the book

Save your file.

Lesson 9 Application 3 Gaming Application

Open the data file **Lesson 9 Application 3 Gaming Application**. Add your name to the title slide and save the file adding your name at the end of the file name. The *Ripple* slide Transition has already been applied, and action buttons have been inserted. The presentation consists of two slides. Slide 2 looks like figure 9–28

Figure 9–28

You need to use the skills you learned in this lesson related to spinning on pivots to animate the planes so that the planes at the top and right of the circle on the left in figure 9–28 Spin twice Counterclockwise, then Disappear and then Appear on the circle to the right, Spin Clockwise twice, and then exit one to the top and one to the bottom of the screen. *Hint: Instead of making a duplicate copy of the plane picture in order to create a pivot at the center of both images, you could just use a rectangle shape the same size as the plane image.* Figure 9–29 shows how the slide looks in Slide Show view when the two planes are circling the shape at the right of the screen. Save your presentation.

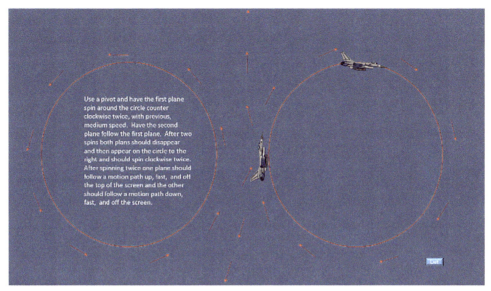

Figure 9–29

LESSON 10

Advanced Drawing, Mouse Over Game

Data Files

Lesson 10 Mouse Over Game
Lesson 10 Adding Video

Overview

In Lesson 10 you will continue to learn advanced drawing techniques, and you will learn to add video to your presentations. You will continue to learn to develop apps and games.

Cell Phone Menu

Open a new PowerPoint presentation and add **Lesson 10 Cell Phone Menu** *to the title.* Add your name to the subtitle and save the file. Add a second slide in Blank Layout. Add a black fill to both slides with white text fill. Figure 10–1 shows the cell phone you will prepare on slide 2.

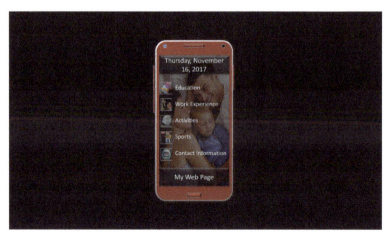

Figure 10–1

Step 1

Draw a rounded rectangle height 5.5" and width 2.75". Fill color of dark red from the standard colors. Drag the yellow adjustment handle to adjust the curve of the edges. Change the outline to white Background 1 darker 25 percent or sliver preset if available or preset gradient Top Spotlight Accent 3 (recommended). Change the line width to 4.5 pt. Add an 8 pt Glow effect the same color used for the phone (dark red), 60 percent transparent. Format the rounded rectangle for the effect, Bevel Circle. Add 3-D Rotation, Perspective Front to the object. Align the object to the center and to the middle. Your slide 2 should look like figure 10–2 at this point.

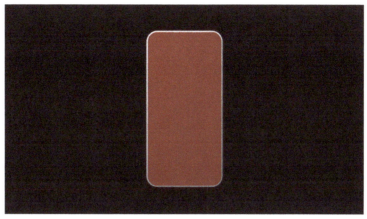

Figure 10–2

Step 2

Draw a rectangle shape on top of the first shape height 4.5" and width 2.5". Align the shape to the center and middle. Add a picture of your choice as the fill for the new shape. Make the picture 50 percent transparent. When you make the photo 50 percent transparent, the color of the phone will show through the picture. Draw another rectangle height 4.5" and width 2.5". Align the shape to the center and middle. Fill the new shape black, Background 1, No Line. Send the shape backward so that it is behind the picture. Your slide 2 should look like figure 10–3 at this point.

Figure 10–3

Step 3

Insert a rectangle height .65" and width 2.5", 50 percent Transparency, Fill black, Background 1, Preset shape effect, Preset 2 (Format/Shape Styles/Preset/Preset 2), even with the top of the picture. Copy and paste it even with the bottom of picture. Align the picture and two shapes at the center.

Use a rounded rectangle height .1" and width .7". Fill and line color the same as phone color, 3-D Format Bevel Circle for the button and top of the phone. Copy and change size to height .15" and width .5" and paste it at the bottom. Center both shapes as shown in figure 10–4.

Use an oval to create the activity light, height .1" and width .1", Fill blue. Add an Emphasis Blinking animation, Very Slow, Repeat Until End of Slide. Create an oval .12"×.12", no fill with the same line color as the phone, and move it over the blue oval. Align the ovals at the center and top. Add another oval .12"×.12", Fill black, Background 1, and Line color the same as the phone. Move it to the right edge of the phone. Align the three objects at the top. Your phone should look like figure 10–4 after this step.

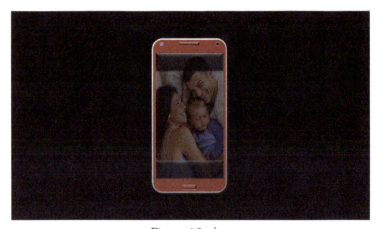

Figure 10–4

Step 4

Insert the date and time in the partially transparent box at the top of the picture. Size the text as needed.

Use the rounded rectangle at the bottom of the phone as a hyperlink to exit the presentation.

Insert a text box in the shape at the bottom of the picture and add the text *My Web Page*. You will use this object to link to your home page in the future.

Insert two rounded rectangles for volume up and down buttons on the left of the phone. Each oval should be height .8" and width .05", 3-D Bevel Circle effect, 3-D Rotation Perspective Front, with the same fill and outline color as the phone. Copy the top volume button and move it on the right side of the phone to represent the power button. Your phone should look like figure 10–5 at this point.

ADVANCED POWERPOINT: MORE THAN PRESENTATIONS!

Figure 10–5

Step 5

Add five rectangles height .4" and width .4". Add the same fill and line color as the phone. Add a 3-D Bevel Circle effect to the boxes and arrange them vertically as shown in figure 10–6. Add the text shown to the right of each box as text boxes. Align the shapes and text boxes.

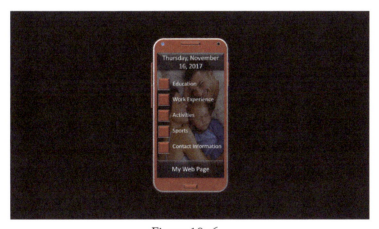

Figure 10–6

Step 6

Fill each of the boxes you created in step 5 with a picture of your choice. Your phone should look like figure 10–7 at the completion of this step. Save your file.

Figure 10–7

Using the Phone Image

You will complete the next step in this job when completing the applications at the end of the lesson. In that step you will use the picture buttons on the phone to hyperlink to information about yourself: your education, work experience, athletics, sports, contact information, etc. It would be a unique way to introduce yourself to your audience using the phone buttons to navigate the presentation. Save your file.

Adding Video to Your Presentation

Adding a video to your presentation is a good way to attract and keep the attention of your audience. However, a video that does not play or that displays a lot of irrelevant advertisements is a good way to lose your audience.

The most common problem associated with inclusion of videos in a presentation is breaking the link—that is, the location of the file has changed or the online address has changed. The second most common problem is linking to an online video that links to a Web site that displays advertisements that are not part of the video you want to use.

One of the most watched YouTube® videos of all time was: Susan Boyle – Britain's Got Talent 2009 Episode 1 – Saturday, 11 April episode. The YouTube link to this video is https://www.youtube.com/watch?v=RxPZh4AnWyk.

You could insert that link in your presentation and in Slide Show view click on the link, and the video will be displayed. However when you access the video through this link a screen similar to figure 10–8 is displayed. The screen displays a lot of information in addition to the video you want to view.

ADVANCED POWERPOINT: MORE THAN PRESENTATIONS!

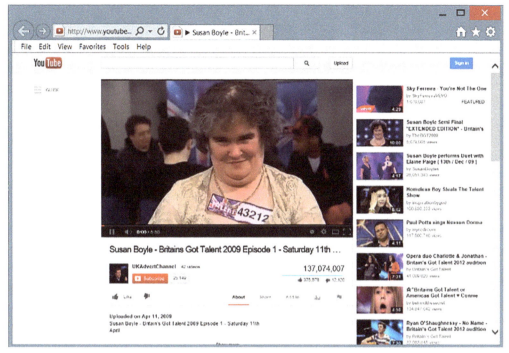

Figure 10–8

Insert Online Video

Recent versions of PowerPoint make it very easy to add videos from the Internet or from your own files. You simply Click *Insert/Media/Video/Online Video* as shown in figure 10–9

Figure 10–9

The dialog box shown in figure 10–10 will be displayed, and you enter the name of the YouTube video, *Louisa Johnson,* you want to search for as shown, and then press Enter. A list of videos on YouTube for Louisa Johnson will be displayed as shown in figure 10–11, and you select the one you want, the first video, *Soul singer Louisa Johnson covers Who's Loving You*, and click *Insert*. An image representing the video will be inserted on your slide as shown in figure 10–12.

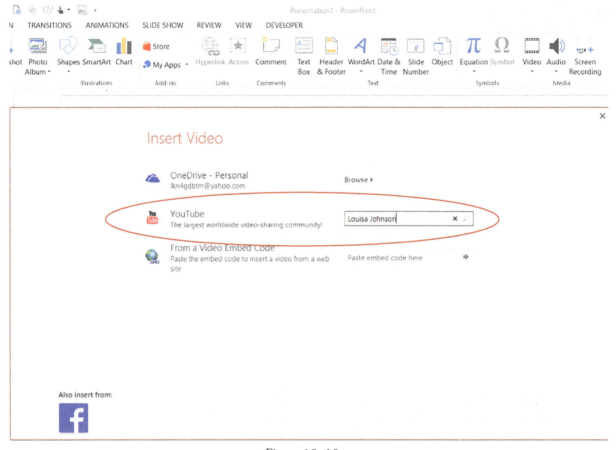

Figure 10–10

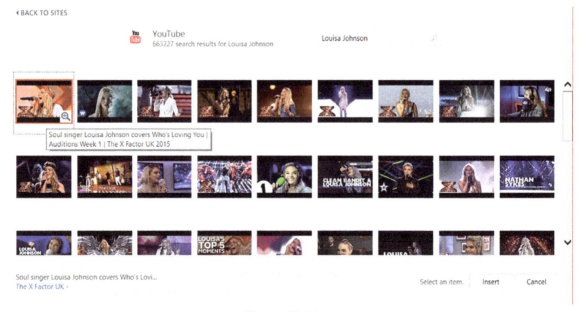

Figure 10–11

ADVANCED POWERPOINT: MORE THAN PRESENTATIONS!

Figure 10–12

Once the image is on your slide, you can size it and select options under the Format and Playback tabs.

Figure 10–13

You could also insert a video from OneDrive or enter the video embed code. The video will be linked to the URL (address) of the file, and it will play when you display the slide.

Insert Video from File

If you have your own videos you want to insert into a presentation, you follow the same steps, but select Video on my PC. Navigate to the location of the file, and click *insert*. Once you insert the video, the *video tools tab* is displayed and you can change the format and/or playback of your video as shown in figure 10–13. You can edit the video once you insert it. Among the many things you can do include applying a style, trim the video, have it fade in and fade out, and have it start playing automatically.

Open the data file **Lesson 10 Adding Video**. The design, transition, and action buttons have already been applied. Add your name to the subtitle placeholder. Go to slide 2, add the YouTube video, *Soul singer Louisa Johnson covers Who's Loving You*. Size and format the image as desired, and have it play automatically when the slide is displayed in Slide Show view. Add your name to the file name, and save the file. View the file in Slide Show view. When in Slide Show view, please wait for the video on slide 2 to start playing. You will probably experience some delay depending on the speed of your Internet connection. When completed, save your presentation.

Mouse Over Game

Figure 10–14 shows the five slides of a game you will create. Open the data file **Lesson 10 Mouse Over Game**. Add your name to the subtitle and save the file again. Slide five provides all the objects you will need to prepare the game. You will delete slide 5 after you complete the game. Your slide 2 is now blank since this will be the game board.

The objective of the game is simple, you need to move your mouse and stay on the black road without hitting any obstacles or touching the green background. There are two cross obstacles that you must move on to and off to get back on the black road. These obstacles will be spinning. Other objects on the slide will be moving. If you go off the road or touch an object on the road, you will lose the game and slide 4 will appear and you will hear a voltage sound. If you get to the winning home at the end of the game, you will win the game and slide 3 will appear and you will hear a chime sound.

Slide 1 has a start (next slide) action button that puts your cursor on the road at the starting point of the game. The *Fracture* Transition has been applied, and action buttons have been added to the slides. Background Style 11 has also been applied. Figure 10–15 identifies all the objects that make up the game and figure 10–16 shows the drawbridge when opened.

ADVANCED POWERPOINT: MORE THAN PRESENTATIONS!

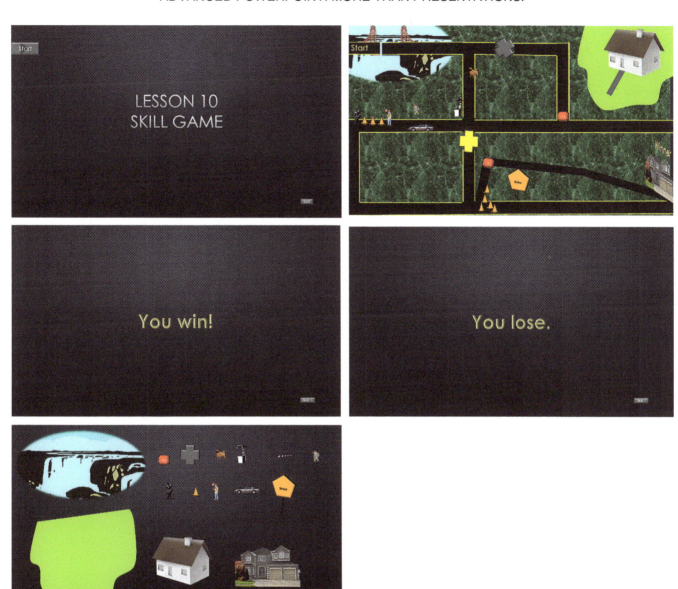

Figure 10–14

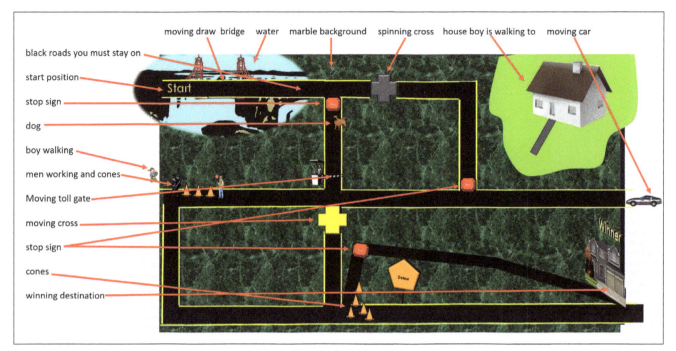

Figure 10–15

Step 1

Move to slide 2 and draw a rectangle that covers the entire slide. Apply the green marble texture fill to the rectangle with no line. Draw the first section of the road using a rectangle height .5" and width 1.5", Fill, black, Background 1, No Line. Add a line boarder, 3 pt, yellow, to both sides of the rectangle as shown in figure 10–15, and place it as shown over the image of the water. Add the word *Start* in yellow WordArt as shown. Leave a space between the first section of the road you just created, and the next horizontal section to represent the location of a drawbridge as shown in figure 10–14. Draw all the roads and add the crosses shown in figure 10–15 keeping the same height, .5", but varying the width as needed. Rotate road sections as necessary.

Copy the objects from slide 5 as shown in figure 10–15. You will need to draw the sidewalk to the house with a rectangle and no outline. A 3-D Rotation, Off Axis, 1 Left has been applied to the house and WordArt in the bottom right corner of the slide.

Click on the rectangle that covers the slide. Click Insert/Links/Action. Click the Mouse Over tab and then click hyperlink to slide 4. Check the sound button and select voltage. Click the image of the water in the top, left corner, and apply a Mouse Over action, hyperlink to slide 4 and play the voltage sound. Click on the image of the house at the bottom, right corner of the slide. Apply a Mouse Over action, hyperlink to slide 3, and play the chime sound. *Note: Be sure you click the Mouse Over tab in the Action settings dialog box and not the Mouse Click tab.*

Go to slide 1 and click the Slide Show view button. Click the Start button on slide 1 and you should move to the road on slide 2. Move your cursor off the road, and you should be taken to the lose slide and the voltage sound should play.

Step 2

The road leading to the winning house should be narrower than the other roads with no border since this will be a detour.

Animate the gray cross to Spin Clockwise, Slow, With Previous, Repeat Until End of Slide. Animate the yellow cross to spin Counterclockwise, With Previous, Medium, Repeat Until End of Slide.

A section of the road covering the water is missing. We will add a section of the road that moves right to left to represent a drawbridge as shown in figure 10–16. Create the section of the road with the width slightly wider than the broken area of the road, and place it on top of the open break in the road. Animate the shape for a Motion Path Right, With Previous, Smooth Start and Smooth End, Very Slow, Auto-reverse, Repeat Until End of Slide. View slide 2 in Slide Show view to make sure the new section of road touches each side of the existing road when it is moving; then move it down to cover the missing piece of the road as shown in figure 10–17.

Figure 10–16

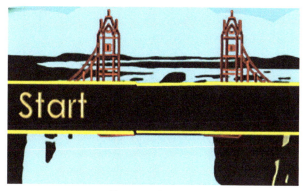

Figure 10–17

Go to slide 1 and view the presentation in Slide Show view. Click the Start button on slide 1 and you will be at the starting point of the game on slide 2. Move your mouse along the road. If you go off the road or touch the water or green background, you will lose the game.

Step 3

In step 3 we will add other obstacles to the game. Copy the stop sign and place it in the three locations as shown in figure 10–15. Add an Action to hyperlink to the losing slide if the mouse is moved over any of the three stop signs. Add the Voltage sound.

Moving from the top of the screen down, animate the first stop sign to Appear, With Previous, Delay 2 seconds. Animate the same stop sign to Disappear With Previous, Delay 6 seconds.

Animate the second stop sign to Appear, With Previous, Delay 4 seconds. Animate the same stop sign to Disappear, With Previous, Delay 12 seconds.

Animate the third stop sign to appear, With Previous, Delay 8 seconds. Animate the same stop sign to disappear With Previous, delay 18 seconds.

Copy the dog onto the game board as shown in figure 10–15. Add an Action to hyperlink to the losing slide if the mouse is moved over any of the dog. Add a Voltage sound.

Copy the gateman and the gate to the location shown in figure 10–15. Note the gate is in two sections, one visible and one transparent, so that you can rotate it from the center. Add an Action to hyperlink to the losing slide if the mouse is moved over the gate. Add the Voltage sound. Animate the gate to Spin Counterclockwise, 180°, With Previous, 10 seconds, Auto-reverse, Repeat Until End of Slide.

Copy the image of the boy and paste it to the left of the slide. Add an Action to hyperlink to the losing slide if the mouse is moved over any of the boy. Add the Voltage sound. Animate the boy for a Custom Path across the screen and to the house, With Previous, Delay 6 seconds, Duration 15 seconds, Repeat Until End of Slide.

Copy the image of the car and paste it to the right of the slide so that it is aligned with the horizontal road across the slide. Add an Action to hyperlink to the losing slide if the mouse is moved over the car. Add the Voltage sound. Animate the car for a Motion Path Left and off the left side of the slide, With Previous, Medium, Repeat Until End of Slide.

Copy and paste the detour sign to the location shown in figure 10–15.

Copy the remaining objects, cones, lady holding the stop sign, and man working to the locations shown. Add an Action to hyperlink to the losing slide if the mouse is moved over any of the objects. Add the Voltage sound.

Step 4

Your game should be complete. Go to slide 1 and view the presentation in Slide Show view. Click the Start button on slide 1 and your mouse pointer will be on the road. Move the pointer, staying on the black road and moving over the spinning crosses. Don't touch any of the objects or you will be taken to the lose slide. You can click the slide 1 button on the lose slide to return to slide 1 and play the game again.

If you are able to get to the winning house, you will be taken to the win slide, and can click the button to return to slide 1 to play the game again or exit Slide Show. Once you are sure your game works accurately, you can delete slide 5. Save your presentation.

ADVANCED POWERPOINT: MORE THAN PRESENTATIONS!

Lesson 10 Applications

Lesson 10 Application 1 Presentation Application

Open a new presentation. Select a topic of your choice such as sports, hobbies, movies, television, etc. Add the title to the title slide and your name in the subtitle. Select a design of your choice.

Add two additional slides and add video related to the topic from YouTube.

Add appropriate action buttons to navigate the presentation and save it as ***Lesson 10 Application 1 Presentation Application your name.***

Lesson 10 Application 2 Instructional Materials Application

Open your file ***Lesson 10 Cell Phone Menu***. Save the file again as ***Lesson 10 Application 2 Instructional Materials Application*** *with your name* added to the end of the file name.

The presentation should contain two slides: the title slide and a slide with a cell phone image that you prepared for this lesson.

Step 1

Add five additional slides to the presentation with Title and Content Layout. Add the content for each slide as shown in figure 10–18.

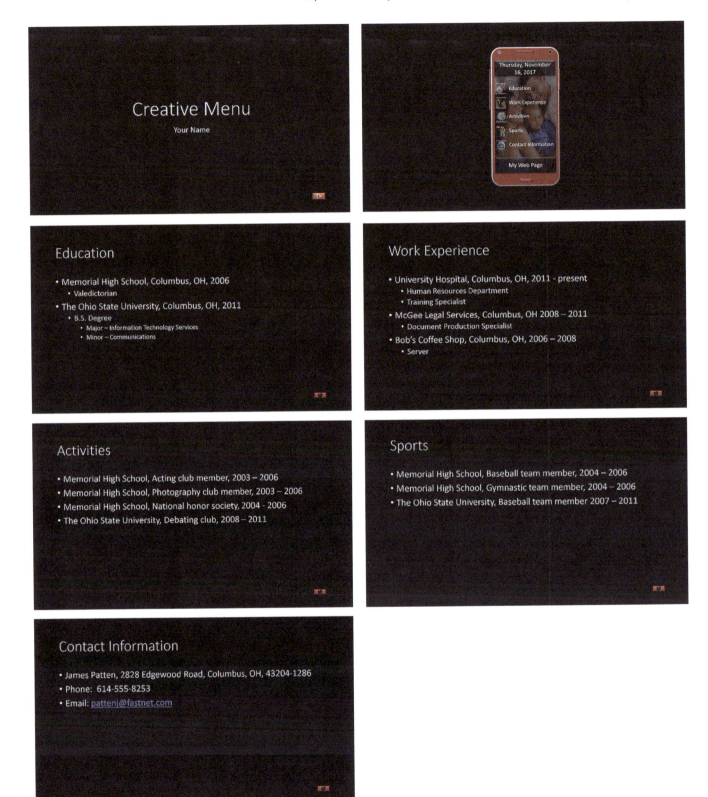

Figure 10–18

Step 2

Create a link from each of the pictures on the cell phone to the appropriate slide. If a Web page were available, you would also create a link from the text *My Web Page* to the appropriate web page.

Step 3

Add an Exit button to the slide with the cell phone. Add a Return button to each of the five new slides you added. Set up the presentation to be Browsed at a Kiosk. Save your presentation. View the presentation in Slide Show view to make sure everything is working properly. Make any necessary changes and save the presentation again.

Lesson 10 Application 3 Gaming Application

Apply the techniques you learned in this lesson to create an original game using the mouse over technique. Your presentation should include the title slide, a game slide, a win slide, and a lose slide. Add appropriate action buttons to navigate the Slide Show.

Save the presentation as ***Lesson 10 Application 3 Game Application Your Name***.

LESSON 11

More VBA, Advanced Animation, and Mazes

Data Files

Lesson 11 Animation
Lesson 11 Mazes
Lesson 11 VBA 5
Lesson 11 Application 1 Presentation Application
Lesson 11 Application 2 Instructional Materials Application
Lesson 11 Application 3 Gaming Application

Overview

In Lesson 11 you will learn more VBA coding related to declaring variables, variable types, inputting data, and calculating. You will also learn more animation techniques, and you will create animated mazes as well as other apps and gaming applications.

VBA

In some of the previous VBA applications we did not declare variables. It is recommended that you declare variables using the Dim statement at the beginning of the code.

Option Explicit

This statement, Option Explicit, requires that all variables be declared using a Dim statement. This procedure helps reduce coding errors and can reduce the amount of reserved storage for each variable. For example, a variable declared as an *Integer* requires 2 bytes of space, a variable declared as a *Date* requires 8 bytes of space, and a variable declared as a *Decimal* requires 14 bytes. If you don't declare a variable, VBA considers it a *Variant* type variable and requires 16 bytes. In addition, if you declare variables and then misspell a variable name in the code, VBA will alert you of the error. Table 11–1 shows the space allocated for different variable types. Table 11–2 shows a partial inventory table. Figure 11–1 shows the code for the macro you will write in this job.

In this job we are going to write a macro that will calculate the cost of specific purchases. Open the data file ***Lesson 11 VBA 5.*** Add your name to the subtitle placeholder and save the file again.

ADVANCED POWERPOINT: MORE THAN PRESENTATIONS!

The presentation consists of four slides: the title slide, slide 2, which shows the code you will need to write, slide 3 where you will prepare the partial inventory table, and slide 4 where you will indicate the items purchased, calculate the cost for each purchase, and enter the total cost in an ActiveX Text Box.

A slide transition, slide numbers, and action buttons have already been added.

Data Type or Subtype	Required Memory
Integer	2 bytes
Long integer	4 bytes
Single	4 bytes
Double	8 bytes
Currency	8 bytes
Fixed string	String's length
Variable string	10 bytes plus the number of characters
Object	4 bytes
Boolean	2 bytes
Variant	16 bytes
Decimal	14 bytes
Byte	1 byte
Date	8 bytes

Table 11–1

Sample Inventory Items		
Product Number	**Product Name**	**Cost**
P1811	Executive High-Speed Copy Paper	59.99/carton
P1827	Kelly Copy Plus MP Paper	50.99/case
P1832	Sterling Office Paper	51.99/case
W1622	SureWrite Bold Retractable Ball Pens	8.29/pack of 8
W1692	Rand Retractable Ballpoint Pens	11.49/dozen
N1705	Office Spiral Notebook	4.49/each
N1735	Office Wirebound Notebook	4.39/each
C4218	Office Brand Paper Clips	1.29/box
C4263	OIC® Gold Tone Paper Clips	1.69/box
M1903	SureWrite Permanent Fine-Point Markers	8.29/dozen
M1982	SureWrite Ballpoint Stick Pens	1.99/dozen
F1912	Office Color End-Tab Folders	44.99/box
F1933	Office End-Tab Folder	33.99/box

Table 11–2

```
Option Explicit
Sub CostCalculation()

  'Declare variables
  Dim ProductNumber As String
  Dim ProductName As String
  Dim QuantityPurchased As Integer
  Dim Cost As Currency
  Dim Taxrate As Single
  Dim Subtotal As Currency
  Dim Tax As Currency
  Dim Total As Currency


  'Input data
  ProductNumber = InputBox("Number: ")
  ProductName = InputBox("Name: ")
  QuantityPurchased = InputBox("QuantityPurchased: ")
  Cost = InputBox("Cost: ")

  'Calculations
  Subtotal = QuantityPurchased * Cost
  Taxrate = 0.055
  Tax = Subtotal * Taxrate
  Total = Subtotal + Tax

  'Display results
  MsgBox ("Name: " & ProductName & vbNewLine & "Number: " & ProductNumber & vbNewLine &
  "Quantity: " & QuantityPurchased & vbNewLine & "Cost: " & Cost & vbNewLine & "Subtotal: " &
  Subtotal & vbNewLine & "Tax: " & Tax & vbNewLine & "Total: " & Total)

End Sub
```

Figure 11–1

Step 1

Open the Visual Basic Editor and add a new module. Type the code required for the macro used to calculate the cost of a specific purchase. You could copy and paste the code from slide 2.

Run the *CostCalculation* macro and enter this data to make sure the macro is working properly—Item: *P1827*, Produce Name: *Kelly Copy Plus MP Paper*, Quantity: *5*, Cost: *51.99* a case. The total cost should be: *274.25*.

Prepare slide 4 as shown in figure 11–2. Create the four-column table as shown. Add the title *Total Cost* as a text box. Below the Total Cost heading, insert five ActiveX Text Box Controls aligned with the top of each of the five rows in the table. Insert a rounded-rectangle with the word Calculate as shown. Add an Action so that when you click on Calculate in Slide Show view, the CostCalculation macro is run. In Slide Show view run the *costcalculation* macro to determine the total cost for each item. Place your answers in the Total Cost column for each item. Save your file.

ADVANCED POWERPOINT: MORE THAN PRESENTATIONS!

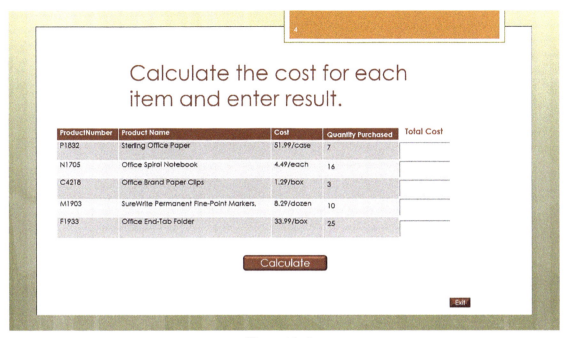

Figure 11–2

Animation

Open the data file ***Lesson 11 Animation***. Add your name to the title slide and save the presentation. The Berlin theme has already been applied to the presentation.

Step 1

On slide 2, you are going to draw a caterpillar using oval shapes. Use the smiley shape to draw the head. The size should be height .5" and width .5", gradient fill, radial from center, 0 percent Position light gray, at the 50 percent Position, red, and at the 100 percent Position, Black Background 1, No Line. Apply the 3-D Format, Bevel Circle to the top and bottom of the shape and change the height and width for the top and bottom to .20 pt. Change the 3-D Rotation to Perspective Contrasting Right. Change the Material to Warm Matte and the Lighting to Balance.

Use the oval shape height .4" and width .4" for the next five objects that make up the caterpillar. Use the same 3-D Format and Rotation, but change the gradient colors to white, Text 1, standard yellow, and black, Background 1 for the next four shapes. Change the oval used for last shape to height .2" and width .4", use the same 3-D Format and Rotation as the other objects. Change the color to white, Text 1; purple, Background 2, Darker 50 percent, and black, Background 1. Drag the caterpillar to the top left of the screen as shown in figure 11–3. Align the shapes at the middle and distribute horizontally.

Figure 11–3

Step 2

In step 2 you will apply a number of animations to the caterpillar shapes.

Animation 1

Select all the shapes that make up the caterpillar and add a Motion Path, Wave Animation, Very Slow, With Previous, to all the shapes. Beginning with the second shape, delay the animation .1 seconds, .2 seconds, .3 seconds, .4 seconds, and .5 seconds respectively. Your animation should look similar to figure 11–4.

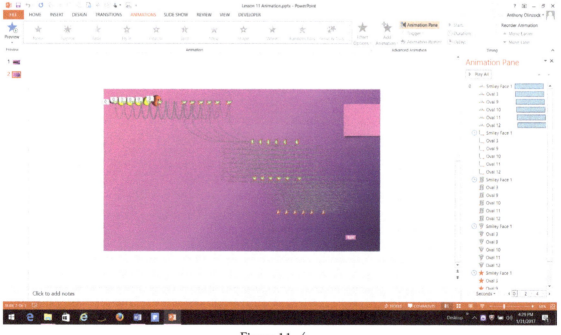

Figure 11–4

Animation 2

Select all the shapes that make up the caterpillar. Add a Motion Path animation, Turn Down Right, Very Slow. Use the directional arrows to move the green starting point for the new animation on top of the red ending point for the previous animation as shown in figure 11–4. Change the first animation, the head, to After Previous, the rest should be With Previous. Delay all the animations *With Previous animations*, to .1 seconds to .5 seconds respectively. See figure 11–4.

Select all the shapes that make up the caterpillar. Add a Motion Path animation, Spring, 10 seconds. Use the directional arrows to move the green starting point for the new animation on top of the red ending point for the previous animation as shown in figure 11- 4. Change the first animation, the head, to After Previous, the rest should be With Previous. Delay all the animations, With Previous animations, to .1 seconds to .5 seconds respectively. See figure 11–4.

Animation 3

Select all the shapes that make up the caterpillar. Add a Motion Path animation, Funnel, 10 seconds. Use the directional arrows to move the green starting point for the new animation on top of the red ending point for the previous animation as shown in figure 11- 4. Change the first animation, the head, to After Previous, the rest should be With Previous. Delay all the animations, With Previous animations, to .1 seconds to .5 seconds respectively. See figure 11–4.

Animation 4

Select all the shapes that make up the caterpillar. Add an animation Exit, Boomerang, Very Slow. Change the first animation, the head, to After Previous, the rest should be With Previous. Delay all the animations, With Previous animations, to .1 seconds to .5 seconds respectively.

Complete the Presentation

Add an action button to move from slide 1 to slide 2. Add an Exit action button on slide 2. Add a slide transition to all slides, and set up the presentation to be Browsed at a Kiosk. Save the presentation.

Mazes

Open the data file **Lesson 11 Mazes**. Your presentation will look similar to figure 11–5. Add your name to the title slide and save the presentation. Most of the presentation is completed. Slides 1 and 3 are complete. A maze game is on slide 2. When you click on the next button on slide 1, you are at the start position of the game. You need to move your mouse along the black maze and try to get to the end position within one minute to win the game. If you touch the yellow part of the slide a mouse over action will take you to the *Lose* slide and you will hear a laser sound. If you click the word *end*, the word *Winner* will appear in WordArt on top of the game board as a Zoom Entrance animation.

Your slide 2, however, is not compete. The end section of the maze is not complete, and the clock is not animated. Also, when you view slide 2 in Slide Show view, you can see that some of the sections of the maze are moving, and you will need to add two moving sections when you compete the maze. Your slide 2 looks like figure 11–5. The sections you need to add are shown in figure 11–6.

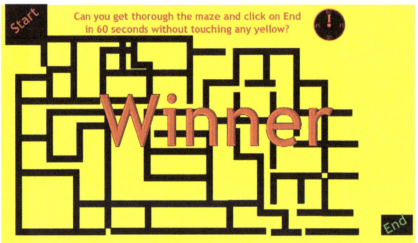

Figure 11–5

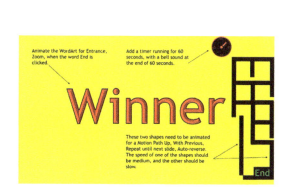

Figure 11–6

Step 1

Because slide 2 contains a timer that runs for one minute, it will be necessary to create a Custom Show consisting of slides 2 and 3. Create a Custom Show named *Slides 2 and 3*. Create a link from the next action button at the top of slide 1 to the Custom Show *Slides 2 and 3*. Be sure to click the *Show and Return* button in the Custom Show dialog box. If you don't use a Custom Show, the clock will not start over each time you return to slide 1 to play the game again. Create an End Show action from the Exit button on slide 1.

Step 2

Add the 1-minute timer shown in figure 11–6 at the top of slide 2. The timer should start With Previous. The clock is made, but you will need to animate the clock hand that has a visible and transparent section. Animate the bell sound, already on the slide, to play after 60 seconds. Add the section of maze shown in figure 11–6, and animate the two sections specified. The animation should start With Previous. Animate the WordArt *Winner* to Zoom in when the word *End* is clicked.

Step 3

Run the presentation in Slide Show view from slide 1. Make sure that clicking the next button takes you the Custom Show, *Slides 2 and 3*. If you move the pointer over a yellow section of the screen, you should be taken to the Lose slide and pressing ESC will take you back to slide 1. If you move through the maze and click End, the word *Winner* will appear in WordArt. Make any necessary corrections and save your presentation.

Lesson 11 Applications

Lesson 11 Application 1 Presentation Application

Open the data file ***Lesson 11 Application 1 Presentation Application***. Add your name to the title slide and save the file again. The Drop Entrance animation has been added to the Slide Title, With Previous, and the Drop Entrance animation has been added to the Subtitle, After Previous. The presentation includes the three slides shown in figure 11–7.

Figure 11–7

Slide 2

Slide 2 includes five shapes representing a worm. Your job is to animate the objects.

Select the five objects representing the worm. Add a Motion Path Zigzag, With Previous, Very Slow to the objects. Display the Animation pane and delay the second object for .2 seconds, the third for .4 seconds, the fourth for .6 seconds, and the fifth for .8 seconds. Change the effect options for all Motion Path animations in this application to Smooth Start and Smooth End. Figure 11–8 shows slide 2 and the animation pane.

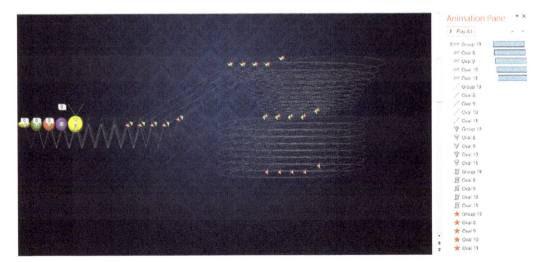

Figure 11–8

Select the five objects that make up the worm again. Add a Motion Path, Diagonal Up Right, Very Slow. *Note: The green arrow indicates the starting point of the animation, and the red arrow indicates the ending point of the animation as shown in figure 11–8.* While the five objects are still selected using the directional arrows (left/right and up/down) to position the green arrows for the objects on top of the red arrows for the first animation. Change the first new animation to After Previous, the others will stay With Previous. Display the animation pane and delay the second object for .2 seconds, the third for .4 seconds, the fourth for .6 seconds, and the fifth for .8 seconds.

Select the five objects that make up the worm again. Add a Motion Path, Funnel, very slow. While the five objects are still selected, use the directional arrows (left/right and up/down) to position the green arrows for the objects on top of the red arrows for the previous animation. Change the first new animation to After Previous; the others will stay With Previous. Display the animation pane and delay the second object for .2 seconds, the third for .4 seconds, the fourth for .6 seconds, and the fifth for .8 seconds.

Select the five objects that make up the worm again. Add a Motion Path, Spin, Very Slow. While the five object are still selected, use the directional arrows (left/right and up/down) to position the green arrows for the objects on top of the red arrows for the previous animation. Change the first new animation to After Previous; the others will stay With Previous. Display the Animation pane and delay the second object for .2 seconds, the third for .4 seconds, the fourth for .6 seconds, and the fifth for .8 seconds.

Select the five objects that make up the worm again. Add an Exit Animation, Pinwheel, Very Slow. Change the first new animation to After Previous, the others will stay With Previous. Display the Animation pane and delay the second object for .2 seconds, the third for .4 seconds, the fourth for .6 seconds, and the fifth for .8 seconds.

Slide 3

As you can see in figure 11–9 a figure is drawn to help you in preparing the animation. You will delete the green figure after you have the animation working properly. The worm animation is off to the left of the screen. Select all the objects that make up the worm, and add a Motion Path Right animation, With Previous, Very Slow. Drag the red ending arrow for each animation so that the worm is touching the left side of the large oval as shown in figure 11–9. All animations are With Previous. Display the Animation pane and delay the second object for .2 seconds, the third for .4 seconds, the fourth for .6 seconds, and the fifth for .8 seconds.

Select the five objects that make up the worm again. Add a Motion Path, Circle, Very Slow, Repeat Twice. Change the first animation to After Previous. The others should already be With Previous. Delay the animation for the second to fifth object as you did for the previous animation. Use the direction arrows to position the green arrows at the top and to the left of the center of the green oval as shown in figure 11–9, then size the ovals so that they are the same size as the green ovals. You will have to adjust the size of the circle for the head of the worm because it is larger than the other objects. Change the first new animation to After Previous, the others will stay With Previous. Display the Animation pane and delay the animation for the second to fifth object as you did for the previous animation.

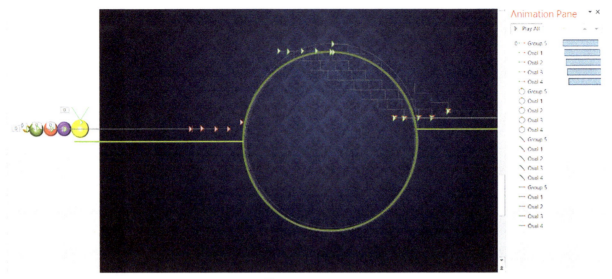

Figure 11–9

Select the five objects that make up the worm again. Add a Motion Path, Stairs Down, Very Slow. Change the first animation to After Previous. The others should already be With Previous. Delay the animation for the second to fifth object as you did for the previous animation.

Select the five objects that make up the worm again. Add a Motion Path, Right, Very Slow. Change the first animation to After Previous. The others should already be With Previous. Delay the animation for the second to fifth object as you did for the previous animation. Use the direction arrows to position the green arrows on top of the red arrows for the previous animation.

View slide 3 in Slide Show view and make any necessary adjustments. When the animation is working properly, delete the green objects that you used as a guide to prepare the animation.

Complete the Presentation

Add a slide transition of your choice to all slides, and add necessary action buttons to navigate and exit the presentation. Save your file.

Lesson 11 Application 2 Instructional Materials Application

Open the data file *Lesson 11 Application 2 Instructional Materials Application*. Add your name to the title slide and file name and save the presentation again as a PowerPoint Macro-Enabled presentation. Figure 11–10 shows the eleven slides that make up the presentation. The Dividend theme, a slide transition, slide numbers, and action buttons to navigate the presentation have already been applied. View presentation in Slide Show view to become familiar with it. The second slide contains a table that shows the memory used when you declare different data types for variables. Slide 3 shows the formula for making different types of mathematical calculations. Slide 4 shows suggested ways to declare the variables used in this job.

In this activity, you will need to write a macro for seven different calculations.

ADVANCED POWERPOINT: MORE THAN PRESENTATIONS!

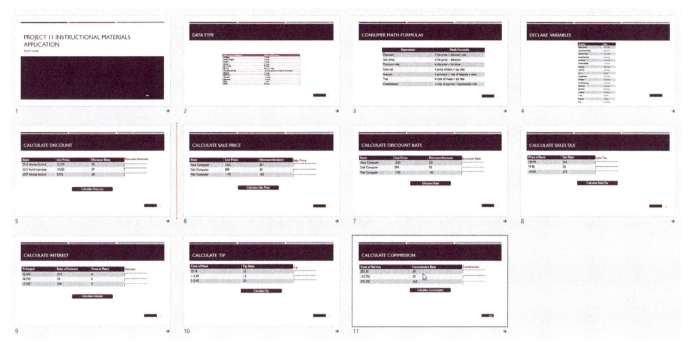

Figure 11–10

Step 1

Open the Visual Basic Editor and add a module. Add notes that indicate the current date and indicate that seven macros will follow.

Step 2

Declare the variables shown on slide 4.

Step 3

Go to slide 5. Slide 5 contains a table that shows an Item, the List Price, and the Discount Rate. You need to write a macro that will determine the Discount. Sample code is shown in figure 11–11. The macro is named *CalculateDiscount*. The user will input the Name of an item, the Discount Rate, and the List Price. The Discount is calculated by multiplying the List Price by the Discount Rate. (The formula was shown on slide 3.) A message box will display the Name of the Item, the List Price, the Discount Rate, and the Discount.

```
'Input data and calculate discount

Sub CalculateDiscount()
Name = InputBox("Name: ")
DiscountRate = InputBox("Discount Rate: ")
```

ListPrice = InputBox("List Price: ")
Discount = ListPrice * DiscountRate
MsgBox ("Name " & Name & vbNewLine & "List Price " & ListPrice & vbNewLine & "Discount Rate " & DiscountRate & vbNewLine & "Discount " & Discount)

End Sub

Figure 11–11

Return to PowerPoint and in the Code group and click Macros. Click on the CalculateDiscount macro and run it to make sure it is working properly. Correct any errors you find.

Click on the Rounded Rectangle on slide 5, Calculate Discount, to select it. Click the Insert tab and in the Links group click Action. Click Run Macro and select the CalculateDiscount macro to select it and click Ok. View slide 5 in Slide Show view and run the macro to calculate the discount for the three items listed. Record your answer in the ActiveX Text Box to the right of each item. *Note: vbNewLine code is used to have each item display on a new line in the message box.*

Step 4

Follow step 3 to write the necessary macros needed to make the calculations of slides 6 to 11. You will need to select a name for each of your macros. Be sure that you can click the rounded rectangle on each of the slides to run the macro. Perform the calculations and enter the solutions in the appropriate text boxes on each slide.

Step 5

Set up your presentation to be Browsed at a Kiosk. Save the presentation.

Lesson 11 Application 3 Gaming Application

Open the data file ***Lesson 11 Application 3 Gaming Application***. Add your name to the title slide and save the presentation again. The presentation contains four slides as shown in figure 11–12. The *Crush* Transition has been applied to the slides, the slides contain buttons that you will apply actions to.

Figure 11–12

ADVANCED POWERPOINT: MORE THAN PRESENTATIONS!

The second slide contains four objects: an image of a school, an image of a house, and an image of the background to be used for the design, and an image of a helicopter. Your job is to develop a maze mouse over game where the user has to move on a maze from the school to get to the house.

Step 1

Save the image to be used as the background design of the slides as a picture. Make the picture the background of all slides. Size the image of the slide background so that it covers the entire slide. On slide 2, size the design image (the original picture you used as the background) so that it covers the entire slide, and send it to the back. The school, house and helicopter should be on top of the background image you sized. Apply a mouse over action to the large image that covers the entire slide to the losing slide, slide 3. Have the Whoosh sound play with the action.

Step 2

Create a mouse over maze game leading from the school to the home image (a path and objects that cover the background image that take the user to the winning slide). Figure 11–13 is just an example. You should create your own maze. Remember that you adjust size and speed to change the difficulty level. Create a mouse over link from the image of the home to the winning slide. Play a Chime sound with this link.

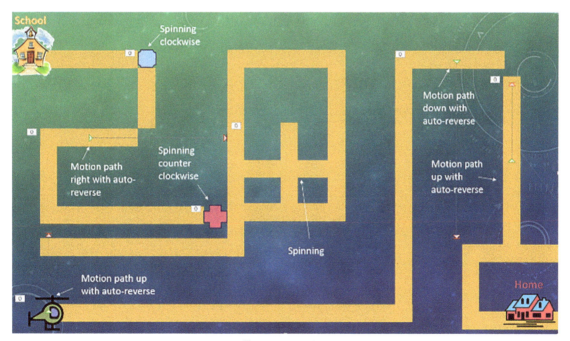

Figure 11–13

Step 3

Go to slide 1 and create a hyperlink on the next button at the top of the screen to the next slide. Create a hyperlink from the Exit button to end Slide Show. Create a hyperlink from the slide 1 buttons on slides 3 and 4 to slide 1. Set up the show to be Browsed at a Kiosk.

Step 4

View and play the game in Slide Show view to make sure everything is working. Make any necessary corrections, and save your presentation.

LESSON 12

More VBA, Embedding Presentations, and Shape Tools

Data Files

Lesson 12 Dogs
Lesson 12 Fish
Lesson 12 Embed Presentations
Lesson 12 Drawing Tools
Lesson 12 VBA Continued
Lesson 12 Application 1 Presentation Application
Lesson 12 Application 2 Instructional Materials Application
Lesson 12 Application 3 Gaming Application

Overview

In Lesson 12 you will learn additional VBA coding. You will also learn techniques for working with shapes and lines.

VBA Continued

Open the data file *Lesson 12 VBA Continued*. Add your name to the title slide and save the file again as a PowerPoint Macro-Enabled presentation. The presentation consists of three slides as shown in figure 12–1. The *Austin* Design theme and *Flip* Transition have been applied, and action buttons have been added to navigate the presentation.

Slide 2 shows the VBA code you need to write and that you can add to instructional materials when you want to be able to interact with the user. The code lets you ask the user to enter a name, and then a question is asked that requires a yes/no answer. Based on the answer input, different messages are displayed in a message box. The name of the macro is *InteractWithUser*.

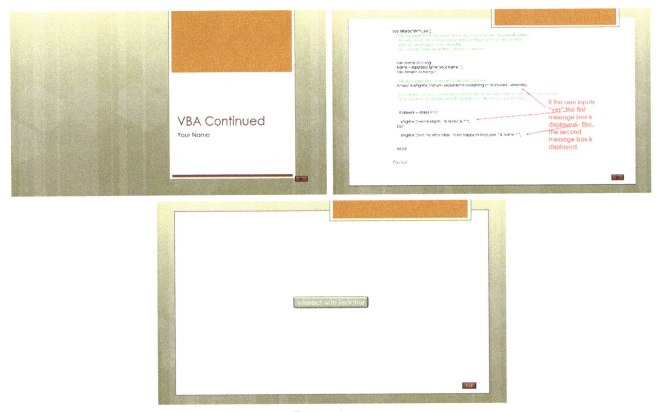

Figure 12-1

Step 1

Open the Visual Basic Editor and add a module. Enter the code shown on slide 2 in the module. You can copy and paste the code.

Step 2

Go to slide 3 and use the rounded rectangle with the text *Interact with Teacher* to run the macro with the name InteractWithUser.

Step 3

View the presentation in Slide Show view. Go to slide 3 and click Interact with Teacher button and enter your name. In response to the next prompt, answer *No*. Repeat the process, but answer *Yes*.
Make any necessary corrections and save the file.

ADVANCED POWERPOINT: MORE THAN PRESENTATIONS!

Embed a Presentation Within a Presentation

Open the data file ***Lesson 12 Embed Presentations***. The file consists of four slides. Add your name to the title slide and save the presentation again. The Apex theme has been applied to the presentation and the *Vortex* Transition. The transition is set to move to a new slide every four seconds.

Slides 2 and 3 explain the procedures for embedding a presentation within a presentation. Slide 4 contains a button you will use to run a presentation you will embed on that slide.

Step 1

Go to slide 4. Click Insert/Text/Object. Select *Create from file* and navigate to your data files for Lesson 12. Click on the presentation named *Dogs* and click *OK, OK*. The presentation is embedded on slide 4.

Step 2

Click on the embedded object to select it, and click the *Animation tab*, and then click *Add Animation*, *OLE Action Verbs* as shown in figure 12–2. From the Add OLE Action Verb dialog box, click on *Show* and then click *OK* as shown in figure 12–3.

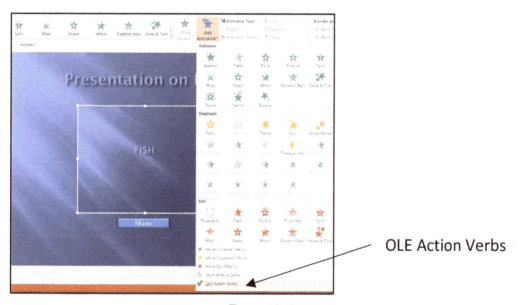

Figure 12–2

215

Figure 12–3

The new animation will be shown in the Animation pane as shown in figure 12–4. Select Timing and use the rectangle with the word *Show* in it as the trigger to start the animation.

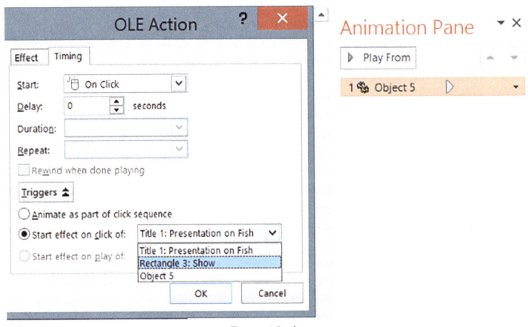

Figure 12–4

Step 3

View the presentation from the beginning in Slide Show view. When slide 4 is displayed, click on the show button to see the *Dogs* presentation. Make any necessary corrections and save the file again.

Drawing Tools

Add the following commands to the QAT (Quick Access Tool Bar): *Combine Shapes, Fragment Shapes, Intersect Shapes, Subtract Shapes, and Union Shapes. Hint: You can click the Customize Quick Access Toolbar button to the right of the toolbar and then click More Commands to locate the commands you want to add.* See figure 12–5.

Figure 12–5

Open the data file **Lesson 12 Drawing Tools.** Add your name to the Title slide and save the presentation again. A design has been applied to the presentation, and page numbers have been added. The *Curtain* Transition has been applied to all the slides for a duration of 3 seconds.

Union Shapes

Slide 2 contains an image made from *moon* and *oval* shapes as shown in figure 12–6. Select and copy the large oval that represents the face and the two ovals that represent the ears and paste them on slide 3 as shown in figure 12–6. Delete the text from the shapes. While the shapes are still selected, click the Union Shapes button on the QAT. Your slide will look like figure 12–7.

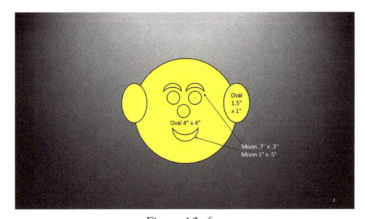

Figure 12–6

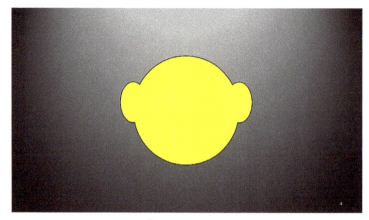

Figure 12–7

Subtract Shape

Copy the shapes that represent the eyebrows, eyes, nose, and mouth from slide 2, and arrange them on the shape. Once you have the face arranged, *in order click* the large shape the represents the face and ears, then hold down the *Ctrl* key and select the eyebrows, eyes, nose, and mouth. With all the shapes selected, click the Subtract Shapes button on the QAT. Your slide 3 should look like figure 12–8.

Figure 12–8

Go to slide 4 and create two orange stars, one height 4" and width 4" and one height 2" and width 2". Place the small star on top of the large star as shown in figure 12–9. Duplicate the stars and move the new stars to the right as shown in figure 12–9. Click on the large star to select it and hold down the *Ctrl* key and select the small star. While both stars are selected click the Subtract Shapes button on the QAT. Your slide 4 should look like figure 12–9.

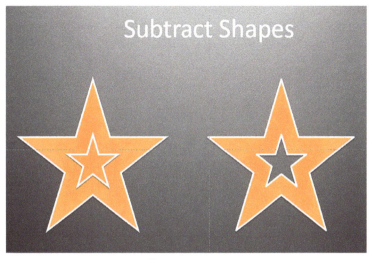

Figure 12–9

Go to slide 5. Your slide 5 has two red hearts. You want to create a broken heart as shown in figure 12–10. Duplicate the hearts. Draw two shapes on the heart using the curve tool as shown. The shapes have been made transparent so that you can see the procedure. Make two additional copies of the red heart and place the new left shape on top of one heart and the right shape on top of another heart. Use the Subtract Shapes tool to create the broken heart (select the heart object first) as shown at the bottom of figure 12–10.

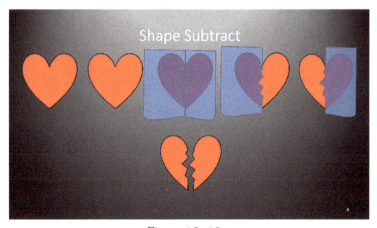

Figure 12–10

Go to slide 6. Your slide 6 contains two shapes as shown in figure 12–11, an oval and a shape drawn and placed on top of it. Subtract the blue shape from the yellow oval. Use your shape and drawing tools to create the image shown in figure 12–12.

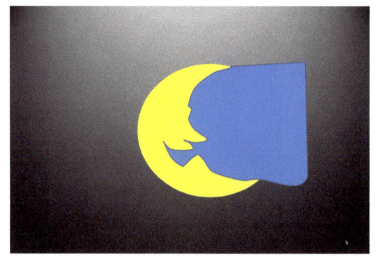

Figure 12–11

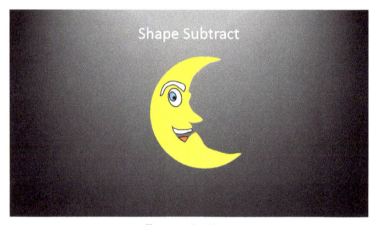

Figure 12–12

Union Shapes

Go to slide 7. Your slide 7 includes the four shapes shown at the top of the slide in figure 12–13. Arrange the two brown shapes to create a handle. While the two shapes are still selected, click the Union Shapes button. Follow the same procedure to combine the arrow and heart as shown in figure 12–13.

Figure 12–13

Combine Shapes and Intersect Shapes

Go to slide 8. Your slide 8 contains two images made up of four red ovals, and two hearts with one of the hearts flipped vertically. Arrange the four red ovals as shown in figure 12–14. While the ovals are still selected, click the Combine Shapes button on the QAT to create the shape shown in figure 12–14.

Click on the two yellow hearts to select them and then press the Intersect Shapes button on the QAT. The shape remaining will be used to make the glasses shown in figure 12–14. The Bevel Convex 3-D Format was applied to the shape, and the Perspective Front 3-D Rotation was applied. The weight of the outline was changed. The sides for the glasses were created with rectangles and an appropriate 3-D Rotation was applied. Create the glasses on your slide 9.

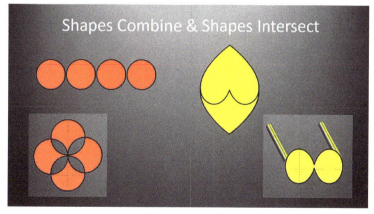

Figure 12–14

Fragment Shapes

Go to slide 10. Slide 10 is blank. Create five heart shapes height 4" and width 4", height 3" and width 3", height 2" and width 2", height 1" and width 1" and height .5" and width .5" and center them on top of one another as shown in the top right of figure 12–15. Select all the shapes and press Ctrl+D to duplicate them and move them to the right of the original shape. While the shapes are all selected, press the Fragment Shapes button on the QAT. Drag the heart shapes to create the five images shown in figure 12–15.

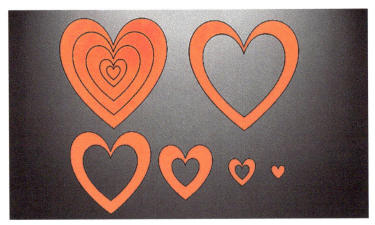

Figure 12–15

Go to slide 11. Slide 11 contains a rectangle shape with three stars inserted on top of it as shown in the top left portion of figure 12–16. Select all the shapes and press Ctrl+D to duplicate them and move them to the right of the original shape. While the shapes are all selected, press the Fragment Shapes button on the QAT. Drag the star shapes to create the four images shown in figure 12–16.

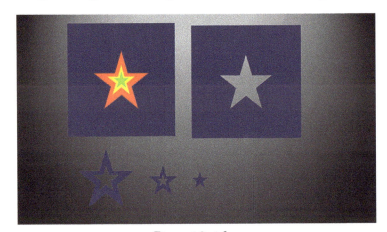

Figure 12–16

Lesson 12 Applications

Lesson 12 Application 1 Presentation Application

Open the data file ***Lesson 12 Application 1 Presentation Application***. Add your name to the subtitle and save the file again. The *Apex* theme and *Vortex* Transition have already been added.

Your job is to embed the presentation ***Lesson 12 Fish*** that is located in your data files on slide 2. Use the rectangle with the word *Show* on it on slide 2 to trigger the Slide Show to run. Save your presentation.

Lesson 12 Application 2 Instructional Materials Application

Open the data file ***Lesson 12 Application 2 Instructional Materials Application***. Add your name to the subtitle and save the file again as a PowerPoint Macro-Enabled presentation. The *Custom* theme, the *Flip* Transition, and action buttons to navigate the presentation have already been added.

Your job is to open the Visual Basic Editor, insert a Module, and write the code that will let the user interact with the teacher regarding performance on a review quiz for Lesson 1. Sample code is shown on slide 2.

Once you have written the code. Go to slide 3 and use the rounded rectangle with the words *Interact with Teacher* as a hyperlink to run the macro. Make sure that you can run the macro and that a correct message box is displayed if the user selects *yes* or *no*. Save the presentation.

Lesson 12 Application 3 Gaming Application

Open the data file ***Lesson 12 Application 3 Gaming Application***. Add your name to the subtitle and save the file again. The background Style 10, the *Glitter* Transition and action buttons to navigate the presentation have already been added. Figure 12–17 show slides 2 and 3 of the presentation showing examples of characters created from different shapes using various shape tools you learned in Lesson 12. On slides 4 and 5 create two original characters from different shapes as well as free-form shapes you might create. Use various shape tools as needed.

Figure 12–17

LESSON 13

Logic and Triggers, Morphing and Animation, and Artistic Effects

Data Files

Lesson 13 Artistic Effects
Lesson 13 Morphing
Lesson 13 Structured Cabling Standards
Lesson 13 Application 1 Presentation Application
Lesson 13 Application 2 Instructional Materials Application
Lesson 13 Application 3 Gaming Application

Overview

In Lesson 13 you will use triggers and image mapping to create an interactive presentation. You will also be introduced to morphing, a technique to transform one object into another object. Finally, you will learn to use artistic effects to create attractive images.

Logic and Triggers

In this job you want to test engineering students' knowledge of structured cabling standards. The TIA/EIA structured cabling standards define how to design, build, and manage a cabling system that is structured, meaning that the system is designed in blocks that have very specific performance characteristics. The numbers at the right of each term represent those locations on the illustration in figure 13–1 that show a transparent view of a building and its cabling.

Terminology you should know related to cabling include the following:

1. Demarc (#2)
2. Horizontal cross connect (#8)
3. Intermediate distribution frame (#4)
4. Line from local exchange carrier, LEC (#1)
5. Main distribution frame (#3)
6. Vertical cross connect (#7)
7. Wiring closet (#5)
8. Work area (#6)

ADVANCED POWERPOINT: MORE THAN PRESENTATIONS!

Open the data file ***Lesson 13 Structured Cabling Standards***. Add your name to the title slide and save the file again. The *Office* theme and *Fall Over* Transition have been applied to the slides. Action buttons have been added to navigate through the Slide Show. Slide 3 looks like figure 13–1.

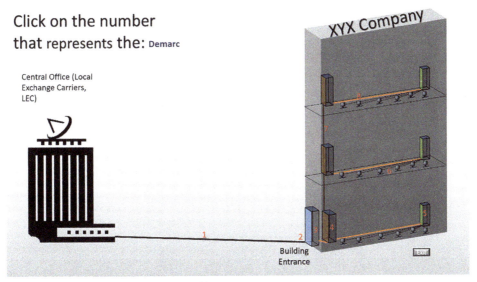

Figure 13–1

You want to develop a simulated activity on a slide 3 where one of the eight terms related to structured cabling is displayed after the text *Click on the number that represents the:*, and the user must click on the correct number in the illustration that represents that term. If the correct number is clicked, then the word *Correct* in dark blue will be displayed below the term. After two seconds *Correct* will disappear, the term *Demarc* will disappear, and the next word will appear. If a wrong number is clicked, then the message *Incorrect, try again!* will be displayed below the term in red for two seconds and then disappear, and the user can try again. This step will be repeated until the correct answer is selected. The terms will be displayed in the order shown by the number at the left of each term in the numbered list shown above.

Figure 13–2 shows how the simulation will work. The image of the first slide shows the display when the user clicks on the correct number. The second slide shows the display when the user clicks an incorrect number. The third slide shows the next term displayed in dark blue after a correct answer. The number 2 is no longer visible because it was the correct answer, and can't be selected again.

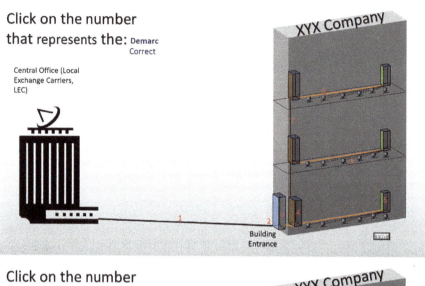

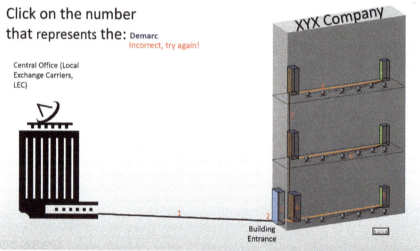

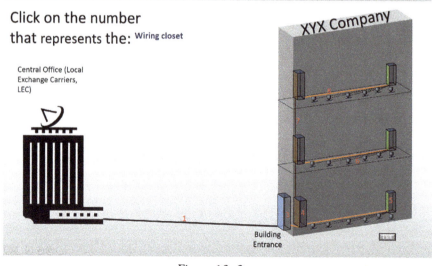

Figure 13–2

Step 1

Go to slide 3 and type the word *Correct* in 20 pt dark blue below the word *Demarc*. Trigger the word *Correct* to appear when the #2 is clicked. Have the term *Demarc* Disappear With Previous, but Delay for 2 seconds. Have the word *Correct* Disappear With Previous. Have the #2 Disappear With Previous. Have the term *Wiring Closet* Appear in the same location as *Demarc* With Previous. All the terms and the word *correct* are in dark blue.

Step 2

The user should not be able to click any number except #2. To prevent the user from clicking any other number, draw a small rectangle box height .3" and width .3", With Previous, and make it 100 percent transparent with No Line. You might want to name the rectangle, *incorrect box 1*. Place the box on top of #1. Add the text *Incorrect, try again!* in 20 pt red font and place it on top of the word *correct* below the term. Trigger the text to Appear when you click on the *incorrect box 1* you just created. Have the text disappear With Previous, but delay 2 seconds.

Copy the transparent box and rename it *incorrect box 2* and place it on #3, which represent a wrong answer. Copy the text *Incorrect, try again!* and have clicking on *incorrect box 2* trigger the text to Appear. Have it Disappear With Previous, but Delay 2 seconds. Repeat this procedure to cover all the numbers except for the #2.

Step 3

At this point, only clicking on the #2 when in Slide Show view will display *Correct*. Clicking on any other number will display *Incorrect. Try again!* The final step is to remove incorrect box covering the next correct term. The next correct term is *Wiring Closet*, represented by #5. Click on the box and click Exit Disappear, With Previous, and move the animation in the animation pane after the animation that made the term *Wiring Closet* appear. Complete slide 3 testing users' knowledge of the eight terms.

View the presentation in Slide Show view to make sure the presentation works, and save the presentation.

Morphing

In this job you will use the process of *morphing*, the transformation of one object into another. Morphing can be a good attention-grabbing technique. Open the data file **Lesson 13 Morphing**. Add your name to the title slide and save the file again. The *Parallax* Design theme and *Dissolve* Transition have already been applied to the slides. Action buttons have been added to navigate the presentation.

Your presentation consists of five slides. Slides 2 to 5 already have images inserted on them. Figure 13–3 shows how each slide will look before, on the right, and after on the left, animation and morphing have been applied to the slides.

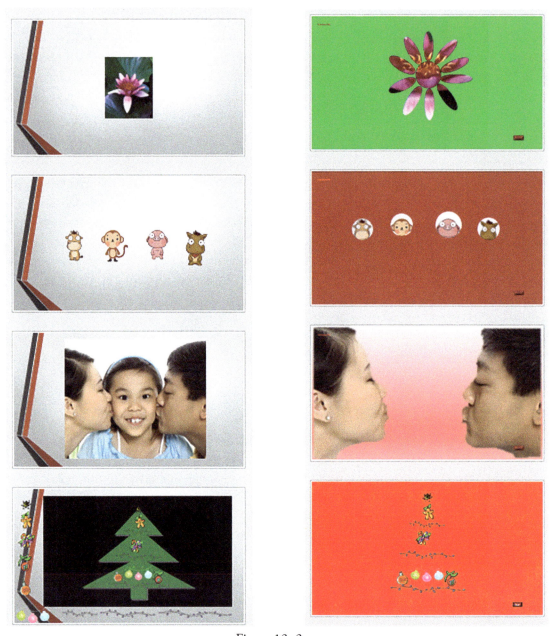

Figure 13–3

Slide 2

Your slide 2 has a photo of a flower inserted on it.

Step 1

Right-click on the photo and save it in your data files for Lesson 13 with the name *flower* in PNG format, and then delete the photo from slide 2. Click on the Design tab and in the Customize group click Format background. From the Format Background pane that is displayed, click on Picture or Texture fill, click File, navigate to the *flower* picture you saved, click on the file, and click open. The picture will now be the background for slide 2. The picture is in the background, and anything you add will cover the background.

Step 2

Draw a large rectangle that covers the entire slide and change the fill color to green with No Line. Since the rectangle covers the entire slide, you no longer can see the background. Drag the rectangle down so that you can see most of the background as shown in figure 13–4. Using the oval shape, draw an oval height 1.5" and width 1.5" on top of the center of the flower as shown in figure 13–4. Do not change the weight of the outline, it was only increased to make it easier for you to see it. Draw a pedal for the flower using the oval shape approximately height 1.7" and width .6". Copy and rotate this shape to form the outline of a flower as shown in figure 13–4. Move the green rectangle back onto the slide as shown in figure 13–5. If necessary, send the rectangle to the back so that the objects you drew on the flower are on top of the green rectangle as shown in figure 13–5.

Figure 13–4

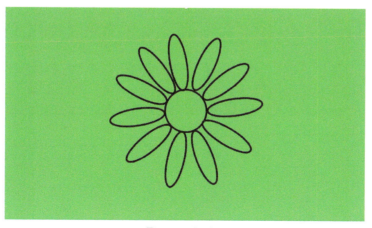

Figure 13–5

Step 3

Right-click on the oval shape that represents the center of the flower, and select Format Shape. From the Format Shape pane, select slide Background Fill. The shape will be filled with the background of the slide, which is behind the green rectangle. Remove the outline. Repeat this process for each of the shapes that make up the flower you drew with shapes as shown in figure 13–6.

Figure 13–6

Step 4

In step 4, you are going to animate the flower shapes you created. Select all the shapes that make up the flower and click Animation, Advanced Animation, Add Animation, Emphasis, Grow/Shrink, With Previous, Medium Speed, 150 percent, and Auto-reverse. View the slide in Slide Show view to see the animation.

Select all the shapes again and add a Spin animation. Change the first new animation for After Previous, the others will already be With Previous. Click on the second new animation, hold down the Shift key, and click on the last of the new animation. Change the rotation of these animations (the pedals) to 360º Counterclockwise. Repeat the animation three times.

Select all the shapes again and add a Grow/Shrink animation, 150 percent. Change the first new animation to After Previous. All the others will already be With Previous. Do not add an Auto-reverse to this Grow/Shrink animation.

Finally, click on the large green rectangle and add an Exit animation, Fade, After Previous, Very Slow. View the slide in Slide Show view again to see the animation. As you can see, the flower shape you created animates changing its shape and look but keeping the background, and morphs into the background of the slide, the original photo you used as background.

Slide 3

Go to slide 3. Your slide contains four images: a cow, a monkey, a pig, and a horse. You want to use the entire slide as a background for the slide.

Step 1

To do this click File, Save As, and navigate to your data files for Lesson 13. Save the file as **Slide 3** and as a JPEG file as shown in figure 13–7.

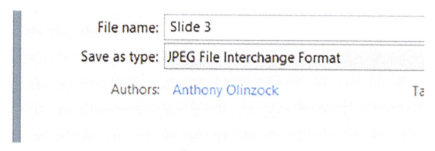

Figure 13–7

A prompt will appear asking if you want to save all slides or *Just This One*. Select *Just This One* as shown in figure 13–8.

Figure 13–8

Delete the four images from the slide and then use the image of slide 3 you saved as the background. Once you do this, you will not be able to click on anything on the slide since the background is the picture of the slide.

Step 2

Next, we want to use the heads of the animals to create an animation that includes the morphing effect. First, draw a rectangle that covers the entire slide. Use the Fill, red, Accent 1, and No Line. Move the rectangle down so that it covers approximately one-fourth of the slide as shown in figure 13–9.

Figure 13–9

Draw an oval over the cow's head. Size the oval as needed. Change the Fill to Slide Background Fill, and No Line. Repeat this process with the other three images. Slide the rectangle back on top of the slide, and your slide should look like figure 13–10.

Figure 13–10

The ovals are filled with the slide background at specific locations on the slide. If you animate the ovals to move, the oval fill image will remain the same.

Step 3

Next, we want to animate the heads that fill the oval shapes. Select all four shapes and add an animation Emphasis Spin, With Previous, Medium. Have the ovals on the end spin Clockwise and the two inside ovals should spin Counterclockwise.

Click on the first oval at the left, and add a Motion Path Right, After Previous, Auto-reverse. Drag the red ending point so that it goes all the way to the center of the horse's face.

Click on the last oval at the right, and add a Motion Path Left, With Previous, Auto-reverse. Drag the red ending point so that it goes all the way to the center of the cow's face.

Click on the second oval, add a Motion Path Right, With Previous, Auto-reverse. Drag the red ending point so that it goes to the middle of the pig's face.

Click on the third oval, add a Motion Path Left, With Previous, Auto-reverse. Drag the red ending point so that it goes to the middle of the monkey's face.

Select all four shapes and an animation Emphasis, Grow/Shrink, Auto-reverse. Change the first animation to After Previous, the others should already be With Previous.

Select all four shapes and add a Motion Path, Circle. Change the first animation to After Previous, the others should already be With Previous.

Select all four shapes and add an animation Emphasis, Pulse. Change the first animation to After Previous, the others should already be With Previous.

Select the red rectangle and add an animation Exit, Fade, Very Slow, After Previous.

Slide 4

Go to slide 4. Your slide 4 contains a photo. Right-click on the picture and save it as Couple, in PNG format with your Lesson 13 data files. Use the picture you just saved as the background for slide 4.

Step 1

You need to trace the image of the woman as one shape, and the image of the man as another shape. Use the curve tool to trace the shapes. The tracing does not have to be perfect because we will make some adjustments to accommodate poor tracing. Three sides of the shape can be straight lines as shown in figure 13–11.

Figure 13–11

Draw a rectangle that cover the entire slide and apply a Gradient Fill, Linear Down, and shades of light red. Send the rectangle to the back. Your slide should look like figure 13–12.

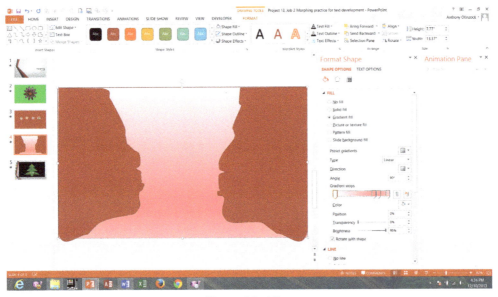

Figure 13–12

Step 2

Click on the traced image of the female, and use a Slide background fill, with No Line. Add a 10-point soft edge effect. Repeat this process for the male image. Your images should look similar to figure 13–13.

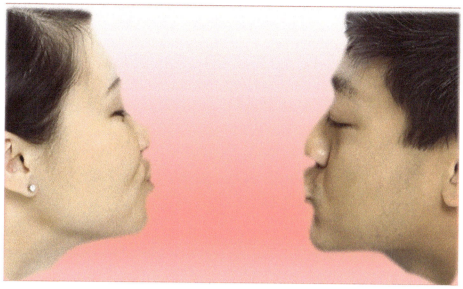

Figure 13–13

Step 3

Click on both the image of the female and the image of the male. Add an animation, Emphasis, Grow/Shrink, Very Slow, With Previous, Auto-reverse. Change the effect size to 200 percent.

Select the image of the female, the image of the male, and the rectangle covering the background. Add an animation Exit Fade, Very Slow. The first new animation should be After Previous, the others will be With Previous.

View slide 4 in Slide Show view. Correct any errors you find.

Slide 5

Go to slide 5. Your slide 5 has an image of a Christmas tree with images of decorations around the edges of the slide. View slide 5 in Slide Show view. As you can see, some of the images are animated .gif files which you will learn to make in a future lesson.

Step 1

Right-click on the picture and save it as Tree, in PNG format with your Lesson 13 data files. Delete the tree picture. Use the picture you just saved as the background for slide 5. Take all the decorations and place them on top of the same decoration used as background for the slide. Use the Curve tool and trace the image of the tree. Remember if you click and hold down the *Ctrl* key when using the Curve tool, the line will remain straight. Remove the Shape fill and change the outline to red, 4 ½ pt. Animate the outline for an Emphasis, Complementary Color, With Previous, Repeat Until End of slide. Your slide 5 should look like figure 13–14 after this step.

Figure 13–14

Step 2

Draw a rectangle to cover the entire slide. Use a red fill with No Line. Send the rectangle shape to the back. The outline of the tree should be behind the red rectangle, also. Only the tree ornaments should be visible as shown in figure 13–15.

Figure 13–15

Step 3

Click on each ornament and draw a random Custom Path around the screen, With Previous, 7 seconds, Smooth Start and End, Auto-reverse.

Repeat the above steps for each ornament on the slide. When you view the slide in Slide Show view, the ornaments will be moving about the screen for seven seconds and will return to their starting point.

Step 4

Select the red rectangle that covers the screen. Animate it to Exit, Fade, After Previous, Very Slow. View slide 5 in Slide Show view to make sure it is working properly. Add the *Origami* Transition to all slides, and action buttons to navigate through and to exit the Side Show. Save your presentation.

Artistic Effects

In an earlier lesson, you applied different artistic effects to pictures. In this lesson, you will combine a variety of picture artistic effects with other effects to create slides or printed material that attracts attention. Open the data file ***Lesson 13 Artistic Effects***. Add your name to the title slide and save the presentation again. The presentation contains five slides. Slides 2 to 5 have a picture inserted on them. Figure 13–16 shows slides 2 to 5 when completed.

Slide 2

Your slide 2 shows a photo of a girl working on a laptop with the ocean as a background. We want to create a slide that looks like the first slide in figure 13–16.

Make a copy of the picture. Right-click on the original picture of the girl. Click the Format picture and change the Line width to 20 pt. Change the line color to orange, Accent 6, Lighter 40 percent. Change the Cap type to Square and the Join type to Miter (see figure 13–17). Add an orange, Accent 6, Lighter 40 percent, Glow 11 pt, 60 percent Transparency. Move the photo to the upper left edge of the screen.

Size the copy of the picture so that it covers the entire slide, and sent it behind the photo that is in the upper left corner of the slide. Add the Artistic effect, Texturizer, to the photo.

Draw a rectangle height 2.5" high that stretches from the left edge to the right edge of the screen. Add a Gradient Fill, Linear, Down. At stop 0 percent position, white, Background 1, 60 percent Transparency; at 50 percent position, orange, Accent 6, Lighter 40 percent, 80 percent Transparency; at the 100 percent positon, white, Background 1. Remove the outline from the shape, and position it as shown in figure 13–16. Send the new shape behind the picture, but in front of the image of the girl covering the entire slide.

Use WordArt to add the text shown. Change the font to 54 pt French Script. Change the font color to orange, Accent 6, Darker 25 percent.

Figure 13–16

Slide 3

Your slide 3 shows a photo of a boy working on a laptop with a park as the background. We want to create a slide that looks like the second slide in figure 13–16.

Click on the original picture of the boy to select it and press Ctrl+D to duplicate the picture. Size the picture to cover the entire slide. Try to keep it proportional. If necessary, bring the original photo to the front. Make sure the image of the boy that covers the entire slide is selected and apply the Cutout Artistic Effect and Color Washout.

Right-click on the original picture of the boy. Click the Format tab and change the width of the line to 20 pt. Change the color olive green, Accent 4, Lighter 40 percent. Change the Cap type to Square and the Join type to Miter (see Format Picture Pane shown in figure 13–17). Add a glow olive green, Accent 4, Lighter 40 percent, 11 pt, 60 percent Transparency. Add an Inside Center Shadow. Add a Soft Edge, 5 pt. Move the photo to the upper right edge of the screen.

Figure 13–17

Draw a rectangle height 3.7" that stretches from the left edge to the right edge of the screen. Add a Gradient Fill, Linear, Up, with positions at 0 percent, 50 percent, and 100 percent, Angle 270°. At position 0 percent, add the color olive green, Accent 3, darker 25 percent, 25 percent Transparency. At the position, 50 percent, add the color olive green, Accent 3, Darker 25 percent, 50 percent Transparency. At position 100 percent add the color olive green, Accent 3, darker 25 percent, 75 percent Transparency. Remove the outline from the shape, and position it as shown in figure 13–16. Send the new shape behind the picture, but in front of the image of the boy covering the entire slide.

Use WordArt to add the text shown. Change the font to Magneto, 54 pt. Change the font color to olive green, Accent 3, Darker 25 percent.

Slide 4

Your slide 4 shows a photo of a girl wearing a graduation hat. We want to create a slide that looks like the third slide in figure 13–16.

Click on the photo of the girl to select it and press Ctrl+D to duplicate the picture. Size the picture to cover the entire slide. Try to keep it proportional. If necessary, bring the original photo to the front. Make sure the image of the girl that covers the entire slide is selected and then add the artistic effect Chalk Sketch.

Draw a rectangle that covers the entire slide. Remove the outline. Add a Gradient Fill, Linear Diagonal, Top Left to Bottom Right, with positions. The position 0 percent should be white, Background 1. The position 50 percent should be orange, Accent 6, Lighter 60 percent, 60 percent Transparency. The position 100 percent should be orange, Accent 6, Lighter 40 percent, 75 percent Transparency.

Right-click on the original picture of the girl. Click the Format tab and change the width of the line to 20 pt. Change the color to orange, Accent 6, Lighter 60 percent. Change the Cap type to Round and the Join type to Round. Add an orange, Accent 6, Lighter 40 percent, glow 11 pt, 50 percent Transparency. Add an Inside Center Shadow. Add a Soft Edge 5 pt. Move the photo to the upper left edge of the screen.

Use WordArt to add the text shown. Change the font to Script MT Bold ,54 pt. Change the font color to orange, Accent 6, Lighter 40 percent and the outline to orange, Accent 6, Darker 50 percent.

Slide 5

Your slide 5 shows a photo of a boy wearing a birthday hat and an image of three children at a birthday party. We want to create a slide that looks like the fourth slide in figure 13–16.

Click on the picture of the three children to select it, and press Ctrl+D to duplicate it. Size the picture to cover the entire slide. Try to keep it proportional. If necessary, bring the photo of the boy to the front. Make sure the image of the three children that covers the entire slide is selected and then apply the Washout Color Effect.

Draw a rectangle that covers the entire slide. Remove the outline. Add a Gradient Fill, Radial, from center. At the position 0 percent white, Background 1, 80 percent Transparency. At the position 50 percent dark blue, Text 2, Lighter 60 percent, 80 percent Transparency. At the position 100 percent dark blue, Text 2, Lighter 40 percent, 60 percent Transparency. Bring the picture of the boy in front of the rectangle.

Click on the original picture of the boy. Click the Format tab and change the width of the line to 15 points. Change the color green, Accent 3, Lighter 60 percent. Change the Cap type to Square and the Join type to Miter. Add an orange, Accent 6, Lighter 40 percent, Glow 11 pt, 50 percent Transparency. Move the photo to the upper left edge of the screen.

Use WordArt to add the text shown. Change the font to Comic Sans MS, 28 pt. Change the font color to olive green, Accent 3, Darker 50 percent.

Add the *Vortex* slide Transition to all the slides, and add action buttons to navigate and exit the presentation. Save the presentation.

Lesson 13 Applications

Lesson 13 Application 1 Presentation Application

Open the data file *Lesson 13 Application 1 Presentation Application*. Add your name to the title slide and save the presentation. Slide 2 contains one image, and slide 3 contains two images.

Go to slide 2. Use artistic effects to prepare slide 2. The image provided should be the focus of the slide.

Go to slide 3. Use artistic effects to prepare slide 3. The images provided should be the focus of the slide. Figure 13–18 shows an example of how slide 3 might be prepared. Do not use this example.

Add a transition of your choice and action buttons to navigate the presentation. Save your presentation.

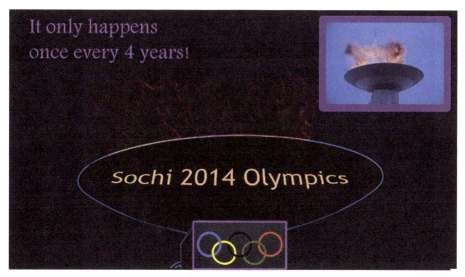

Figure 13–18

Lesson 13 Application 2 Instructional Materials Application

Open the data file *Lesson 13 Application 2 Instructional Materials Application*. Add your name to the title slide and save the presentation. The presentation contains four slides. The second slide gives the instructions for completing slide 4. Slide 3 displays a picture of the human heart with some of the parts named. Slide 4 displays a picture of the human heart with none of the parts named. You need to complete slide 4.

Go to slide 4 and use the skills you learned in this lesson to drill the user on naming the parts of the heart shown on slide 4. The parts have already been numbered, and the numbers and names are shown on slide 3 as shown in figure 13–19. You should display the name of a part, and the user should have to identify that part by clicking on a number, receiving a prompt, correct, or incorrect. Correct or incorrect should disappear after two seconds. When the part is properly identified, a new name of a part is displayed and the number of the previous part disappears.

Add a slide transition and action buttons to navigate the presentation.

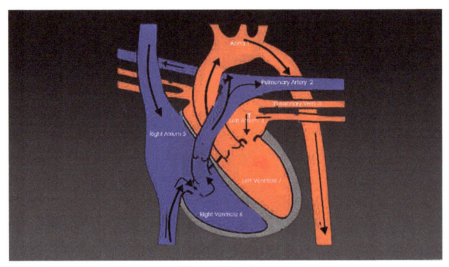

Figure 13–19

Lesson 13 Application 3 Gaming Application

Open the data file *Lesson 13 Application 3 Gaming Application*. Add your name to the title slide and save the file. Slides 2 and 3 each contain a picture. On each slide make the picture the background of the slide and develop a series of animations that morph into the slide background. Add a transition of your choice and action buttons to navigate the presentation. Save your presentation.

LESSON 14

Keyboarding Tutor Simulation and Advanced Animation

Data Files

Lesson 14 Advanced Animation
Lesson 14 Dominos
Lesson 14 Keyboarding Tutor Simulation
Lesson 14 Application 1 Presentation Application
Lesson 14 Application 2 Instructional Materials Application
Lesson 14 Application 3 Gaming Application

Overview

In Lesson 14 you will learn to create interactive simulations. You will also learn more advanced animation techniques.

Creating the Keyboarding Tutor Simulation

Open the data file ***Lesson 14 Keyboarding Tutor Simulation***. Add your name to the title slide and save the presentation. The *Rotate* Slide Transition and action buttons have already been applied to the presentation. The presentation consists of five slides. The second slide contains a drawing of the standard keyboard with the letter keys, the space bar, and the Enter key. Hands have been drawn to show the placement of the fingers on the keyboard. Slide 3 shows the content of the first lesson. Slide 4 gives the instructions for using the keyboarding tutor you will create on slide 5. Most of your work for this lesson will involve slide 5 where you will animate the keyboard to pace the students in typing the keys learned in Lesson 1. You will also add an ActiveX Text Box Control so that the student will be able to use the keyboard to type while being paced by the keyboarding tutor you will create.

Slide 2

On slide 2, move the hands off the keyboard so that you can color-code the keyboard to indicate which fingers control specific keys as shown in figure 14–1.

Figure 14–1

Step 1

Draw a rounded rectangle height .9" and width .9", over the letter *Q* which is controlled by the fourth finger on the left hand. The fill color for all keys controlled by the fourth finger should be blue, Accent 1, No Line, 50 percent Transparency. Copy and paste the transparent shape on top of all keys controlled by the fourth finger on the left and right hands as shown in figure 14–1. The size of the cover on the Shift key and Enter key is height .9" and width 1.33". Repeat this process for the other fingers. The color used for the third finger is dark red, Accent 2, No Line, 50 percent Transparency. The color used for the second finger is olive green, Accent 3, No Line, 50 percent Transparency. The color used for the first finger is orange, Accent 6, No Line, 50 percent Transparency. The color used for the space bar is Gradient, Radial, From Center, Position 0 percent is white, Background 1 and Position 100 percent is black, Text 1, lighter 50 percent, No Line, 50 percent Transparency. *Note: The colors used to cover the letters, Shift key, Enter key, and space bar should all be 50 percent transparent.*

Step 2

Group all objects that make up the left hand. Group all the objects that make up the right hand. Position the hands so that the fingers of the left hand are on the keys *a s d f* and the fingers on the right hand are on the keys, *j k l ;*.

Slide 5

On slide 5 you will create a keyboarding tutor that will guide and pace students in learning to keyboard.

ADVANCED POWERPOINT: MORE THAN PRESENTATIONS!

Step 1

Go to slide 5 and add an ActiveX Text Box Control above the keyboard as shown in figure 14–2. The text box should be height 1" and width 6". Adjust the *properties* to enable the EnterKeyBehavior, allow for MultiLines, enable ScrollBars, and enable WordWrap as shown in figure 14–3.

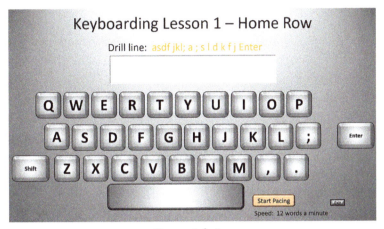

Figure 14–2

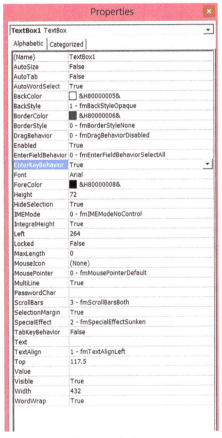

Figure 14–3

Step 2

In step 2 you will create an animation that paces users in typing the drill line shown above the ActiveX Text Box. The pacing will be at the rate of twelve words per minute.

1. Click on the key on the keyboard that represents the first letter in the drill, *a*.
2. Animate the object for an animation Emphasis, Color Pulse, With Previous, Fast, Delay 2 seconds and play a click sound. This animation is delayed to give users the time to click in the ActiveX Text Box during Slide Show view before the animation begins. The user will type in the Text Box.
   - The animation speed indicates fast, but in reality it means you will be displaying each animation at the rate of one per second, or 60 animations in 60 seconds. When calculating keyboarding speed, five keystrokes equals one word. Sixty animations a minute divided by 5 equals the rate of 12 wam (words a minute).
   - 60 strokes at .9 speed would =13.3 wam
   - 60 strokes at .8 speed would = 15 wam
3. Click on key that represents the second letter in the drill, *S*. Add an animation Emphasis, Color Pulse, With Previous, Fast, and play a *click* sound. Move it after the previous animation in the animation pane.
4. Repeat step 3 for all the keys used in the drill including the *space bar* and the *Enter key* as shown in figure 14–4.

Figure 14–4

If you want to use a sound from the Internet instead of the click sound, you would have to insert the sound after each character in the animation pane and have it play With Previous.

Step 3

The last step is to set a trigger to start the pacing drill. Select the first letter *a* in the animation pane, the beginning of the drill. Click the arrow to the right of *a* and select timing. Use the rectangle with the text *Start Pacing* as the trigger. Move all other animation effects in the Animation pane below the trigger effect. View your simulation in Slide Show view to test it. Go to slide 5. Click the *Start Pacing* button. Click in the text box, and type the letters, press the space bar, and press the Enter key when they are highlighted and you hear the click sound. Correct any errors you locate in the animation, and save the presentation as a PowerPoint Macro-Enabled presentation.

Advanced Animation

Open the data file ***Lesson 14 Advanced Animation.*** Add your name to the title slide and save the presentation. The Couture theme has already been applied and action buttons have been applied to navigate the two-slide presentation.

Slide 2

Slide 2 already contains two pictures and a sound file. Two small ovals have been inserted on the projector to represent Start and Stop buttons. You are going to create animations that: turns on the projector so that it appears to be projecting images, a curtain covering the movie screen will rise up, the room will darken, and images will be projected onto the screen. An audio file will play throughout the animation. When your slide 2 is completed, it will look similar to figure 14–5.

Figure 14–5

Step 1

Animate the audio file to start playing when you click the green button on the projector and stop playing after current slide. Move the sound icon off the screen to the right.

Step 2

Draw a shape that represents the white portion of the movie screen as shown in figure 14–6. Fill the image with black, Text 1, lighter 5 percent, and No Line. Duplicate the shape and fill it with dark red, No Line. Move the red shape down so that you can see both shapes. Animate the red shape to Exit, Wipe, With Previous, Up, Very Slow. Have the black shape Exit, Fade, After Previous, Very Slow. Move the red shape on top of the black shape and test the first three animation for the sound, red shape wiping up, and black shape is disappearing.

Figure 14–6

Step 3

Draw a rectangle that covers the entire slide. Add black, Text 1, 35 percent transparent. Animate the shape to Fade In, Very Slow, After Previous. This will provide the effect of dimming the lights.

Step 4

Draw a shape to represent the image from the projector to the screen as shown in figure 14–7. The image at the top shows the shape with a black background so that you can see it. The Image at the bottom is how it will look when the curtain is raised and the lights are dimmed.

Figure 14–7

Draw the shape with a Free-form, add a Gradient Fill, Linear, Right, with three positions, 0 percent white Background 1 Darker 5 percent; 50 percent white Background 1, and 100 percent yellow, 60 percent Transparency. Add a soft edge to the shape. Have the new shape appear After Previous with an animation Emphasis, Teeter, Very Fast, Repeat Until End of Slide.

Step 5

Insert two pictures of your choice. Have the first picture Fade In, Very Slow, After Previous. Have the same picture Exit, Fade, Very Slow, After Previous. Repeat the same animation for a second picture.

Step 6

Bring the green and red ovals to the front. Use the green button as the trigger to start the first animation, the audio file. The next animation should be With Previous. All other animations should be After Previous. Use the red button to end the Slide Show. Save your file.

Dominos

Open the data file **Lesson 14 Dominos**. Add your name to the title slide and save the presentation again. Slide 2 of the presentation looks like figure 14–8. In this job, you are going to format and arrange the dominos so that when you click, the first domino will fall, cause the other dominos to fall in order. In order to make the animation work, you need to have the pivot point of each domino at the bottom.

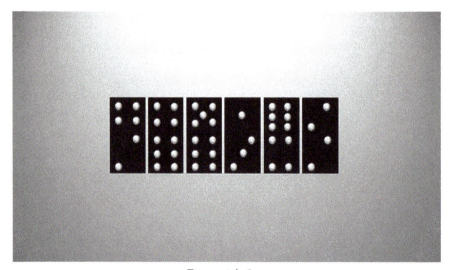

Figure 14–8

Step 1

Click on the first domino and apply a 3-D Rotation, Off Axis 1 left. Apply Background Style 5. Duplicate the domino and place the copy at the bottom of the first domino as shown in figure 14–9. Make the copy 100 percent Transparency. Group the two objects. Repeat this process for the remaining dominos.

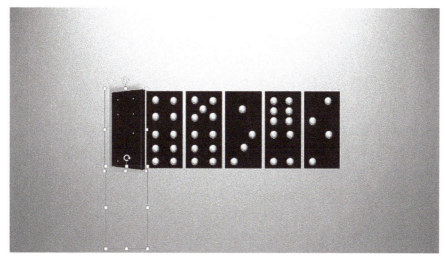

Figure 14–9

Step 2

Add a rectangle height 7" and width 9". Add a Texture Oak fill and a Bevel Riblet effect. Format the shape for Off Axis, 1 Top. Send the rectangle to the back of all the dominos as shown in figure 14–10. Make sure each domino is behind the domino in front of it.

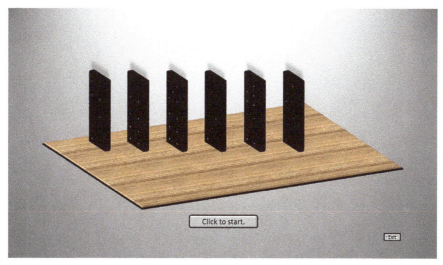

Figure 14–10

Step 3

Animate the first domino for a Spin, Clockwise, 90°, Medium, On Click. Animate all the other dominos for a Spin, Clockwise, 90°, With Previous. Delay the second domino .5 seconds, and each of the remaining an additional .5 seconds (1, 1.5, 2, and 2.5). Your dominos should be arranged as shown in figure 14–10. Add a shape that can be clicked to start the animation.

Step 4

Add action buttons to navigate and exit the presentation. Save the presentation.

Lesson 14 Applications

Lesson 14 Application 1 Presentation Application

Open the data file *Lesson 14 Application 1 Presentation Application*. The file consists of two slides. Slide 2, as shown in figure 14–11, has examples of images of a birthday party. Use these and/or other images to create an animation on slide 2 that represents a birthday party. Add any audio or video you wish to add. Add a transition of your choice, and action buttons to navigate through the presentation. Save your presentation.

Figure 14–11

Lesson 14 Application 2 Instructional Materials Application

Open the data file *Lesson 14 Application 2 Instructional Materials Application*. The presentation consists of three slides as shown in figure 14–12. The illustration on slide 2 represents a data network consisting of a connecting device, hub, and four hosts (computers) as shown in figure 14–13. Hubs have multiple ports where you can connect a device to the hub. When a hub is used as a connecting device, a message sent by one host is sent to all devices connected to the hub. The host that the message was addressed to accepts the message, and all other hosts just discard it. A *frame* is a digital data transmission unit in computer networking and telecommunication.

We want to create a simulation that demonstrates how a frame is sent and received in a network where a hub is used as the connecting device. We will use slide 2 to create our simulation as shown in figure 14–13.

ADVANCED POWERPOINT: MORE THAN PRESENTATIONS!

Figure 14–12

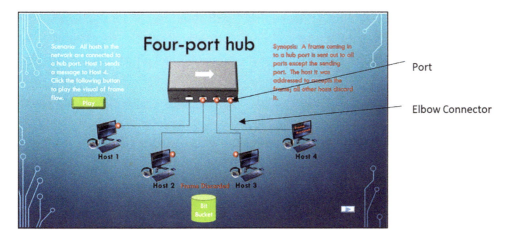

Figure 14–13

Slide 2

Step 1

Use the line elbow connector shape (a line shape) to create the wired connection from each host (computer) to the hub as shown in figure 14–13.

Step 2

Animate the red 3-D shape next to host 1 to Appear and, set the *Play* object as the trigger. Animate the red oval for a Custom Path following the elbow connector from the host to the hub, After Previous, Very Slow. Animate the red Oval to Disappear, After Previous. View this step in Slide Show view. The red shape should appear and move along the path to the hub and disappear once it reaches the port.

Step 3

Animate the red 3-D shape at Port 2 to Appear, After Previous. Animate the red 3-D shapes at Ports 3 and 4 to Appear, With Previous. Add a Custom Path to the 3-D object at Port 2 to move along the path of the elbow connector to Host 2 as shown, Very Slow, After Previous. Add a Custom Path to the 3-D object at Ports 3 and 4 to move along the path of the elbow connector to Hosts 3 and 4, Very Slow, With Previous. Animate the red 3-D shapes at Ports 2, 3, and 4 to Disappear; the first shape After Previous, and the others With Previous. View this step in Slide Show view and make any corrections necessary.

Step 4

Animate the 3-D shape to the right of Host 2 to Appear, After Previous. Animate the 3-D shape to the left of Host 3 to Appear With Previous. Animate the text above the Bit Bucket to Appear, With Previous. Draw a Custom Motion Path from the 3-D shape to the right of Host 2 to the Bit Bucket, After Previous. Draw a Custom Motion Path from the 3-D shape to the left of Host 3 to the bit bucket, With Previous. Animate the 3-D shape to the right of Host 2 to Disappear, After Previous. Animate the 3-D shape to the left of Host 3 to Disappear, With Previous. Animate the text *Frame Discarded* to Disappear, With Previous. View this step in Slide Show view, and make any corrections necessary.

Step 5

Animate the text on the monitor of Host 4 *Frame Accepted*, to Appear, After Previous. Have the same text Blink, After Previous, Repeat 5 times.

Step 6

Have the red text representing the synopsis Appear, After Previous. View this slide in Slide Show view and test the animation. Correct any errors you find. Save the presentation.

Slide 3

Slide 3 is very similar to slide 2. However, when a switch is used as a connecting device, a message sent to the switch is only sent out to the host to which it is addressed. No frame is discarded. Using the objects provided on slide 3, create a simulation that shows how a message moves from a host to the switch to the receiving host. View slide 3 in Slide Show view and correct any errors you find. Save your presentation.

Lesson 14 Application 3 Gaming Application

Open **Lesson 14 Application 3 Gaming Application**. The presentation already has the transition and action buttons added. You are only going to work on slide 2. From the dominos provided on slide 2, create an animation similar to figure 14–14.

ADVANCED POWERPOINT: MORE THAN PRESENTATIONS!

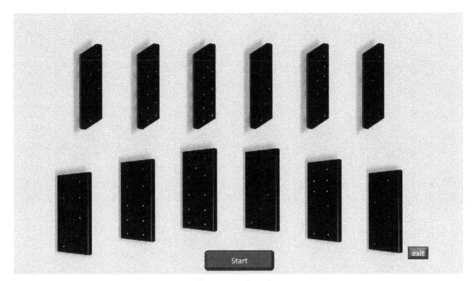

Figure 14–14

Create and format dominos as shown in figure 14–14. When you click the Start button, the dominos in the bottom row will fall left to right with a click sound added to each domino, knocking the domino following it down. The top row will fall right to left with a click sound, knocking the domino following it down. View your presentation in Slide Show view, and make any necessary corrections. Save your file.

LESSON 15

.gif Files and Advanced Animation

Data Files

Lesson 15 Advanced Drawing and Animations
Lesson 15 Creating a .gif File
Lesson 15 Application 1 Presentation Application
Lesson 15 Application 2 Instructional Materials and Gaming Application

Overview

In Lesson 15 you will learn to create animations by creating your own .gif files. You will learn additional advanced drawing and animation techniques. You will create original games and apps.

Creating a .gif File

A .gif file, Graphics Interchange Format, can support multiple images that can be strung together to create simple animations. There are many free gif animation programs available online, a simple one you will use to begin learning to create .gif animations is called UnFREEz®. You should download it to complete this job. The link is http://www.whitsoftdev.com/unfreez/.

Open the data file **Lesson 15 Creating a .gif File**. Add your name to the title slide and save the file again. The presentation consists of three slides. Slides 2 and 3 have an object on them. Go to slide 2.

Slide 2

Duplicate the image of the fish in a fish tank. Click on the copied image of a fish in a fish tank to select it.

Step 1

Ungroup the second image of the fish in a fish tank (Format/Arrange/Group/Ungroup). Click *yes*. Click ungroup again and the image will be ungrouped as shown in figure 15–1.

ADVANCED POWERPOINT: MORE THAN PRESENTATIONS!

Figure 15-1

Step 2

Click to the left of the image and above the fish, drag down and to the right to select only the fish as shown in figure 15–2. Use the right directional arrow to move the selected parts to the right of the picture. While all the parts of the fish are selected, group the fish image.

Figure 15-2

Step 3

While the fish is still selected decrease its size by dragging one of the corner handles as shown in figure 15–3.

Figure 15-3

Step 4

Move the fish back into the fish bowl and group all parts of the image as shown in figure 15-4. When you click on the image, it should be selected as one object.

Figure 15–4

Step 5

Create a new folder in your Lesson 15 data files titled Fish Images. Right-click on the new grouped picture of the fish in the fish bowl. Select *Save As Pict*ure. Navigate to your Lesson 15 Data Files and select the Fish Images folder in the Save As Picture dialog box. Name the file *Fish 1*, and the *Save as type to GIF* as shown in figure 15–5.

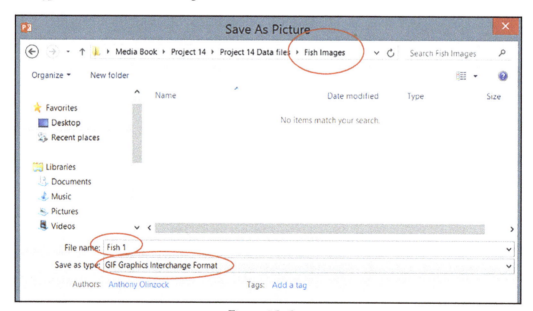

Figure 15–5

Step 6

Click on the Fish 1 image and ungroup it. Move the fish to a location slightly to the right as shown in figure 15–6. Group the image again, and save it as Fish 2 in your Fish Images folder as a GIF file. Repeat this process six more times, each time moving the fish to a different location as shown in figure 15–6. The additional images should be saved as GIF files with the names Fish 3, Fish 4, Fish 5, Fish 6, Fish 7, and Fish 8.

Figure 15–6

Step 7

Open the UnFREEz program you downloaded, and open the Fish images folder. Drag each of the eight fish pictures, in order, to the drop area of the UnFREEz dialog box as shown in figure 15–7. Place a check mark in the Loop Animation box, and enter 25 in the Frame delay box. *Note: The lower the number, the faster the animation.* Click Make Animated GIF and save it as **Fish Animation** in the Fish Images folder. In UnFREEz, 100 is approximately one second, but the actual speed will vary based on your computer.

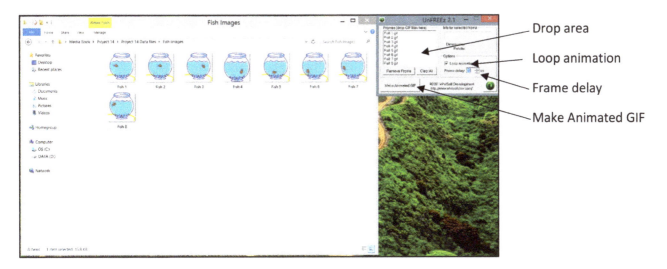

Figure 15–7

Step 8

Go to slide 2, and insert the **Fish animation** picture you saved as a GIF file next to the original picture. View the slide in Slide Show view, and the picture you inserted should be animated.

Slide 3

Create an Animated GIF from the image of the dog on slide 3. Your animation should have the dog jumping through the hoop with the body of the dog under the hoop on one side of the hoop and over the hoop on the other. *Hint: You might need to save the hoop as a picture and crop it into two pieces.* Save your presentation.

Advanced Drawing and Animation

Open the data file **Lesson 15 Advanced Drawing and Animations** and add your name to the file name and save it again.

Drawing the Car Shapes

Using the shapes shown on your slide 2 (all shapes were drawn using the various shapes and drawing tools), we are going to create the images shown in figure 15–8 on slide 3. Once we create the images, we will add animation and sound. Figure 15–9 shows the shapes used to create the images shown in figure 15–10. The images on slide 2 are in the background so you will need to trace the images or use shapes to create them. Duplicate shapes as needed. Two sound files are also included on slide 2: engine starting sound and burning rubber squeaking brakes sound.

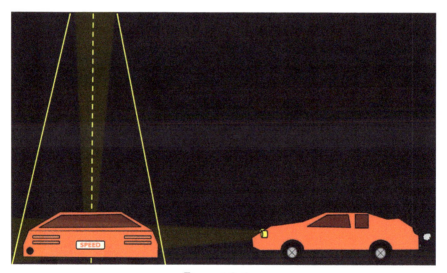

Figure 15–8

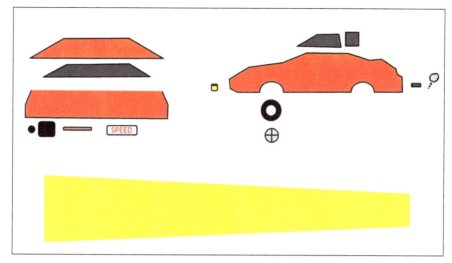

Figure 15–9

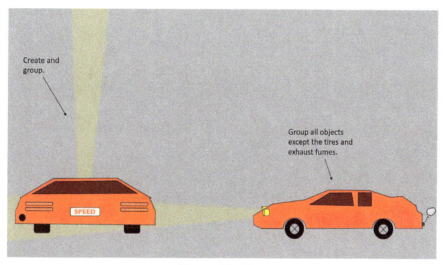

Figure 15–10

Once you have created all the shapes and added the necessary fill and line colors, copy all shapes to slide 3 and group them as shown in figure 15–10. On the side view of the car, the tires and exhaust smoke should not be grouped with the other objects since they will be animated separately. Send shapes to the back or bring shapes to the front as needed.

Add background to this slide, black, Text 1, Lighter 15 percent. Draw the road lines as shown in figure 15–8. Add the yellow to represent the headlights using the yellow shape, and make the color 85 percent Transparency. Arrange the objects to look like figure 15–8. The yellow shape representing the light coming from the headlights should be grouped with the section of the car that does not include the exhaust and side tires.

Adding Sound and Animation

Add an *engine starting* sound, the one on slide 2 or one you download from the Internet. Select a sound that is about ten seconds long or trim to the desired length. Have the engine sound play With Previous, and make sure you keep it as the first animation in the animation pane.

Add the animation Emphasis Teeter to the exhaust object, With Previous, .1 seconds, Repeat Until End of Slide. Select the two tires that are part of the side view of the car. Add an animation Emphasis, Spin, Counterclockwise, With Previous, Repeat Until End of Slide.

Select all objects that make up the side view of the car and add an animation Motion Path Left to them. The first animation should be After Previous and the others With Previous.

Select all objects that make up the side view of the car and add an animation Exit, Disappear, With Previous, Delay 19 seconds. *Note: If you didn't use the .wav file from slide 2, you might need to adjust the amount of the delay.*

Select the image that represents the back of the car. These shapes should already be grouped. Add an animation Entrance, Appear, With Previous, Delay 19.5 scconds. *Note: If you didn't use the .wav file from slide 2, you might need to adjust the amount of the delay.* Add an animation Exit, Zoom, With Previous, Delay 19.5 seconds.

Copy the brake squeaking sound from slide 2 and add it to slide 3. Animate it to play With Previous, Delay 19.5 seconds. *Note: If you didn't use the .wav file from slide 2, you might need to adjust the amount of the delay.* It should be the last object in the animation pane. View the slide in Slide Show view and save your presentation.

Butterfly and Hummingbird Animations

We are going to use the objects on slide 4 to create an animation where the butterfly flies across the screen with wings flapping and the hummingbird is flying in place at the flower with wings flapping as shown in figure 15–11. In order to do this, we must cut the pictures into sections. We will work with the butterfly first.

Figure 15–11

Butterfly

Copy the butterfly from slide 4 onto slide 5. Make two additional copies of the butterfly, and using the crop tool, create the three sections of the butterfly as shown in figure 15–12.

Figure 15–12

Move the three sections close together so that it looks like the original picture. Select the two wings and animate them for Emphasis, Grow/Shrink, Size 150 percent, With Previous, .1 seconds, Repeat Until End of Slide. View your slide in Slide Show view to see the animation.

Select the three sections that make up the butterfly and move them off the slide to the left. While the three shapes are still selected, add an animation Motion Path Right, With Previous, 10 seconds. Move the red ending points for the animations off the slide to the right.

Hummingbird

The first step in animating the hummingbird is to remove the background by clicking on the picture and then clicking Format/Adjust/Remove Background/Mark areas to remove/Keep Changes as shown in figure 15–13. Next, mark any additional areas to be removed and keep changes.

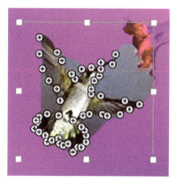

Figure 15–13

In order to animate the hummingbird and have the wings moving in place, you will need to crop the picture into three sections as shown in figure 15–14. Make three copies of the picture and crop or remove sections of the picture to create the three shapes as shown. Once you have done that, put the three sections together and animate the wings for an Emphasis, Grow/Shrink, 150 percent, With Previous, .1 seconds, Repeat Until End of Slide. View the slide in Slide Show view and save your presentation.

Figure 15–14

Pan and Zoom Effect

Slide 6 contains a photo taken in a jungle that shows an animal in a tree. We want to create a pan and zoom effect that looks like you are viewing the scene through a camera lens and then using the zoom effect to zoom in on the Iguana.

Create two yellow rectangles, no outline, to cover a portion of the picture as shown in figure 15–15.

Figure 15–15

Add a third rectangle, no outline, that covers the remaining picture and that stretches about four inches off the left and right side of the screen and shown in figure 15–16.

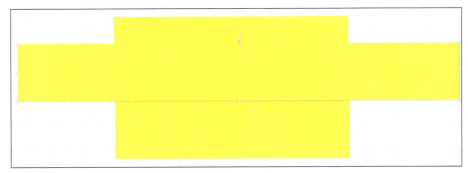

Figure 15–16

Draw an oval shape on top of the last rectangle and use subtract shape tool to remove the section as shown in figure 15–17.

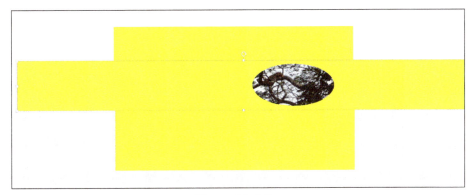

Figure 15–17

Draw an oval on top of the picture shown through the rectangle shape and remove the fill color then add a 10-point yellow border as shown in figure 15–18, and add an effect, Bevel Angle. Group the rectangle and the outline of the oval.

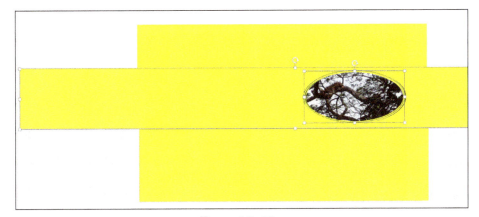

Figure 15–18

Move the rectangle shape with the oval off the screen to the right so that the entire screen is yellow. Add an animation Motion Path Left to the rectangle with the oval shape, 8 seconds, With Previous, Auto-reverse, Smooth Start and Smooth End. Move the red ending point so that the animation moves across about three-fourth of the slide.

Add another animation to the rectangle with the oval for a Motion Path Right, 8 seconds, After Previous, Smooth Start and Smooth End. Adjust the red ending point so that the animation stops over the animal in the tree.

Finally, click on the picture (you might have to temporally move the rectangle), and add an animation, Emphasis, Grow/Shrink, 150 percent, After Previous, Very Slow. Make any adjustments needed. View the slide in Slide Show view and save your presentation.

Trace Map Route

Slide 7 has a picture of a map of Mississippi. Make the picture the background of the slide and use the line tool to create a shape from city to city: Oxford to Tupelo to Columbus to Greenville to Vicksburg to Meridian to Hattiesburg to Natchez to Gulfport to Biloxi to Pascagoula. You should have a separate line shape between each city. Starting with the first shape, Oxford to Tupelo, animate the shape for Entrance, Wipe, With Pervious, Left, Slow. Repeat for the other shapes, each After Previous and either Down, Left, or Right. View the slide in Slide Show view and save your presentation.

Digital Timer

Open a new blank presentation and name it **Lesson 15 Digital Timers**. Add a title to the title slide, *Digital Timers* and *your name* as the subtitle. Apply the *Vapor* Design theme, and the *Curtain* Transition to all slides. Add a new slide, Blank Layout for slide 2.

Slide 2

On slide 2 you are going to create a digital timer that counts down from 15 seconds.

Step 1

Create an image for the digital timer using a rounded rectangle shape, height .73" and width 1.63". Add a Gradient Fill, Radial, From Center. Use 3 positions: at 0 percent Gold, Accent 3, Lighter 40 percent; at 50 percent Lime, Accent 4, Lighter 40 percent; at 80 percent red, Accent 1. Add an effect Bevel Soft Round. Use a black, Background 1 for the Outline, 6 pt. Align the shape to the center and middle. Enter the number 15 in Impact, 24 pt. font as shown in figure 15–19.

ADVANCED POWERPOINT: MORE THAN PRESENTATIONS!

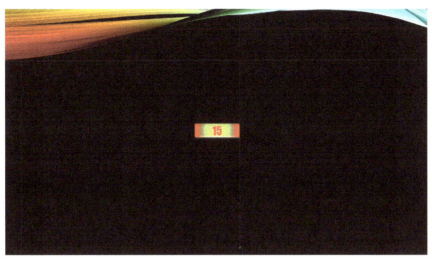

Figure 15–19

Step 2

Save the image as 15, as a GIF file in your data file folder. Change the number to 14 and save the image again as a GIF file. Repeat this process for numbers 13 to 0. Use the UnFREEz program to create a GIF file titled *Fifteen second timer*. Refer to figure 15–7. Adjust the frame delay in the UnFREEz dialog box to a number that represents 1 second when run on your computer. Compare the time it takes to count down 15 seconds to another timer or watch, and decrease the number for frame delay to make it run faster or increase the number to make it run slower. Insert the .gif you created on slide 2, and delete any other objects. Align the image at the middle and center. Save the file in your Lesson 15 folder.

Lesson 15 Applications

Lesson 15 Application 1 Presentation Application

Open the data file **Lesson 15 Application 1 Presentation Application**. Add your name to the subtitle and save the file again.

Your slide 2 should look like figure 15–20.

Figure 15–20

Slide 3

Copy the flag image from slide 2 to slide 3. Use the flag image to create a .gif file that has the flag waving. *Note: You can make multiple .gif images of the flag decreasing and increasing the width, and combine the images to make the .gif file.* Insert the .gif file on slide 3.

Slide 4

Copy the pumping iron image from slide 2 to slide 4. Use the pumping iron image to create a .gif file. *Note: You can cut the image into three sections—the left arm, the body, and the right arm. You can make multiple .gif images, changing the positions of the arms.* Insert the .gif file on slide 4.

Add action buttons to navigate the file, a design, and a slide transition to all the slides. Save your presentation.

Lesson 15 Application 2 Instructional Materials and Gaming Application

Open the data file *Lesson 15 Application 2 Instructional Materials and Gaming Application*. The presentation includes the five slides shown in figure 15–21. Your slides are not complete at this point.

ADVANCED POWERPOINT: MORE THAN PRESENTATIONS!

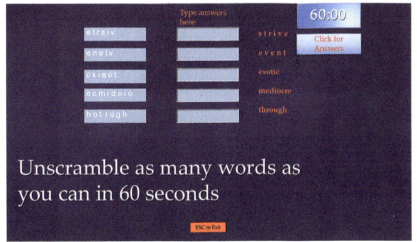

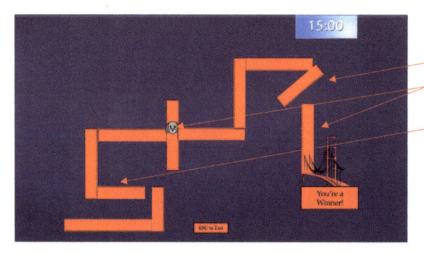

Figure 15–21

Slide 2 – Word Game

On slide 2, you will add the ActiveX Text Box Controls shown. You will add a scrambled version of each word in the left column of boxes. The user will unscramble the words and type them in the column of text boxes at the right. You need to create and add a sixty-second digital timer (.gif file) and have the sound play at the end of sixty seconds. The sound file is inserted on the slide. Move it off the slide. Add a shape named *Click for Answers*, and use the shape as the trigger to display the correct answers. Create a Custom Show consisting of slide 2, and name the Custom Show *Word Game*. Create a link to this Custom Show from the *Word Game* button on slide 1.

Slide 3 – Maze Game

Animate the maze game on slide 3. Refer to slide 3 in figure 15–21. Animate the red rectangles and dog as indicated. If the user goes off the path and touches the blue background or dog before reaching the *You're a winner!* object, the user should be taken to slide 4. If the user is able to touch the rectangle with the words *You're a winner!*, she/he should be taken to slide 5.

Create a fifteen-second digital timer (.gif file), and have buzzer sound play at the end of fifteen seconds. The sound object is already on the slide. Move it off to the right. Set up the Slide Show to be Browsed at a Kiosk.

Create a Custom Show consisting of slides 3, 4, and 5, and name the Custom Show *Maze Game*. Create a link to this Custom Show from the *Maze Game* button on slide 1. Save your file.

LESSON 16

Using VBA to Create an Electronic Calculator in PowerPoint, Tweening, Photos and Graphics

Data Files

Lesson 16 Globe gif
Lesson 16 Tweening
Lesson 16 Application 3 Gaming Application

Overview

In Lesson 16 you will learn to use VBA to create your own apps for presentations and instructional materials. You will be introduced to Tweening, a technique designed to give the illusion of moving an object by creating a Motion Path, sizing, and rotating the object at the same time.

Creating a Calculator

Step 1

Open a blank PowerPoint presentation. Add the *Crop* Design and the *Blinds* Transition. Add the title **Lesson 16 Creating a Calculator in PowerPoint** and add *your name* in the subtitle text box. Add a new slide in Blank Layout.

Click on the Developer tab and in the Code group, click Visual Basic to access the Visual Basic Editor. Click the Insert tab and click on UserForm. A UserForm will be opened along with the Toolbox of controls as shown in figure 16–1. Size the form to approximately 5" long by 3" wide as shown in figure 16–1. Click on the text box control button and draw a text box approximately height .5" and width 2 1/2" across the top of the UserForm.

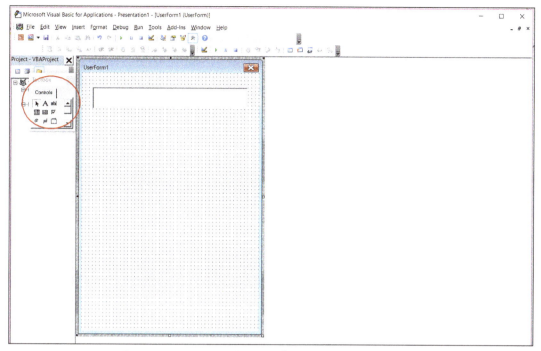

Figure 16–1

While the Text Box is selected the *Properties* box is displayed as shown in figure 16–2. If it isn't displayed, right-click on the Text Box and select *Properties*. Change the font to Calibri, Bold, 20 pt. Change the Text to 0 and the TextAlign to Right as shown in figure 16–2.

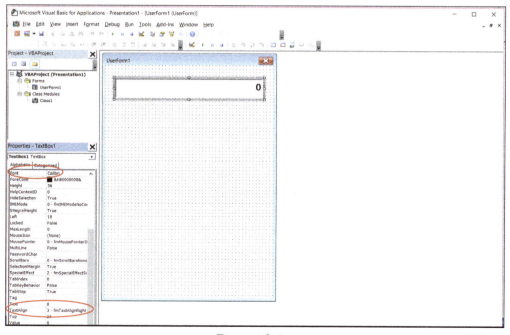

Figure 16–2

Step 2

Click on the command button control in the Toolbox, and insert seventeen command buttons sized as shown in figure 16–3. Use the grid to assist in placement. Change the *properties* for the Command buttons so that the font is Calibri, Bold, 20 pt. Your UserForm should look like figure 16–3.

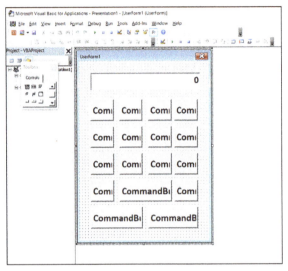

Figure 16–3

Change the caption for each command button as shown, and add a Button Shadow BackColor to the buttons + , -, *, /, Clear, and = as shown in figure 16–4.

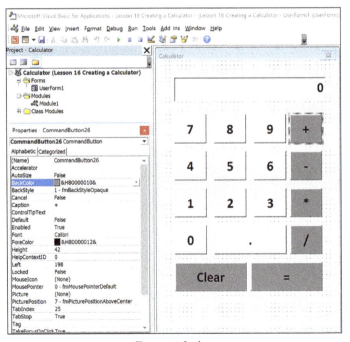

Figure 16–4

Step 3

Double-click on the number *0* on the ten-key pad. When you do this, the visual basic editor opens, and two lines of codes are already written as shown in figure 16–5. *Note: Your CommandButton number will probably be different than that shown in figure 16–5. Private sub* is a keyword that tells visual basic what the access level of the variable or procedure it is declaring will be within your application, and as such what code has permission to read it and write to it (or call it). You will add code between these two lines that will let you click one of the buttons on the calculator and display the results in the text box at the top of the calculator.

Private Sub CommandButton26_Click()

End Sub

Figure 16–5

Add the code shown in figure 16–6 between *Private Sub* and *End Sub*.

```
Private Sub CommandButton13_Click()
If TextBox1.Text = "0" Then
   TextBox1.Text = "0"
Else
   TextBox1.Text = TextBox1.Text & "0"
End If
End Sub
```

Figure 16–6

Note that the number *zero* is displayed in the result box. You can return to the UserForm by clicking on the word UserForm in the left pane. If the left pane is not displayed click the View tab and in the drop-down menu, select Project Explorer.

Copy the code between Private Sub and End sub. Double-click on the number 1 on the calculator and then paste the copied code between the two lines of code already created. You will only need to change the two numbers circled in red shown in figure 16–7. These numbers represent the key you clicked on the keypad. You can repeat this procedure to add code for each of the numbers on the calculator. The *If* statement examines the value of the number you clicked, and if there is no value in Textbox 1, it will put that number in the box. Otherwise, it will put the number you clicked to the right of the value already in Textbox 1 and displays the result in the text box at the top of the screen.

```
Private Sub CommandButton21_Click()
If TextBox1.Text = "0" Then
    TextBox1.Text = "1"
    Else
    TextBox1.Text = TextBox1.Text & "1"
End If
End Sub
```

Figure 16–7

Option Explicit/Declare Variables

Go to the top of your code and enter Option Explicit. The Option Explicit statement requires that all variables be declared using a Dim statement. Coding is more efficient and programs run more efficiently when you declare variable such as string, double, integer, long, etc. You learned the variables types in a previous lesson. If you don't declare variable types, VBA supports the Variant data type that can hold any type of data. Variant is the default type. Using the variant type increases processing time when encountered in code because when the code is run the compiler has to determine what type of data is stored in the variable.

Add the code shown in figure 16–8 at the top your code.

```
Option Explicit
Dim firstnum As Double
Dim secondnum As Double
Dim results As Double
Dim operations As String
```

Figure 16–8

Operations First Number

The next thing you need to do is to add code that enters the number you click on the calculator and defines the operation of the +, -, *, and / as shown in figure 16–9. Double-click on the + key on your calculator and add the code shown between the two lines of code already displayed. You can follow this same procedure to define the operation of the other operator keys. You will only need to change the operation sign to – or * or /. The *firstnum* you entered is saved in the firstnum variable, and the *operations* is defined as +.

```
Private Sub CommandButton26_Click()
firstnum = TextBox1.Text
   TextBox1.Text = ""
   operations = "+"
End Sub
```
Figure 16–9

Operations decimal point

Double-click on the "." key on your calculator to access the code, and add the code shown in figure 16–10 between Private Sub and End Sub. This code examines the string of data in Textbox1 and adds the decimal point.

```
Private Sub CommandButton16_Click()
If InStr(TextBox1.Text, ".") = 0 Then
TextBox1.Text = TextBox1.Text + "."
End If
End Sub
```
Figure 16–10

Clear

Double-click on the "clear" key, and add the code shown in figure 16–11. This code removes any data displayed in the text box at the top of the calculator.

```
Private Sub CommandButton15_Click()
TextBox1 = ""
TextBox1 = "0"
End Sub
```
Figure 16–11

Operations "=" and second number

The next thing you need to do is add code that will let you enter additional numbers (0–9) and operators (+, -, *, and /) and calculate the results. The following code lets you add additional numbers that are saved in the *secondnum* variable, add the operator, and calculates and displays the *results*. See figure 16–12. Double-click on the "=" and add the code between Private Sub and End Sub.

```
Private Sub CommandButton29_Click()
secondnum = TextBox1.Text
If operations = "+" Then
results = firstnum + secondnum
```

```
            TextBox1.Text = results
        ElseIf operations = "-" Then
            results = firstnum - secondnum
            TextBox1.Text = results
        ElseIf operations = "*" Then
            results = firstnum * secondnum
            TextBox1.Text = results
        ElseIf operations = "/" Then
            results = firstnum / secondnum
            TextBox1.Text = results
        End If
End Sub
```

Figure 16–12

Run Calculator in the Visual Basic Editor

To run the code from the UserForm in the Visual Basic Editor while displaying code, click the Run Sub/UserForm. You could also press F5. The calculator will display and you can operate it. Enter a number, enter an operator (+, -, *, or /) and then enter as many other numbers and operators as you want. Click the "=" when done entering numbers and operators, and the result will be displayed in the text box at the top of the calculator. Press *Clear* to enter a new calculation.

Run Calculator in Slide Show View

If you click the Developer Tab in PowerPoint and then click Macros in the Code group, no Macros are listed for you to run. If you look at the bottom of the dialog box, you will see that there are macros in the presentation, but you can't access them directly. In order to be able to display and run the calculator in Slide Show view, you need to write a simple macro as shown in figure 16–13 that will let you run the UserForm. Insert a module and add the code. This macro, since it is not Private, is accessible to use in PowerPoint. You will be able to access this macro and run it from PowerPoint Normal view. You can also assign the macro action to an object and run it during Slide Show view. You can expand the operations of the calculator as desired.

```
Sub ShowForm()
    UserForm1.Show
End Sub
```

Figure 16–13

Slide 2

On slide 2 of your presentation, add two buttons as shown in figure 16–14.

ADVANCED POWERPOINT: MORE THAN PRESENTATIONS!

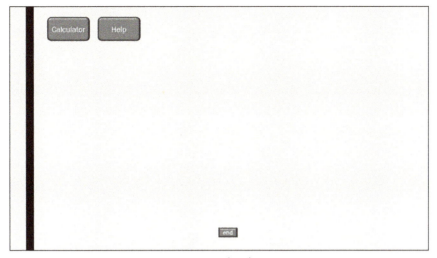

Figure 16–14

Use the Calculator button to launch the ShowForm Macro. Use the Help button to link to the next slide and add the text and action button (return to last Slide Shown) in figure 16–15. Add an End button slide 2 to end the Slide Show and a next slide button on slide 1. Save your presentation as a PowerPoint Macro-Enabled presentation, ***Lesson 16 Creating a Calculator***.

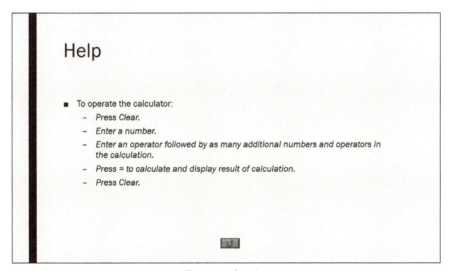

Figure 16–15

Tweening

Tweening as related to animation involves inserting an object between existing objects. The process usually involves a combination of animation techniques such as a Motion Path, a Spin, and Grow/Shrink at the same time. A good example would be drawing a card from a deck of cards and inserting it between other cards in a player's hand. This technique has many applications.

Open the data file ***Lesson 16 Tweening***. There are six slides in the presentation as shown in figure 16–16. At the top right of slides 2–5 is a picture of a series of cards. Below the picture are three cards that are already in the order of the picture shown above. Your job is to locate the missing card from the cards at the right, and animate it to move in place between the existing cards. For example, the first card missing on slide 2 is the Ace of Diamonds. You will locate the Ace of Diamonds, draw a Custom Path to place in between the Ace of Spades and the Jack of Spades. You will also need to add an animation Emphasis Spin, With Previous to turn the card. Once you have the placement accurate, use the More Cards button to trigger the animation. Make sure the spin animation is With Previous and after the Motion Path in the animation pane. Animate the second card, After Previous. Repeat this process for slides 3, 4, and 5. *Note: You might need to bring the cards in the hand forward or backward as needed.*

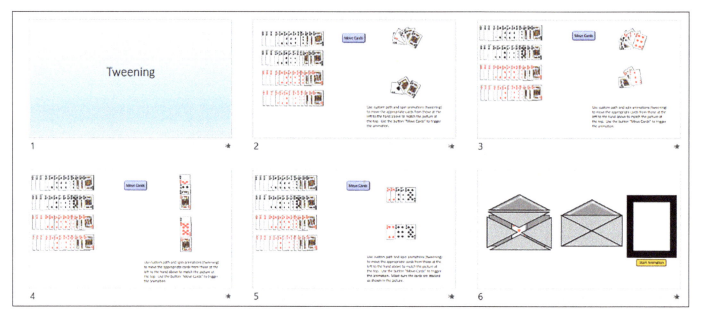

Figure 16–16

On slide 6, you have a card, the Ace of Hearts. You are going to place that card in an envelope, have the envelope open, and animate the card to move into the frame and at the same time increase in size. The envelope is made up of Isosceles Triangles and a rectangle as shown in figure 16–17.

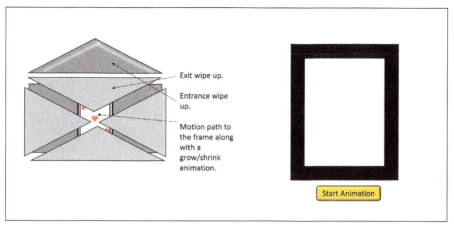

Figure 16–17

Arrange the pieces of the envelope as shown in figure 16–17. The rectangle is the back of the envelope, the ace is on top of the back of the envelope, and all the triangles are on top of the ace as shown.

To open the envelope, animate the section of the envelope numbered 1 to Exit, Wipe, From Bottom. Have the *Start Animation* button serve as the trigger to start the animation. Have the number 2 section Entrance, Wipe, From Bottom, After Previous. The card should now be visible when you run the animation.

Move section 1 off the card so that you can animation the card. Animate the card, Custom Path to the center of the frame, After Previous. Add an animation Emphasis, Grow/Shrink, 200 percent, With Previous. Move section 1 back in place. View your animation in Slide Show view to make sure everything works, then save the presentation.

3-D .gif File

Open the data file **Lesson 16 Globe gif.** Your slide 2 contains two pictures and looks like figure 16–18. Once you complete this job, your slide will look like figure 16–19. Slide 2 is supposed to be the image of earth from another planet. The earth image is a 3-D .gif file that you will create. You will also add stars, a falling star, and moving clouds.

Creating the Globe .gif File

Go to slide 3 of the presentation, it has a flat image of earth. As shown in figure 16–20.

Figure 16–18

Figure 16–19

Crop the picture into there or more equal parts as shown in figure 16–20. Next, crop the three parts (Format/Size/Crop/Crop to shape/Oval) you created to ovals of equal size as shown in figure 16–21. Save the first image as globe 1, a .gif file. Move the second globe on top of the first globe and make sure it is aligned, and save it as globe 2, a .gif file. Move the third image on top of the first two image. Make sure it is aligned, and save it as globe 3, a .gif file. Use the UnFREEz program to create a .gif file from the three images. Set the frame delay to 30, and create a .gif file named *Animated Globe*. Insert the animated globe on slide 2 as shown in figure 16–19. Size as needed.

ADVANCED POWERPOINT: MORE THAN PRESENTATIONS!

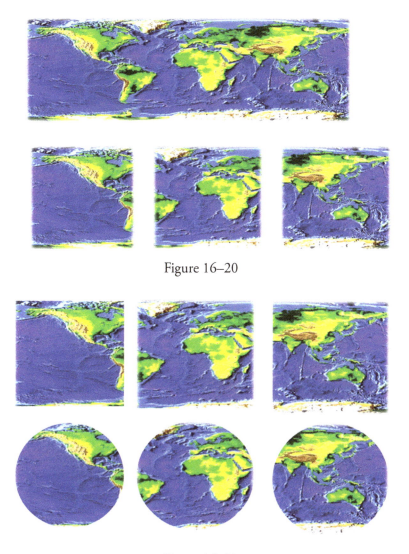

Figure 16–20

Figure 16–21

Creating Stars

Create the stars by using very small ovals of varying size with a gradient fill from the center and different shades of white. Add a white glow to the stars. Add an animation to one of the stars, a Custom Path from above the slide, across the slide, and off the other end of the slide at a slow speed to represent a falling star.

Creating Clouds

Draw two images of different sizes to represent clouds, with a light gray fill and No Line. Make each cloud 60 percent Transparency. Add a 25 pt Soft Edge to each cloud. Animate the clouds to move slowly at different speeds (12 seconds and 15 seconds) from the off the right edge to off the left edge. Delay the second cloud 3 seconds. Repeat both cloud animations Until End of Slide.

Transparent Cover

Draw a rectangle that covers the top picture on the slide, dark blue, No Line. Make the rectangle 80 percent transparent. This layering helps create depth and the 3-D effect. You can even add additional layers of complementary colors to increase the effect.

Add the shape transition, three seconds. Once you have the animation working properly, save your file.

Lesson 16 Applications

Lesson 16 Application 1 Presentation Application

Open a blank presentation and title it ***Lesson 16 Application 1 Presentation Application***. On slide 2 create an image of a spinning oval (.gif file) with a picture or pattern image. Add an appropriate background. Figure 16–22 is only a sample.

Figure 16–22

Lesson 16 Application 2 Instructional Materials Application

Open your ***Lesson 16 Creating a Calculator*** file you completed in this lesson. Add two command buttons to the UserForm as shown in figure 16–23. The Rnd Num button will generate a random number between 0–99. You can make the range anything you want. The SQRT button will calculate the square root of any number you enter. The code you will need for each operation is shown in figure 16–24.

ADVANCED POWERPOINT: MORE THAN PRESENTATIONS!

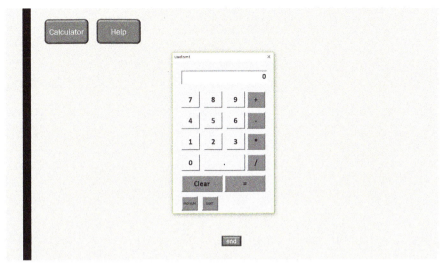

Figure 16–23

```
Private Sub CommandButton30_Click()
    Randomize
  TextBox1.Text = ""
  TextBox1.Text = TextBox1.Text & Int(100 * Rnd)
End Sub

Private Sub CommandButton31_Click()
If TextBox1.Text = "0" Then
  TextBox1.Text = "0"
  Else
  MySqr = Sqr(TextBox1.Text)
  TextBox1.Text = MySqr
  End If
End Sub
```

Figure 16–24

Make sure your UserForm is working properly, and save your file as *Lesson 16 Application 2 Instructional Materials Application*.

Lesson 16 Application 3 Gaming Application

Open the data file *Lesson 16 Application 3 Gaming Application*. Your slide 2 looks like figure16-25.

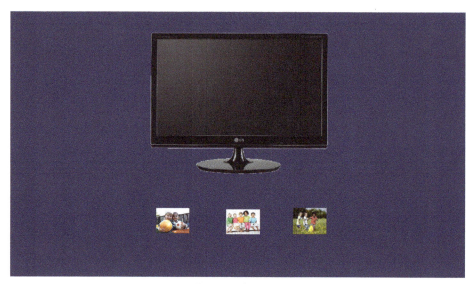

Figure 16–25

Animate each of the pictures below the monitor to move up onto the screen of the monitor, grow 350 percent, and Exit Fade, Delay 2 seconds. Each animation should be Very Slow. Use each of the pictures as the trigger to start the animation. Save your presentation.

LESSON 17

Working with Pictures and Videos, Pivots and Animation, UserForm

Data Files

Lesson 17 Music and Animation
Lesson 17 Pictures and Graphics
Lesson 17 Pivots and Animation

Overview

In Lesson 17 you will learn techniques for working with pictures and videos. You will work with pivots to create realistic animation such as having a character walk or a plane maneuver in the sky.

Pictures and Graphics

PowerPoint makes it easy to add pictures to your slides. You simply click Insert/Images/Online pictures to locate pictures online or Insert/Images/Pictures to locate a picture on your computer. You can even capture a screen shot by clicking Insert/Images/Screenshot. Once you begin to accumulate a number of pictures, you can organize them in a photo album by clicking Insert/Images/Photo Album.

Inserting a picture is only the beginning step in working with pictures and graphics. You can add a variety of preset backgrounds, patterns, and original picture backgrounds. You can adjust pictures and add a variety of effects and colors.

Open the data file *Lesson 17 Pictures and Graphics*. Slides 2 and 3 have the pictures shown in 17–1 already inserted on the slides.

Figure 17–1

Slides 2 and 3

Step 1 – Add Background

We want to add a background to slide 2. You can do that by clicking Design/Custom/Format Background. You can add a solid fill, gradient, picture or texture, or a pattern. Many of these options include preset designs that you can use. We are going to create our own gradient background. Go to slide 2 and click Design/Format Background/Gradient. You will need 6 positions set at 0, 20, 40, 60, 80, and 100. Set the gradient for Linear and the direction Down. Using standard colors set the 0 percent red, 20 percent orange, 40 percent yellow, 60 percent green, 80 percent blue, and 100 percent purple. Your background should look like figure 17–2.

Figure 17–2

Step 2 – Add a Style

Click on the first picture at the left, and add a Metal Rounded Rectangle style. Change the border color to dark red. Add a 3-D Rotation Off Axis, 2 Right. Format the remaining two pictures the same as the first picture. Your slide 2 should look like figure 17–3.

Figure 17–3

Step 3 – Adjust Color

Duplicate slide 2. On slide 3, select the first picture and change the color to orange, Accent color 2 Dark. Change the color of the middle picture to blue, Accent color 5 Light. Change the color of the picture at the right to green, Accent color 6 Dark. Your slide 3 should look like figure 17–4.

Figure 17–4

Slides 4 and 5

Step 1 – Add Background

On slide 4 add a Gradient Fill Linear Down for the background with positions at 0 percent, 25 percent, 50 percent, 75 percent, and 100 percent. Add gray-50 percent, Text 1, Lighter 50 percent color to positions 0 percent, 50 percent, and 100 percent. Add gray-25 percent, Background 2 Darker 10 percent, at positions 25 percent and 75 percent. Your slide should look like figure 17–5.

Figure 17–5

Step 2 – Apply a Style

Apply the Reflected Bevel, black style to the three pictures. Add 3-D Rotation to the picture at the left, Perspective Contrasting Right. Add 3-D Rotation to the center picture, Perspective Above. Add 3-D Rotation to the picture at the right, Perspective Contrasting Left. Your slide 4 should look like figure 17–6.

Figure 17–6

Step 3 – Adjust Color

Duplicate slide 4. On the new slide 5, change the color of all the pictures to grayscale. Your slide 5 should look like figure 17–7.

ADVANCED POWERPOINT: MORE THAN PRESENTATIONS!

Figure 17–7

Add a white marble background to slide 1. Add a transition of your choice, and add action buttons to navigate and exit the Slide Show. Set up the presentation to be Browsed at a Kiosk.

Music and Animation

Open the data file ***Lesson 17 Music and Animation***. The presentation contains six slides, and slides 2, 3, 4, and 6 include a picture in the upper left corner of the slide to show you what the slide will look like when completed, and the various objects you will need to complete the slide. Add your name to the title slide. A slide transition, music, and action buttons have already been added.

Slide 2

Slide 2 when completed will look like figure 17–8. Use the objects on the slide to create the boy and girl sitting on a stool. Create an animation so that their arm moves to their mouth slowly with an auto-reverse simulating their taking a sip from the wine glasses they are holding. Have the music play until the next slide. You can substitute other music if you prefer to do that. Once you complete the slide, delete the picture from the upper-left corner as well as the other objects on the slide you no longer need.

Figure 17–8

Slide 3

Slide 3 when completed will look like figure 17–9. Use the objects on the slide to create an animation where the boy is throwing a basketball through the basket repeatedly. Have the music play until the next slide. You can substitute other music if you prefer to do that. Once you complete the slide, delete the picture from the upper-left corner as well as the other objects on the slide you no longer need. *Note: The ball needs to go through the basket, not on top of it.*

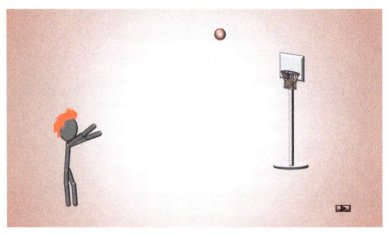

Figure 17–9

Slide 4

Slide 4 when completed will look like figure 17–10. Use the objects on the slide to create an animation on slide 5 where the boy's head is moving back and forth repeatedly as though he were moving to music. Have the music play until the next slide. The wheels should be turning, and the exhaust fumes should be teetering. You can substitute other music if you prefer to do that. Once you complete the slide, delete slide 4.

Figure 17–10

Slide 5

Note: Complete the next section of this lesson entitled Pivots and Animation before you complete slide 5. Slide 5 when completed will look like figure 17–11. Use the objects on the slide to create an animation on slide 5 where the stick figure bends over to pick up the money and then hands it to the policeman. You can substitute other music if you prefer to do that. Once you complete the slide, delete any objects that are no longer needed.

Figure 17–11

Pivots and Animation

Open the data file **Lesson 17 Pivots and Animation**. Add your name to the title slide and then go to slide 2. Your slide 2 should look like figure 17–12. Click on any shape except the head, and note that the shape is in two parts, a visible and a transparent section. As you learned in earlier lessons, when you spin an object, it spins in place from it center point. To have it spin form another pivot point such as at the bottom of or top of a shape, you create a duplicate copy of the shape, make it transparent, and then group the two shapes. As you can see from figure 17–12. A stick figure has been created and a transparent portion of each shape (except the head) has been added and grouped.

Figure 17–12

Step 1

Copy all sections of the stick figure and paste them to slide 3. On slide 3, arrange the stick figure as shown in figure 17–13. Place the tablet in the stick figure's hands as shown.

Figure 17–13

Step 2

Copy the stick figure from slide 3 to slide 4, and remove the tablet. On slide 4, you are going to make the stick figure stand up and take a step forward. In order to make the figure stand up, you will move each part of the figure at the same time (With Previous) and Very Slow. The object will move using a Motion Path (to right, left, up, down), and as needed a Spin (clockwise or counterclockwise). After you make the figure stand up, it should look similar to figure 17–14.

Figure 17–14

Select one of the objects (bottom section of the right leg) to use as the major pivot around which all objects will move. Animate the bottom section of the right leg for a Motion Path Right, With Previous, Very Slow, Smooth Start and Smooth End. Click on the red ending point to change the distance to the desired length. If you hold down the Shift key while you do this, the direction will remain straight. Add an animation, Emphasis, Spin, With Previous, Very Slow, Counterclockwise, 15°. Repeat this process until your stick figure looks like figure 17–15 before the animation is played and figure 17–14 after the animation is played. *Note: All animations should be With Previous, Very Slow.*

Bottom right section of the leg, Motion Path Right, With Previous, Very Slow, Smooth Start and Smooth End.

Also add an Emphasis, Spin, Counterclockwise, 15°, With Previous, Very Slow.

Top right section of the leg, Motion Path Right, With Previous, Very Slow, Smooth Start and Smooth End.

Figure 17–15

Step 3

Select all the objects in the animation and animate them for Exit, Disappear. Set the first new animation for After Previous, and the rest should already be set for With Previous. View the animation in the animation pane. The stick figure should get up from the bench and then disappear.

Step 4

In step 4 you want to make the stick figure take another step. Copy the stick figure from slide 5, and place it in the position where the previous animation ended (the stick figure standing up). You can move the shapes to reflect the way your stick figure looked. Animate all the new figure to Appear. The first object should be After Previous and all the other new animations With Previous. At this point when you run the animation, your figure will stand up, disappear, and then appear again. Animate the new stick figure to take one step forward. Your slide will look like figure 17–16 at the conclusion of step 4.

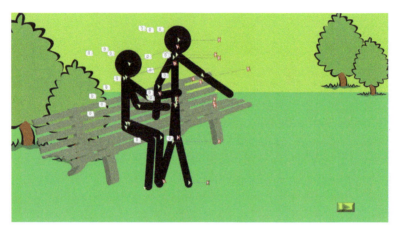

Figure 17–16

Figure 17–17 shows how your animation will look at the end of the first animations in Slide Show view. Figure 17–18 shows how your animation will look at the end of the second animation in Slide Show view.

Figure 17–17

Figure 17–18

You can now return to Lesson 17 Music and Animation and complete slide 5. Make any necessary changes and save your presentation.

Lesson 17 Applications

Lesson 17 Application 1 Presentation Application

Open a new blank PowerPoint presentation. Create a presentation consisting of four slides. Insert three related videos from YouTube on slides 2, 3, and 4. Add an appropriate transition, and add action buttons to navigate the presentation. Save the presentation as ***Lesson 17 Application 1 Presentation Application***.

Lesson 17 Application 2 Instructional Materials Application

Open a new blank presentation and name it ***Lesson 17 Application 2 Instructional Materials Application.*** Add the title ***VBA Social Media Quiz*** to the title slide. Add your name to the title slide as shown in figure 17–19.

Figure 17–19

Step 1

Add a new blank slide. Open the VBA editor. *Note: Refer to Lesson 16 to review the steps required to complete a UserForm.* Add a UserForm as shown in figure 17–20, and on the form create a social media quiz. The title is a Text Box Control. The numbers 1 to 10 are command buttons. Add the captions to the command buttons 1 to 10. When you double-click on one of the command buttons, you are taken to the code window and can write code between Private Sub and End sub. Double-click on the Command Button with a number 1 on it and enter the following code:

Private Sub CommandButton1_Click()
MsgBox "Which page has the most Facebook® fans? President Obama, Texas Hold 'Em Poker, or Starbucks?"
End Sub

Figure 17–20

Repeat this process for the other command buttons. The text for questions 2–10 is shown in table 17–1.

Step 2

Insert a module and add code to run UserForm1 as shown below. You will be able to run the UserForm1 macro while in Slide Show view.

Sub UserFrom1()
UserForm1.Show
End Sub

Add an Answer section to the user form as shown in figure 17–20. The answer to each question is shown in table 17–1.

Social Media Quiz		
Number	Question	Answer
1	Which page has the most Facebook fans? President Obama, Texas Hold 'Em Poker, or Starbucks?	Texas Hold 'Em Poker
2	The character limit for posting on Twitter is? 142, 200, 140, 130.	140
3	"Me at the Zoo" is the millionth video upload to YouTube? The first video uploaded to YouTube? The most unpopular video uploaded to YouTube? Not a Video?	The first video uploaded to YouTube?
4	Facebook founder Mark Zuckerberg founded the site while a student at Harvard, Yale, Stanford, or Columbia?	Harvard
5	Foursquare can be used for everything but restaurant reservations, tracking friends, buying movie tickets, unlocking badges.	Buying movie tickets
6	The first sign something went wrong in Twitter is a whale, a monkey, a bird, or a sad face.	A whale
7	What can you no longer do on Facebook? Poke someone, give them a gift, suggest a page to them, tag them in a photo?	Give them a gift
8	Which media site helped launch Susan Boyle's career— Twitter, Facebook, YouTube, or My Space?	YouTube
9	Where did Chartroulette start? England, India, United States, or Russia?	Russia
10	Conan O'Brien follows how many people on Twitter? 1, none, 1542, 10?	1

Table 17–1

Step 3

On slide 2, add a rectangle with the text *Social Media Quiz*. Format the rectangle as desired. Use the rectangle to run the UserForm1 macro.

Step 4

View slide 2 in Slide Show view. You should be able to click on the button *Social Media Quiz* and display the UserForm. You should be able to click on any of the buttons on the UserForm and a new question will be displayed. You can click on any of the numbers and the answer for that question will be displayed.

Make sure your slide 2 is working properly and save your presentation.

Lesson 17 Application 3 Gaming Application

Open a new blank presentation. Create a stick figure and then create an animation in which the stick figure moves. Add an appropriate transition, and add action buttons to navigate the presentation. Save the presentation as *Lesson 17 Application 3 Gaming Application*.

LESSON 18

Capstone Lesson: Advanced Animation, Graphics, and Sound

Data Files

Lesson 18 Making a Slot Machine
Lesson 18 Challenge Application 1 Five in a Row, ppsm Format
Lesson 18 Challenge Application 1 Five in a Row, pptm Format
Lesson 18 Challenge Application 2 One Slide, 3–5 Minute Animation, ppsx Format
Lesson 18 Challenge Application 4 Multiple Column Slot Machine, ppsm Format
Lesson 18 Challenge Application 4 Multiple Column Slot Machine, pptm Format

Overview

In Lesson 18 you will use the many animation skills you have learned throughout the lessons to create a working slot machine. In these application activities, you are given the opportunity to create additional application for presentations, instructional materials, and gaming with little or no instructions.

Making a Slot Machine

In this lesson, you will make a traditional three-wheel slot machines as shown in figure 18–1.

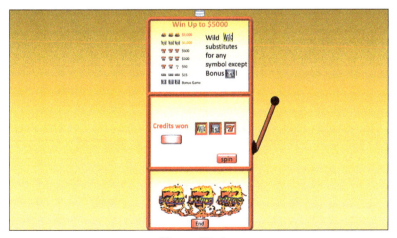

Figure 18–1

Go to your data files and open the file ***Lesson 18 Making a Slot Machine***. Slides 2 to 4 show the basic components needed to construct the slot machine as shown in figure 18–2. The images on slides 2 and 3 are in the background of the slide and are shown as examples, except for the symbols and win amounts. The top row of images on slide 4 is also in the background, but the other images are available for you to use as you build your slot machine. You will delete slides 2, 3, and 4 once your slot machine is complete.

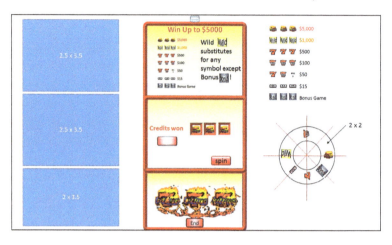

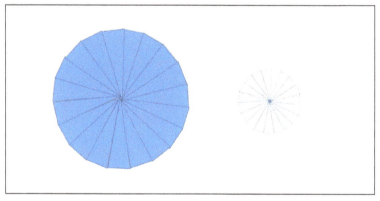

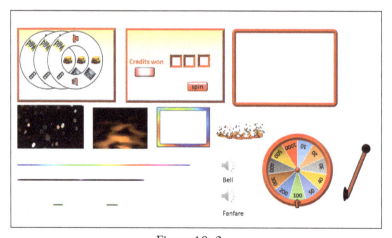

Figure 18–2

ADVANCED POWERPOINT: MORE THAN PRESENTATIONS!

Step 1 – Drawing and Creating the Slot Machine

Add a new blank slide after slide 4. Create three rectangles as shown on the example on slide 2, size them as shown. Add a Gradient Fill to the rectangle, Linear Up with positions at 0 percent, 50 percent, and 100 percent. (Suggested colors of white, Background 1; Gold Accent 4, lighter 80 percent; Gold Accent 4, lighter 40 percent) Center all rectangles. Apply the Bevel Angle effect to each rectangle, and add a 3 pt red line color to each of the shapes. Your slide will look like figure 18–3.

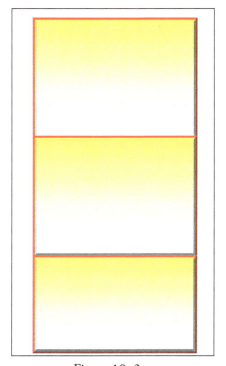

Figure 18–3

Add a text box, *Win up to $5000* in Calibri font, 20 pt, red, bold; and center it at the top center of the top rectangle as shown in figure 18–1. Copy the symbols and win amounts from slide 2 and paste them in the top rectangle as shown in figure 18–1. Size as necessary. Set the transparent color to remove the background.

Add the text box shown in figure 18–4. The text is in 18 pt black text. You will need to crop the symbols from the picture on slide 2:

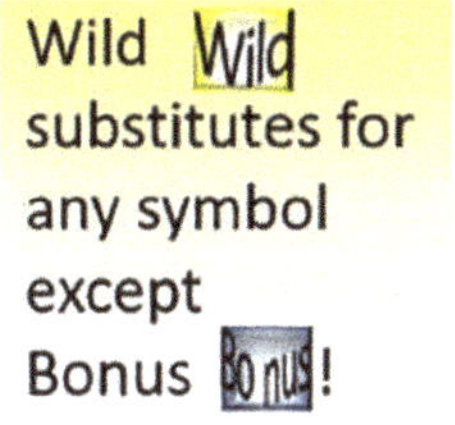

Figure 18–4

In the middle section of the slot machine, add the text *Credits won* in Calibri font, 18 pt, red, and bold. Add the two rounded rectangles height .3" and width .7" with a Gradient Fill, Radial, From Center, in shades of red and white. Add an effect Bevel Circle to both rectangles. Add the text *Spin* in black on the rectangle at the bottom right of the section as shown in figure 18–5.

In the bottom section of the slot machine, crop one of the fiery sevens from the symbols shown on slide 2 to create the images in the bottom section of the slide. Copy the .gif animation from slide 4, and size it and place it as shown in figure 18–5. Add a rounded rectangle height .3" and width 7", Gradient Fill, Radial, From Center, in shades of red and white to the bottom section of the slot machine. Add the word *End* to the rectangle. Add the effect Bevel Circle.

At the conclusion of this step, your slide 5 should look like figure 18–5.

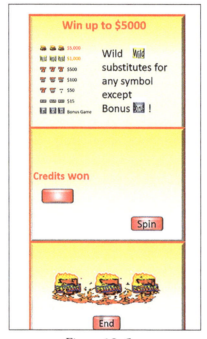

Figure 18–5

Step 2 – Creating the Wheels

In step 2, you are going to create three wheels containing the symbols shown in the middle section of the slot machine. Draw a donut shape height 2" and width 2", white fill and black outline, as shown in figure 18–6. When you click on the donut shape, you will see the handles at each corner and in the horizontal center and vertical center of the object. Use these guides to draw a straight line from handle to handle as shown in figure 18–6. Each line represents 45°. If you place the slot machine symbols on each of the lines, you would have a symbols at 45°, 90°, 135°, 180°, 225°, 270°, 315° and 360°. You would have a possibility of 512 combinations of symbols with three wheels and eight possible symbols or blank on each wheel. Adding more symbols on the wheel increases the number of combinations. *Note: Use the yellow adjustment handle to increase the width of the donut shape to accommodate all symbols if needed.*

Crop Symbols

Copy the picture with symbols from slide 2, and crop the first symbol. Keep the symbols to approximately height .4" and width .5". Duplicate the picture and crop the other five symbols. Arrange the symbols on the wheel you created as shown in figure 18–7. *Note: Do not add the numbers.*

When your wheel looks like the figure 18–7, delete the lines and group the shape. It should look like figure 18–8. Duplicate the shape two times and arrange the shapes as shown in figure 18–9. Bring objects forward or send objects backward as necessary to make your slide look like figure 18–9. Add two can shapes to the tops of the machine to represent lights one blue and one white, .2"×.4". Duplicate the can shapes and place the copies on top of the original can shapes.

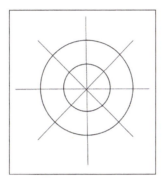

Figure 18–6

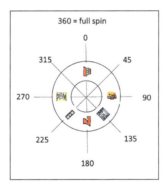

Figure 18–7

Figure 18–8

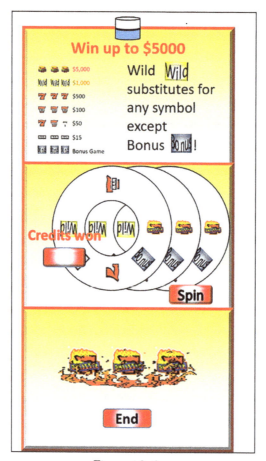

Figure 18–9

Step 3 - Creating the Working Section of the Slot Machine

In step 3 you are going to cover the working section (middle section) and create windows to display symbols through the windows.

1. Draw 3 rectangles height .4" and width .4" and place them as shown in figure 18–10. Align the rectangles at the top and distribute them horizontally. Use No Fill to remove the fill from the rectangle. The three fiery sevens should be outlined by the three rectangles. Once you have the three rectangles aligned properly as shown in figure 18–10, add the blue Fill color to all of them as shown in figure 18–11.

ADVANCED POWERPOINT: MORE THAN PRESENTATIONS!

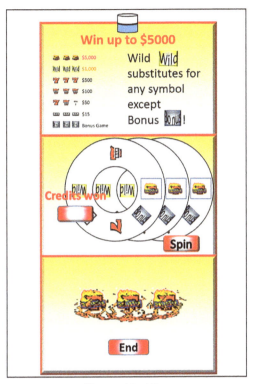

Figure 18–10

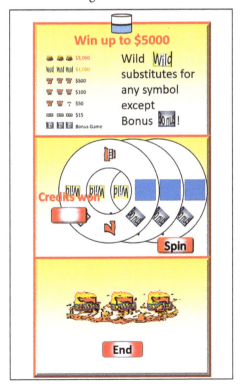

Figure 18–11

2. Copy the rectangle that is the background of the middle section. Align it to cover the entire middle section and send it backward until the three blue rectangles you created are on top as shown in figure 18–12.

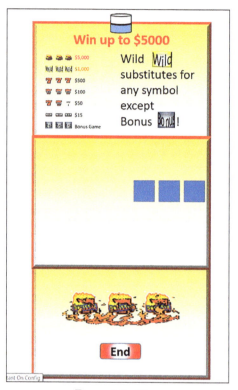

Figure 18–12

3. Use subtract shapes to remove the blue rectangles from the rectangle covering the middle section. To remove the first shape, click on the large rectangle shape and then hold down the Shift key and click on the first blue square. Click Subtract Shape and it will be cut out. Repeat this step to cut the remaining two rectangles. Your slide should look like figure 18–13. *Note: You can add the subtract shape button to the Quick Access Tool Bar in the upper-left corner of the ribbon.*

ADVANCED POWERPOINT: MORE THAN PRESENTATIONS!

Figure 18–13

4. Send the large rectangle covering the middle section of the slot machine to the back until you can see all the objects you have added to the middle section, except the three wheels, as shown in figure 18–14.

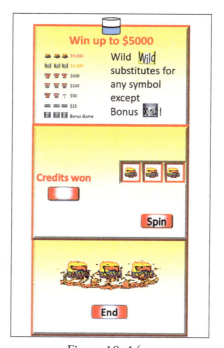

Figure 18–14

5. Add a frame, height .5" and width .5" around each of the three windows as shown in figure 18–15. The shape outline should be 2 ¼ pt. Change the Outline Color to red, and add an effect Bevel Angle. Align the frames at the top and distribute them horizontally.

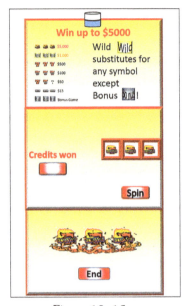

Figure 18–15

6. Draw a 4 ½ pt. frame shape around each of the three sections of the slot machine. Format the shape for effect Bevel Slope. Align the three rectangles at the left as shown in figure 18–16. Bring the objects that represent the light at the top of the machine to the front.

Figure 18–16

ADVANCED POWERPOINT: MORE THAN PRESENTATIONS!

7. Copy the slot machine handle from slide 4 and paste it onto the slot machine as shown in figure 18–17.

Figure 18–17

Step 4 - Animating the Slot Machine Wheels

If you added a spin action to each of the slot machine wheels, the wheels would spin 360° and stop displaying the same symbols in the same place. Real slot machines spin the wheels when you press the spin button, and each wheel randomly stops on one of the symbols or a blank space. When you press the Spin button, the amount each wheel will spin is randomly determined, and the amount you won, if any, is displayed. With a little more skill in VBA, you could write code to do just that. We are going to do the same thing at this point without using any VBA code.

Spinning the Wheels

Notice the wheel displayed on figure 18–18. A symbols or blank space is located every 45° on the wheel. The fiery seven is displayed in the box window. If we wanted the *first wheel* to spin *once* and stop on a blank space, you would spin the wheel 405°, 360° + 45°. Because we cut windows so that the symbols would show through the windows, you can click on the symbol or blank shown in the window to select the wheel, and then animate the wheel to spin. If you wanted the *second wheel* to spin *twice* and then land on *Wild*, you would spin the wheel 900°, 360° + 360° + 180°. If you wanted the *third wheel* to spin the wheel *three times* and then land on *Wild*, you would spin the wheel 1260°, 360° + 360° + 360° + 180°.

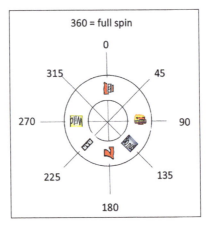

Figure 18–18

Table 18–1 shows the spin rotation needed to spin a wheel completely around once (360°), twice (720°) or three times (1080°) from the fiery seven position and then land on a specific symbol. The sound to be played with each symbol is also shown. In order to hear each sound, the second wheel spin is delayed .2 seconds, and the third wheel spin is delayed .4 seconds. All the spin animations are very fast.

Required Spin Rotations All spins – very fast				
Symbol	Rotation Wheel 1 – one spin (360°) +	Rotation Wheel 2 – two spins (720°) + Delay .2 seconds	Rotation Wheel 3 – three spins (1080°) + Delay .4 seconds	Sound
Blank	405°, 360° + 45°	765°, 720° + 45°	1125°, 1080° + 45°	click
BAR	450°, 360° + 90°	810°, 720° + 90°	1170°, 1080° + 90°	click
Blank	495°, 360° + 135°	855°, 720° + 135°	1215°, 1080° + 135°	click
Wild	540°, 360° + 180°	900°, 720° + 180°	1260°, 1080° + 180°	hammer
BAR	585°, 360° + 225°	945°, 720° + 225°	1305°, 1080° + 225°	click
7	630°, 360° + 270°	990°, 720° + 270°	1350°, 1080° + 270°	click
Bonus	675°, 360° + 315°	1035°, 720° + 315°	1395°, 1080° + 315°	laser
(cash)	720°, 360° + 360°	1080°, 720° + 360°	1440°, 1080° + 360°	cash register

Table 18–1

Slide 5

1. On your slot machine on slide 5, click on the window for the first wheel to the left to select it. A rectangle with handles will be displayed indicating you selected the object.
2. Add an animation, Spin, With Previous, Very Fast, 405°, add a Click sound. Play the animation, and your wheel should stop on a *blank space*.
3. Click on the window for the second wheel, and add an animation, Spin, With Previous, Very Fast, Delay .2 seconds, 990°, and a Click sound. The delay allows enough time for the sound associated with the spin animation to play. The wheel should stop on a *red seven*.
4. Click on the window for the third wheel, and add an animation, Spin, With Previous, Very Fast, Delay .4 seconds, 1440°, and a Cash Register sound. The delay allows enough time for the sound associated with the spin animation to play. A *fiery seven* should be displayed.
5. View the slide in Slide Show view, the wheels should stop one after the other with two click sounds and a Cash Register sound. The display will look like figure 18–19.
6. The amount won remains blank because no amount was won.

Table 18–2 shows the animation requirements for slides 5 to 19. You already completed slide 5.

Figure 18–19

Slide 6

1. Duplicate slide 5. (Right-click on slide 5 in the slides pane at the left of the window, and then select duplicate slide from the menu displayed.)
2. Change the spin animation and sound as shown in table 18–2 for slide 6.
3. Since the wheels stop on three *red sevens*, *500* coins are won.
4. Add a text box that shows 500, and place it on top of the rounded rectangle below the text, *credits won*. Size as needed. Animate it to appear After Previous. It should be the last animation in the animation pane. Your slide in Slide Show view will look like figure 18–20. *Note: For each slide you prepare, you will need to make sure that the amount won displays if a winning Combination is spun, or that the you won box is blank if no amount is won.* Your slide 6 should look like figure 18–20.

Complete slides 7 to 19 following the specifications shown in table 18–2.

Figure 18–20

ADVANCED POWERPOINT: MORE THAN PRESENTATIONS!

Slide number	Symbols to be displayed after spin	Sounds	Amount won
5	[ ][7][cash]	click, click, cash register	
6	[7][7][7]	click, click, click	500
7	[ ][ ][ ]	click, click, click	
8	[BAR][BAR][BAR]	click, click, click	15
9	[cash][cash][cash]	click, click, click	100
10	[BAR][Bonus][Bonus]	click, laser, laser	
11	[7][7][Wild]	click, click, hammer	500
12	[7][7][BAR]	click, click, click	50
13	[ ][7][ ]	click, click, click	
14	[cash][Bonus][Bonus]	click, laser, laser	
15	[7][Wild][7]	click, hammer, click	500
16	[7][Wild][Bonus]	click, hammer, laser	
17	[Bonus][Bonus][7]	laser, laser, click	
18	[cash][Bonus][7]	cash register, laser, click	
19	[BAR][ ][Wild]	click, click, hammer	
20	[Wild][Wild][Wild]	hammer, hammer, hammer	1000
21	[Bonus][Bonus][Bonus]	laser, laser, laser	30 (amount varies)
22	[Bonus][Bonus][Bonus]	laser, laser, laser	400 (amount varies)
23	[cash][cash][cash]	cash register, cash register, cash register	5000

Table 18–2

Slide 20

Most slot machines today display some type animation when the user spins a *Big Win*. A *big win* is an amount less than $1,200, the minimum amount that triggers a jackpot, and requires the machine to lock; and the user is paid manually and receives a copy of Form W-2G, which the casino sends to the IRS. The user is responsible for paying taxes on the winnings contained on the form. There is no specific amount that is a *big win*. It depends largely on the denomination of slot machine you are playing such as a penny, quarter, dollar, or five-dollar machine. A *big win* on a dollar slot machine might be $1,000, for example, an amount less than $1,200.

Duplicate slide 19, change the Spin animation for the first wheel to 540° and a Hammer sound, the second wheel to 900° and a Hammer sound, and the third wheel to 1260° and a Hammer sound. All wheels will stop on the *Wild* symbol. Add a text box with the amount one thousand over the shape below *Credits won*. Animate the text to Appear, After Previous. Add a .wav sound such as a *bell* or buzzer or *musical sound* to play After Previous. You can find many free sounds online or you can use the sample .wav on slide 4. If the sound file is short, you might want to repeat it once or twice.

Add a .gif border around the center section of the machine to Appear, After Previous. You can create your own .gif or use sample shown on slide 4 or find one online.

Add another .gif to cover the top section of the machine as shown in figure 18–21. The .gif should Appear after the border has displayed. Add WordArt, *Big win!*, on top of the .gif and have it Zoom In, after the top .gif has displayed. Both .gifs and the WordArt should then Fade Out, Very Slow; Delay the animation for 3 seconds. Your slide 20 should look similar to figure 18–21 when in Slide Show view. The second image shows the top .gif, WordArt, and the .gif around the center section fading out.

Figure 18–21

Slide 21 – Bonus Game

Today's slot machines contain many features not found on older machines such as sounds, video, and a variety of interactive features. Certain symbols cause a sound to be played, and others trigger dynamic features. The slot machine you created has a bonus game that is triggered when three *bonus symbols* are displayed. When three bonus symbols are displayed a game wheel will be displayed, which the user can spin to win an amount from 10 to 1,000 as shown in figure 18–22.

1. Duplicate slide 20 and delete the .gif animations and the WordArt, *Big win!* Change the animation for all three wheels to 675°, 1035°, and 1395° respectively with the Laser sound. When run, bonus will appear in all wheels.
2. Add a sound .wav to be played After Previous.
3. Copy the rectangle black and orange .gif from slide 4, and paste it on the top section of the slot machine as shown in figure 18–22. Size as needed. Animate the .gif for an animation Entrance Wipe, With Previous, From Top, Slow.
4. Copy and paste the wheel and arrow from slide 4, and paste it on top of the slot machine shown in figure 18–22. Size the wheel to height 2" and width 2". Align the wheel and arrow in the center of the top section of the slot machine. Animate the wheel and arrow for an animation Entrance, Dissolve In, After Previous, Medium, Drum Roll sound. Size the wheel if needed, but make sure the height and width are the same. Align the arrow and the wheel at the center.
5. Add a text box, *Click arrow to spin!,* in 24 pt, red, bold text as shown in figure 18–22. Animate the text to Appear, After Previous, Very Fast.
6. Animate the wheel to Spin 1910°, Fast. It should stop on 30. Use the arrow as the trigger to start the animation.
7. Have the text, *Click to spin!,* Disappear, after the Spin animation. Move the animation after the Spin animation in the animation pane.
8. Have *30* appear in the *Credits won* box, After Previous. Move the animation after the Disappear animation in the Animation Pane.

Figure 18–22

Slide 22 – Bonus Game

Making additional Bonus games is easy. Duplicate slide 21. On the duplicate slide, change the Spin animation from 1910° to 2050°. The wheel will stop on *400* so change the win amount to *400*. Of course, you could add a bonus game that would land on each of the amounts shown on the wheel by simply changing the rotation, but we will only add the two bonus slides you created to our sample slot machine on slides 21 and 22.

Slide 23 – Jackpot

A jackpot is any amount $1200 or greater. On the machine you are making the jackpot would be all *Fiery 7s* which is a $5000 win. When a jackpot is triggered sound and animation usually alert the user that a jackpot has been won, the machine is locked, and a casino host will come to your machine to provide you with the W-2G form, and to pay you the jackpot amount.

1. Duplicate slide 20, and move it to the last slide position, slide 23.
2. Change the Spin animation for the wheels to 720°, 1080°, and 1440° respectively, and a Cash Register sound. The machine will display all Fiery 7s when the animation is run.

ADVANCED POWERPOINT: MORE THAN PRESENTATIONS!

3. Add a text box with the amount *5000* in the box below *You won*. Animate it to appear, After Previous.
4. Add a .gif border around the center section of the machine. Animate it to appear With Previous.
5. Add a .gif border around the object containing the amount won. Animate it to appear With Previous.
6. Copy the black and orange .gif the rectangle from slide 4, and paste it on the top section of the slot machine as shown in figure 18–23. Size it as needed. Animate the .gif for an animation Entrance Wipe, With Previous, From Top, Medium speed.
7. Add the WordArt shown in the top section of the slot machine: *Jackpot* on one line and *$5,000* on the next line. Animate the text box for Entrance, Wipe, From Top, Medium, With Previous.
8. Animate the two parts of the slot machine light at the top of the slot machine (move the top blue shape on top of white, and the top white shape on top of blue). Animate the two parts of the lights to Blink, With Previous, Repeat Until End of Slide, at different speeds (fast and medium). Remember you placed a copy of the light on top of the original light. We did this so that when you make the light blink you will still see the bottom images.
9. Copy and paste the Bell sound from slide 4, animate it to play With Previous. Move the sound icon off the screen.

Your slide should look like figure 18–23.

Figure 18–23

Step 5 – Creating Custom Shows

You have created nineteen slides with slot machines, slides 5–23. You need to save each slide as a Custom Show, beginning with the first slide that contains a slot machine, slide 5, naming it *one*. The next slide with a slot machine will be *two*. Repeat this procedure until you have completed 19 Custom Shows: *one* to *nineteen*. If you click the Slide Show tab and in the Start Slide Show group click Custom Slide Show, your screen should look like figure 18–24 when you complete step 5.

Figure 18–24

Step 6 – Random Wheel

You need to create a random wheel consisting of nineteen sections as shown on slide 3. Once you create the wheel, you can group it and size it as needed. The wheel will need to be sized to fit

ADVANCED POWERPOINT: MORE THAN PRESENTATIONS!

over the Spin Button as shown in figure 18–25. The outline of each piece has been removed, and the fill color has been change 38 percent transparent at this point. *Hint: You can trace one section of the wheel on slide 4 and then copy and paste it eighteen times. Then arrange the nineteen sections into a wheel, group the wheel, and size the wheel.*

Figure 18–25

Step 7 – Link Wheel Sections to Custom Shows

Double-click on the first section of the wheel. Make sure it is selected (handles will appear around the section) as shown in figure 18–26. Click Insert and in the Links group click Action. Hyperlink to Custom Show, *One. Do not click Show and Return.* Figure 18–27 shows the Action Settings dialog box. Repeat this procedure to link each section of the wheel to a different Custom Show.

Figure 18-26

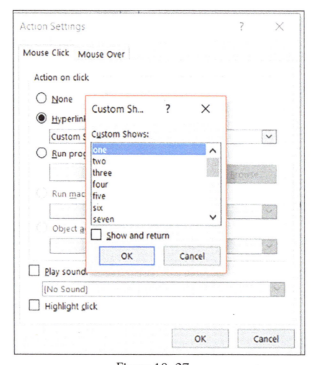

Figure 18-27

Once you have the links completed and the wheel is placed over the spin button on slide 5 as shown in figure 18–25, animate the wheel to spin, speed very slow, With Previous, Repeat Until End of Slide. Copy the wheel onto each slide that contains a slot machine. Rotate the copies at a different location on each wheel. (Rotate it so that it doesn't always start at the same point.) Make the fill color 100 percent transparent so that you can't see the wheel.

Step 8 – Set Up Slide Show to Be Browsed at a Kiosk

Set up your Slide Show to be Browsed at a Kiosk. When you do this, you lock off the keyboard except for the ESC key, which takes you back to the last slide viewed and eventually will let you exit Slide Show view, and you must include hyperlinks (you created hyperlinks on the wheel) to move from slide to slide. Go to slide 5, the first slide with a slot machine. Click Slide Show view and click the Spin button. You will randomly go to another slide containing a slot machine. Continue clicking the Spin button and you will randomly jump from slide to slide. The slot machine is now working and you are randomly jumping from one Slide Show to another, and the user does not know there are multiple slides. It looks like a single slide. *However, pressing ESC once will not let you exit Slide Show view. It takes you to the previous slide viewed and you would have to press ESC the number of times you pressed Spin to exit Slide Show view because when you use a Custom Show. ESC takes you back to the last slide viewed and only exits Slide Show view when you press ESC enough to reach the first slide. Using the End button at the bottom of the slot machine to exit Slide Show view also will not work. Like ESC, it will take you back to the last Custom Show viewed instead of exiting Slide Show view!*

Step 9 – Fixing the Exit Custom Show Problem

The easiest way to fix the exit problem is to write some simple VBA code that will let you exit the slot machine game at any point. Access your visual basic editor, add a new module, and enter the following code.

```
'Macro to exit all running Slide Shows:
Sub ExitAllShows()
    Do While SlideShowWindows.Count > 0
        SlideShowWindows(1).view.Exit
    Loop
End Sub
```

Step 10 – Click End to Run ExitAllShows Macro

Go to the first slide with a slot machine on it. Click on the End button on the slot machine to select it. Click Insert/Links/Action/Run Macro/ExitAllShows/OK. View the slide in Slide Show view and click the End button. You should exit Slide Show view.

Go to each slide containing a slot machine, and have the *End* button run the ExitAllShows macro.

Step 11 – Save as PowerPoint Macro-Enabled Presentation

Since you added a macro to your presentation in step 9, you need to save the presentation as a PowerPoint Macro-Enable presentation.

Step 12 – Test the Game

Go to slide 5 and click the *spin* button. Spin multiple times to see how the slot machine actually works. Click *end* to exit Slide Show view. Correct any errors you find.

Step 13 – Remove Slides Not Needed

Slides 2, 3, and 4 are not need as part of the slot machine game. You can delete those slides. When you delete those slides, your Custom Shows and links are automatically updated to reference the new slide numbers.

Step 14 – Add Action Button to Navigate from Slide 1 to the Slot Machine Game

Since your presentation is set up to be Browsed at a Kiosk, you need to add a link to move from slide 1 to the slot machine game. Insert a next action button on slide 1.

Add your name to slide 1, white font, and add a black background to all the slides. Your slides 1 and 2 should look similar to figure 18–28.

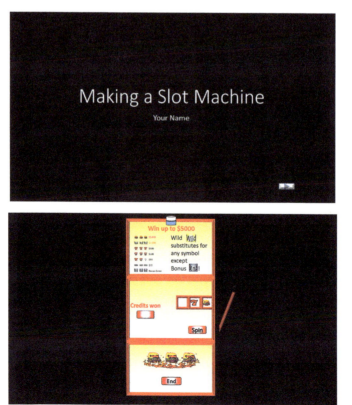

Figure 18–28

ADVANCED POWERPOINT: MORE THAN PRESENTATIONS!

Finish Presentation

Correct any errors you find in your presentation, and save it again as a PowerPoint Macro-enabled presentation.

Challenge Application 1 Five in a Row Game

Open the data file **Lesson 18 Challenge Application 1 Five in a Row**. The presentation is in ppsm format, a PowerPoint Macro-Enabled show format. The file will open automatically, and you can play the game. Close the presentation.

You want to create the game yourself. Open the data file **Lesson 18 Challenge Application 1 Five in a Row**. This presentation is in PowerPoint Macro-Enabled format. Add your name on the title slide. Slide 2 contains the objects, game board, and macros you will need to complete the game. In this game, each player alternately can click on one of the game pieces at the top of the game board to drop the game piece down to the lowest available block in one of nine columns. The first player to align five of her game pieces in a row vertically, horizontally, or diagonally wins the game and can click on the game piece under games won, and click on the number of games won and the piece will move to that location. The game board can be cleared by clicking the *New Game* button. Figure 18–29 shows a completed game where the player using the orange game pieces won the game.

Hints:

1. A *Motion Path down* was used to *drop a game pieces* from its original location to the next available square in the column. For example, if the blue players click the #6 game piece above column 1, it will drop to the bottom box in that column. Since that square is no longer available, the number 6 orange game piece needs to disappear at the same time. There are six game pieces stacked on top of one another for orange and blue above each column.

2. To *clear the game board*, all game pieces need to return to their original position. Apply a *Motion Path up* to the first game piece to its original position and *lock the path* as you did when you learned to teleport an object, and add an *animation Entrance Appear* to the first game piece. Use the *Clear Game object as the trigger* to start the Motion Path Up animation. You will need to repeat this process for each game piece, but all remaining animation will be With Previous and need to be listed below the first Motion Path up that was triggered by the *Clear Game* object.

3. To keep track of *games won*, assign the *move piece macro* to the two game pieces under Games Won. Assign the *new location macro* to all the objects under games won, except the two game pieces. The macros have already been written for you.

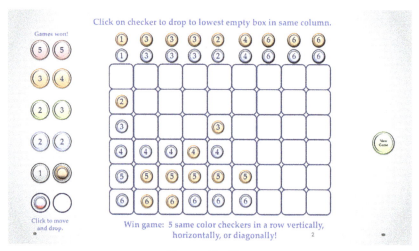

Figure 18–29

When your game is working properly, save it again as **Lesson 18 Challenge Application 1 Five in a Row**, a PowerPoint Macro-Enabled presentation.

Challenge Application 2 One slide 3–5 Minute Animation

For this assignment, you are to use your imagination and the skills you learned to create a 3–5 minute animation all contained on a single slide. The data file **Lesson 18 Challenge Application 2 One slide, 3–5 Minute Animation** is provided in your data files for Lesson 18 in Slide Show view (.ppsm) as an example of the type of animation you might create. The animation on slide 3 was inspired by *Vincent Van Gogh's Cafe Terrace at Night painting* shown in figure 18–30. Save your original presentation as **Lesson 18 Challenge Application 2 One slide, 3–5 Minute Animation.**

Figure 18–30

Challenge Application 3 – Teaching Application

Create an original application of teaching something by playing a game. Review some of the many games you created as you completed this textbook to provide some examples. Save your presentation as ***Lesson 18 Challenge Application 3 Teaching Application.***

Challenge Application 4 – Gaming Application

Open the data file ***Lesson 18 Application 4 Multiple Column Slot Machine*** that is saved in .pptm format indicating it is saved in PowerPoint Macro-Enable presentation format. Slides 2 and 3 show pictures of a five-column slot machine—the opening screen, a help screen, and some sample slides. Slide 4 shows how five columns of picture options were created to move down behind the windows created. The first column is animated with a Motion Path Down, Repeat 3 times, Smooth Start and Smooth End, With Previous, Very Fast. These three slides are only examples from a game that is already created. Your presentation also has a macro written that you can use to *exit* your presentation. You will delete slides 3–4 when you begin creating your own game.

A sample game has been created for you to view and get an idea of what you might do. Open the data file ***Lesson 18 Challenge Application 4 Multiple Column Slot Machine*** in .ppsm, a PowerPoint show that will run automatically.

Create your own five-column slot machine from the data file in .pptm format located in your data files, and save it as ***Lesson 18 Challenge Application 4 Multiple Column Slot Machine.***

Index

3-D 73, 74, 75, 76, 77, 78, 79, 88, 90
3-D Cube 73
3-D format 74, 75, 88
3-D Rotation 73, 78, 79, 90, 99, 122, 183, 184, 192, 201, 221, 250

A

Action buttons 14, 148, 151, 225, 227
ActiveX Controls 9
advanced drawing 182, 256
Alternative text 31
Alt Text 31, 33, 35
analog clock 9, 15
animate photos 162
Animation painter 103
Animation Pane 16, 17, 91, 108, 116, 118, 119, 317
apps 3, 9, 44, 95, 182, 198, 256, 272
artistic effects 224, 237, 241

B

BackColor 13, 274
BorderColor 13
BorderStyle 13
Browsed at a Kiosk 15, 33, 35, 43, 49, 56, 88, 89, 94, 97, 104, 109, 111, 120, 125, 127, 133, 136, 141, 144, 147, 151, 158, 160, 172, 197, 203, 210, 212, 271, 323, 324

C

caption 116, 274
check box 31
code 3, 10, 44, 85, 86, 95, 129, 130, 132, 143, 148, 151, 152, 153, 154, 158, 159, 189, 198, 199, 200, 209, 210, 213, 214, 223, 243, 275, 276, 277, 278, 298, 311, 323
command button 274
contextual tab 116
Crop 76, 97, 272, 282, 305
Custom animation 87
Custom Ribbon 10
Custom Shows 32, 33, 48, 118, 119, 320

D

data files 3, 11, 215, 223, 228, 231, 233, 235, 258, 302, 326, 327

Developer tab 9, 10, 11, 31, 85, 95, 132, 272
digital timer 266, 271
Dim 129, 132, 143, 153, 198, 276
drag and drop 3, 9
DragBehavior 14
drawing 57, 78, 95, 97, 109, 219, 243, 260, 279
Drawing tools 213, 217
Drawing with shapes 97
drop-down menu 10, 158, 275
dynamic squares 119

E

electronic book 162, 172, 179
electronic calculator 272
electronic game board 159
embedding presentations 213
embed object 215

F

font 9, 11, 16, 32, 52, 57, 60, 89, 93, 108, 140, 168, 227, 237, 239, 240, 266, 274, 303, 304, 324
ForeColor 13
Format Background 45, 46, 50, 229
Format painter 125
format shape 17

G

game
checker 159, 160
dominos 250, 251, 254, 255
five in a row 325, 326
maze 203, 205, 211, 271
Tic Tac Toe 57, 58
Wheel of Fortune 55
word 271
game boards 3
game wheel 90
gif 235, 256, 267, 268, 271, 272, 281, 282, 304, 316, 317, 319
Glow 77, 78, 79, 101, 183, 237, 240
graphics 92
gridlines 11, 14, 52, 57, 95, 122
group 10

I
image mapping 3, 224
interactive presentations 3, 9, 44

K
keyboarding tutor simulation 243

L
logic 44, 51, 113, 224

M
macro
MovePiece 115, 119, 121, 123, 127
NewLocation 115, 119, 121, 123, 127
macro-enabled presentation 87, 95, 110, 115, 125, 130, 141, 158, 161, 208, 213, 223, 247, 279, 326
module 85, 132, 143, 154, 158, 200, 209, 214, 278, 298, 323
morphing 3, 224, 227, 231
mouse over 31, 33, 197, 203, 211
MultiLine 13

N
name object 133
Normal view 278

O
OLE Action Verb 215
option button 31, 35
Option Explicit 198, 276

P
pan 99, 264
photos 3, 176, 179
pivot 17, 103, 116, 176, 180, 250
Pivots 162, 176
properties 9, 12, 13, 14, 143, 245, 274
puzzle 52, 53, 55, 56

Q
Quick Access Toolbar (QAT) 10, 31, 145, 217

R
randomization 44
Random wheel 44, 320
reflection 296
Remove Background 263
ribbon 3, 9, 10, 11, 31, 85, 116, 308

S
ScrollBars 13, 245
Selection Pane 97, 105, 117
Set Up Slide Show 15, 323
Shadow 16, 77, 79, 88, 90, 238, 240, 274
Shape
Combine 217, 221
Fragment 217, 222
Intersect 217, 221
Subtract 145, 217, 218, 219
Union 217, 220
Shape Effects 14, 15
shape, fill, and line 261
shape tools 223
shooting at targets 95
simulations 3, 51, 243
slide masters 57, 130, 151
Slide Show view 11, 12, 13, 31, 34, 48, 49, 52, 54, 56, 59, 60, 73, 74, 79, 81, 82, 83, 84, 91, 93, 96, 97, 103, 105, 106, 107, 108, 109, 111, 116, 117, 118, 119, 120, 123, 124, 125, 130, 133, 135, 136, 137, 138, 140, 143, 144, 146, 147, 148, 150, 151, 152, 154, 155, 156, 157, 160, 167, 170, 176, 177, 178, 180, 186, 190, 192, 193, 194, 197, 200, 203, 205, 208, 210, 212, 227, 230, 235, 237, 246, 247, 253, 254, 260, 263, 278, 296, 299, 313, 316, 323, 324
slot machine 301, 302, 304, 309, 310, 311, 313, 316, 317, 318, 319, 320, 323, 324, 327
Soft Edge 73, 78, 79, 81, 173, 174, 238, 240
solution files 3, 4, 5, 7, 10

T
teleport 129, 133, 135, 136, 145, 325
Transparency 50, 59, 81, 93, 103, 125, 175, 177, 184, 237, 238, 239, 240, 244, 249, 250, 261
Triggers 44, 50, 51, 54, 91, 113, 124, 152, 172, 224
Trust Center Settings 9, 10
Tweening 272, 279, 280

U
UnFREEz 7, 256, 259, 267, 282
Ungroup 75, 80, 81, 87, 99, 168, 256
UserForm 272, 274, 275, 278, 298, 299

V
variable 129, 132, 143, 153, 154, 198, 275, 276, 277
variant 133, 276
VBA 3, 31, 44, 85, 87, 95, 129, 130, 148, 151, 198, 213, 272, 276, 297, 298, 311, 323
Visual Basic Editor 132, 143, 154, 209, 214, 223, 272, 278
Visual Basic for Applications 132

W

WordArt 16, 55, 56, 57, 58, 60, 79, 80, 93, 104, 105, 118, 119, 133, 140, 152, 154, 156, 163, 172, 192, 203, 205, 237, 239, 240, 316, 317, 319

WordWrap 13, 245

Z

zoom 79, 87, 264

About the Authors

Wei-Chieh Wayne Yu, PhD

Dr. Yu is an assistant professor in the Department of Instructional Systems and Workforce Development at Mississippi State University. He teaches a variety of courses in the information technology area, such as computer repairs and maintenance, data networks, media for presentations, instruction and gaming, and research in instructional systems and workforce development. His research interests include technology-facilitated learning, computer-assisted language learning, and technology-enhanced learning.

Anthony A. Olinzock, Professor Emeritus

Dr. Olinzock has over thirty-five years of teaching experience at the high school and university levels. He has held teaching and administrative positions at the University of Pittsburgh, the Ohio State University, and Mississippi State University. He has published numerous articles and over twenty textbooks.

Chun Fu Charlie Lin, PhD.

Dr. Lin received his degree in instructional systems, leadership, and workforce development from Mississippi State University. He is currently an assistant professor in the Department of Applied Foreign Languages at the National Formosa University, Taiwan. His teaching and research interests include English as a second language (ESL), English as a foreign language (EFL), and computer-assisted language learning (CALL).

CPSIA information can be obtained
at www.ICGtesting.com
Printed in the USA
LVHW052321131020
668674LV00007B/155